Contents

Abbreviations and Annotations

adj	adjective	n	noun
adv	adverb	NP	Nigerian Pidgin English
AE	American English	pl	plural
arch	archaic	sb.	somebody
BE	British English	sl	slang
derog	derogatory	sth.	something
e.g.	exempli gratia; for example	usu.	usually
fml	formal	v	verb
infml	informal		

The annotations are arranged chronologically; the first time a word is used is where you will find it explained.

Acknowledgements[1]

I wish to thank all those who contributed to bringing this book to reality, too numerous to mention by name. I am particularly thankful to my agents, David Godwin Associates, for their en couragement and support, and my editors, Juliette Mitchell and Donna Poppy, for their invaluable comments and recommendations. And, of course, my wife Susan and the kids, thanks for putting up[2] with me and seeing me through those dark and broody moments of writing.

1 acknowledgement: (here) *Danksagung* **2** put up with sb.: bear sb., get along with sb.'s moods and behaviour

Part One

1

I am walking down a familiar path, with incidents[1] neatly labelled and dated, but when I reach halfway memory lets go of my hand, and a fog rises and covers the faces and places, and I am left clawing about[2] in the dark, lost, and I have to make up the obscured[3] moments as I go along, make up the faces and places, even the emotions. Sometimes, to keep on course, I have to return to more recognizable landmarks, and then, with this safety net under me, I can leap onto less certain terrain.

So, yes, there was an accident, a fire. An explosion in the barn[4] with the oil drums[5]. The fire flew on the wind from house to house, and in a few minutes half the town was ablaze[6]. Many people died, including John's father. They say he died trying to save my sister, Boma, and if it wasn't for him, she'd have died. My father was imprisoned. He doesn't smoke any more since that day. My mother returned to her parents' village, where she still lives. And as my sister burned, and my family disintegrated[7], I was in Lagos[8] listening to lectures, eating dinner in Chinese restaurants and trying to solve the riddle of a mad rapist, and I didn't hear about the tragedy till I returned home with my journalism certificate.

No, it was not a pipeline accident, as I told the white man, as I wrote in my published piece[9]. But it might easily have been one, like in countless other villages. My father is still in prison, Boma and I still go to visit him, and each time he sees her face he turns away and his hands shake, and recently she has stopped going. My mother comes from the village once every month to see him. Occasionally

1 incident: event **2** claw about: search for one's way with one's hands **3** obscured: hidden in the dark **4** barn: building for keeping animals **5** oil drum: metal barrel for oil **6** ablaze: on fire **7** disintegrate: fall apart **8** Lagos: Nigeria's (and Africa's) largest city **9** piece: (here) text, article

I go with her, and I watch them look at each other, and sometimes they have a lot to talk about, and sometimes they just stare at each other in silence. The last time I went with her was over a month ago. I sat away from them, but I could hear what they were saying: she told him about her life in the village, the farm, how the harvest this year had been good. He listened, nodding his head, but all the time he stared at her, trying to catch her eye, but she avoided his eyes as she spoke. And she called to me, Rufus, come here. Why do you stand so far away by the window? The guard pretended to be reading his paper but he watched us all the time. I remember that the room smelled of the roasted peanuts my mother brought for my father. I remember that the guard had a bald spot. My mother looked thinner, darker.

The fog lifts as suddenly as it descended, and the sun shines brightly again, and once more I am on sure ground, but I know the fog can return again, get into memory's eyes, blinding it momentarily.

*

After a while the sky and the water and the dense foliage[1] on the river banks all looked the same: blue and green and blue-green misty[2]. The whole landscape was now a mere trick of light, vaporous[3] and shape-shifting[4], appearing and disappearing behind the fog. It was early morning, but already we had been in the boat for over two hours, leaving the sea and heading up a tributary[5], going west. Irikefe Island[6], also known as Half-Moon Island because of its distinct crescent-shaped[7] coastline, had long since disappeared, swallowed by the distance and the darkness cast by the mist that rose like smoke from the river banks. Mid-river the water was clear and

1 foliage: layers of leaves and branches **2** misty: foggy **3** vaporous: misty, foggy **4** shape-shifting: constantly changing its appearance **5** tributary: river feeding a larger river **6** Irikefe Island: fictional island in the Niger Delta
7 crescent-shaped: having a form like the moon shortly after new moon

mobile, but towards the banks it turned brackish and still, trapped by mangroves in whose branches the mist hung in clumps like cotton balls. Ahead of us the mist arched clear over[1] the water like a bridge. Sometimes, entering an especially narrow channel in the river, our light wooden canoe would be so enveloped in the dense grey stuff that we couldn't see each other as we glided silently over the water. I was wet and cold and hungry, and not for the first time I asked myself if going in search of the kidnapped British woman with Zaq was wise after all. This was our ninth day on her trail. The other journalists had long since returned to Port Harcourt[2], and I was sure the whole adventure – or rather misadventure – was now to them nothing but a memory, anecdotal currency to trade for a drink on a lazy day in the press clubroom.

Zaq dismissed[3] them with a wave of his hand. – That is the difference between great reporters and average ones.

He was no doubt one of the best this country ever produced, and because of that I respected his opinion, but right then I'd have settled for food, dry clothes and shelter over greatness, or opinion, for that matter.

– Tell me, Rufus my friend, what do we seek?

It wasn't a question, but I answered anyway.

– The woman, and the Professor.

– I said 'what', not 'whom'. Forget the woman and her kidnappers for a moment. What we really seek is not them but a greater meaning. Remember, the story is not always the final goal.

– Then what is?

– The meaning of the story, and only a lucky few ever discover that. But I think you know that instinctively, otherwise you wouldn't be here. Everything will turn out fine, you'll see.

His shirt was wet under the arms and at the back. He was still fighting the sudden fever that had dogged[4] him since we left Port

1 arch over sth.: cover sth. like an arch **2** Port Harcourt: one of the Niger Delta's largest cities **3** dismiss sth.: (here) drop a topic because it has no importance **4** dog sb.: follow sb. closely

Harcourt, and the more his health had deteriorated[1] the more he had taken to philosophizing over almost anything: a bat flying overhead, a dead fish on the oil-polluted water, a gathering of rain clouds in the clear sky. But I was glad his mind was still capable of philosophizing. The further we ventured into the forest, the more I found myself turning to him with questions. I had no idea what he meant about the story and its meaning, but perhaps I would find out before this trip was done. Right now my only hope was that he would continue to hold on till we were back in Port Harcourt, on dry land. Ultimately, things didn't turn out fine, as I hoped, and as he promised, especially for him, but then maybe he was talking not about himself but about me. He might have felt that he had drifted past a point in his river that was beyond return.

In the boat was a bag of dried fruit and a plastic bottle full of water, all of which the old man said were from the priest, Naman. Zaq took out his last bottle of whisky and, with a heavy sigh, opened it and sipped.

– Isn't it a bit too early?

– Never too early. Take a sip, Rufus. It'll keep you warm. I pushed away the bottle, almost knocking it out of his weak grip.

– Can't you wait till we're a bit surer of where we are? We could be lost, you know ...

– We'll be fine. The old man here will take care of us.

The old man smiled his big, encouraging smile, nodding his gnomish[2] head eagerly. Beside him his son was shrouded[3] in the dense smoke produced by the boat's outboard motor, his figure appearing and disappearing with the play of the wind on the mist. The boy looked no more than ten years old, but he might have been older, his growth stunted by poor diet. His hair was reddish and sparse[4], his arms were bony like his father's. They were both dressed in the same shapeless and faded homespun[5] shirts and trousers,

1 deteriorate: become worse **2** gnomish: small **3** shroud sb./sth. in sth.: wrap sb./sth. in sth., cover sb./sth. with sth. **4** sparse: *spärlich* **5** homespun (adj): (textile) produced at home

their hands looked rough and callused[1] from sea water, they smelled of fish and seemed as elemental as seaweed. They were wet from water spray coming off the sides of the boat. The boy saw me looking at him and returned my gaze[2] without self-consciousness, his eyes guileless[3] and full of curiosity, forcing me to turn away. We chugged along into the narrowing river, followed by the motor's droning roar.

– Do you know where the militants are?

– No, sah[4]. People say dem fit be[5] near Abakiri.

It was all guesswork. The militants always concealed[6] the locations of their camps, because their life depended on that, and on the ability to pick up their tents and move with the first hint of trouble from the federal patrols[7] that were in constant war with them. Whenever they invited the press to view hostages, or to give lengthy interviews about their reasons for fighting the government, they did so in a village or on a deserted[8] island far from their camps. What was certain, though, was that they always returned to the pipelines and oil rigs[9] and refineries[10], which they constantly threatened to blow up, thereby ensuring for themselves a steady livelihood. If the old man was able to take us to an actual camp, and if we were able to come back safely, we would be among the very few reporters who had done so. My instinct told me to get down at the next village and make my way back to Port Harcourt; to forget the white woman, because the militants would free her, eventually; to forget the perfect story, because there was no such thing as a perfect story anyway, and I already had enough paragraphs to make my editor welcome me with open arms; to forget Irikefe Island, where we had been holed up[11] for the past five days before the old man and his son came to get us; but, most importantly, to forget Zaq and his desperate, long-shot[12] ambitions. Let life continue as it once did: simple,

1 callused [ˈkæləst]: hardened **2** gaze (n): long and steady stare **3** guileless: having no bad intentions **4** sah (NP): Sir **5** dem fit be (NP): they can be **6** conceal sth.: hide sth. **7** federal patrols: federal police **8** deserted: left by everyone **9** oil rig: oil platform **10** oil refinery: construction for processing oil **11** hole up: hide, seek refuge **12** long-shot (adj): not very likely to succeed

predictable, full of its own myriad[1] concerns. But what journalist doesn't hunger for the perfect story, and this one, as Zaq explained, and I totally agreed, was as close to it as any reporter could ever get. The very thought of turning back made me realize how barren[2], how diminished, life would be after the excitement of the past few days, and as we went deeper and deeper upriver, and further and further away from the sea, I made no move to stop. I felt hope and doubt alternating in my chest. I felt a stirring of some hunger inside me, something I had never felt before, a conviction[3], almost, that I was meant to be here, on this boat, on this trail. It was like a breeze blowing through some long-forgotten section of my mind. I knew Zaq could see this stirring hope in my eyes; he could give it a name and describe how irresistible was its pull.

Far ahead, appearing suddenly out of the water, like a mirage[4], was a huge cliff with uneven steps cut into the rock face, leading up to a dense thicket[5] of trees that marked the beginning of a village. We left the boat and climbed up the tricky stone steps, stopping often to catch our breath.

– Who lives here?

The old man shrugged. – Nobody.

– Where did the people go?

– Dem left because of too much fighting.

The village looked as if a deadly epidemic had swept through it. A square concrete platform dominated the village centre like some sacrificial altar. Abandoned oil-drilling paraphernalia[6] was strewn around the platform; some appeared to be sprouting[7] out of widening cracks in the concrete, alongside thick clumps of grass. High up in the rusty rigging[8] wasps flew in and out of their nests. A weather-beaten signboard near the platform said: oil well no. 2. 1999. 15,000 metres. The houses began not too far away from the derelict[9] plat-

1 myriad (adj): many **2** barren: empty **3** conviction: strong belief **4** mirage: optical effect that lets people see things that are not there (often at sea or in the desert) **5** thicket: *Dickicht* **6** paraphernalia: articles of equipment **7** sprout (v): grow **8** rigging: (here) structure **9** derelict: left by everyone

form. We went from one squat[1] brick structure to the next, from compound[2] to compound, but they were all empty, with wide-open windows askew[3] on broken hinges[4], while overhead the roofs had big holes through which strong sunlight fell. Behind one of the houses we found a chicken pen with about ten chickens inside, all dead and decomposing, the maggots[5] trafficking beneath the feathers. We covered our noses and moved on to the next compound, but it wasn't much different: cooking pots stood open and empty on cold hearths; next to them stood water pots filled with water on whose surface mosquito larvae thickly flourished. It took less than an hour to traverse[6] the little village, going from one deserted household to the next, taking pictures, hoping to meet perhaps one accidental straggler[7], one survivor, one voice to interview.

We left. Zaq looked as if he was about to throw up, his face was sweaty, and he raised the bottle to his lips many times before the alertness returned to his eyes. We often stopped to rest, and the river grew narrower each time we set out again. Soon we were in a dense mangrove swamp; the water underneath us had turned foul and sulphurous[8]; insects rose from the surface in swarms to settle in a mobile cloud above us, biting our arms and faces and ears. The boy and the old man appeared to be oblivious to[9] the insects; they kept their eyes narrowed, focused on burrowing[10] the boat through the gnarled[11], hanging roots that grew out of the water like probosces[12] gasping for air. The atmosphere grew heavy with the suspended stench of dead matter. We followed a bend in the river and in front of us we saw dead birds draped over tree branches, their outstretched wings black and slick with oil; dead fishes bobbed white-bellied between tree roots.

1 squat (adj): low **2** compound (n): fenced-in or walled-in area with a group of buildings **3** askew: open **4** hinge [hɪndʒ] (n): piece of metal a window or a door is attached to so that it can be opened and closed **5** maggot: *Made* **6** traverse sth.: move through sth. **7** straggler: *Nachzügler* **8** sulphurous (BE): containing / smelling of sulphur (*Schwefel*) **9** oblivious to sth.: unaware of sth. **10** burrow sth. through sth.: (here) push sth. through sth. **11** gnarled (adj): twisted **12** proboscis (pl: probesces): long nose (e.g. of elephants)

The next village was almost a replica[1] of the last: the same empty squat dwellings, the same ripe and flagrant[2] stench[3], the barrenness, the oil slick, and the same indefinable sadness in the air, as if a community of ghosts were suspended above the punctured[4] zinc roofs, unwilling to depart, yet powerless to return. In the village centre we found the communal well. Eager for a drink, I bent under the wet, mossy pivotal beam and peered into the well's blackness, but a rank[5] smell wafted[6] from its hot depths and slapped my face; I reeled[7] away, my head aching from the encounter. Something organic, perhaps human, lay dead and decomposing down there, its stench mixed with that unmistakable smell of oil. At the other end of the village a little river trickled towards the big river where we had left our boat. The patch of grass growing by the water was suffocated by a film of oil, each blade covered with blotches[8] like the liver spots on a smoker's hands.

We felt drained just standing there, and so we left. We pushed the boat into deeper water and scrambled in. By now Zaq seemed to have lost even the energy – and the will – to lift the bottle to his mouth; it lay neglected by his feet, the piss-coloured liquid in it sloshing[9] back and forth with the movement of the boat. He sat with his hands spread wide on either side of his seat, holding on for dear life, and with each motion of the boat I waited for the vomit to come spewing out of his mouth, but somehow he kept it down.

– Do you want to stop at the next village?

– No, no more villages.

I felt tired and listless, and I wondered when the old man would stop and dig in his heels and demand to go back, but he said nothing, just kept going forward, deeper and deeper. In some places the river was so shallow and the swamp so thick we had to kill the motor and push the boat through, ignoring the cold dirty water that seeped into our shoes and shirts and trousers, and the foul smell

1 replica: copy **2** flagrant: (here) clearly perceptible **3** stench: unpleasant smell **4** punctured: containing holes **5** rank (adj): (here) smelling unpleasantly **6** waft: float **7** reel: *taumeln* **8** blotch: mark, spot **9** slosh: *schwappen*

that clung to our hair, and the itch on our grime-smeared[1] faces. When we came once more to open water, the old man turned the head of the boat and picked up speed. I did not ask where he was going, I only hoped that it was close by and inhabited.

– I get friend for next village. Na[2] good man. We go stop rest small, maybe we fit[3] sleep there tonight. Na good man.

– How far is it from here?

– Not too far, but e far small[4].

We were as soundless as a ghost ship, the roar of our motor muffled[5] by the saturated[6] air. Over the black, expressionless water there were no birds or fishes or other sea creatures – we were alone. When we arrived, a group of urchins[7] welcomed us with shouts and curious stares. We left the boy in charge of the boat and headed for the rust-red roofs that formed this tiny riverside village. After a few minutes the boy got out of the boat and joined the boys, who were now kicking an old and patchy leather ball in the sand. The old man led us down an open street that cut the village in two. On either side were similar box-like houses looking down on the central street with something like a sneer[8]. The houses seemed to belong more to the trees and forest behind them than they did to a domestic human settlement. Women and children stared out at us inquisitively[9], but they quickly closed their doors or turned to some task when we waved or called out to them. Now we were in front of a cluster of open sheds and huts and stalls separated from each other by narrow passages. Inside the sheds and huts and sometimes out in the passages, all sorts of consumer goods were displayed – from bath soaps and detergents[10] to tins of sardines nestling next to tins of milk and packs of biscuits; there were crates of Coca-Cola and Fanta on shelves and under tables; there were second-hand clothes,

1 grime: dirt **2** Na (NP): he is **3** fit (v, NP): can **4** e far small (NP): it is still a little far **5** muffle: drown out a noise, make inaudible **6** saturated: (here) full of humidity **7** urchin: small child in poor clothes **8** sneer (n): mocking grin **9** inquisitive: curious, nosy **10** detergent: chemical used for cleaning

radio batteries, plastic toys, and even roofing nails in broken packs. Loud-voiced women with grimy aprons round their wide waists stood in the middle of the sheds, scooping *garri*[1] from iron basins with measuring bowls and pouring it into plastic bags held by customers. This part of the village was so different from the one we had just passed that I wondered if we were still in the same village. The women called out to us as we passed, pointing to their wares to tempt us. The last shed in the cluster was a blacksmith's[2].

– Na my friend Karibi shop be dis.[3]

The old man went inside. Four men stood in a semicircle in a corner of the shed, talking in low voices. In the centre, squatting before a blazing hearth stocked with metal, was a young man who looked up at us briefly before returning to his chore[4]. The men stopped talking and one of them shook hands with the old man; the others nodded at him, then turned to look at us, their faces solemn[5]. The old man talked for a while with the man while the others listened and interjected[6] occasionally, their faces and gestures expressing deep perplexity; then he rejoined us looking troubled.

– Is that your friend?

– Yes. Him say[7] we must go. We no fit stay.[8]

– But we just got here. Is something wrong?

– Yes. Dem hear say soja de come[9] here today. Dem de come find am.

– Find him for what?

The old man shrugged and turned to look at the men in the shed. – Dem say he de[10] help de militants.

– So why isn't he hiding?

1 garri: West African food produced by grinding cassava (*Maniok*) **2** blacksmith: person who makes and repairs iron objects **3** Na my friend Karibi shop be dis (NP): This shop belongs to my friend Karibi. **4** chore: work, task **5** solemn ['sɒləm]: serious **6** interject: put in a remark in a conversation **7** Him say (NP): he says **8** We no fit (NP): we cannot **9** Dem hear say soja de come (NP): they heard that soldiers came **10** he de (NP): he did

– He say he de innocent so he no go run anywhere. Karibi na important man for dis[1] village. Very proud man.

We stood there, unsure what to do. I looked at Zaq. Clearly a newsworthy event was about to unfold and, rather than leaving, shouldn't I be getting my camera ready, and perhaps interviewing the man for some background? But before that thought could transform into action things began to happen. There was a loud noise as of stampeding[2] feet, dust rose and covered the tight passages and the stalls and sheds, people rushed down the passages, knocking down tables and entire sheds as they went. Then a single gunshot rang out. For a moment everyone froze. As I turned to ask the old man what was going on, a terrified market woman suddenly appeared in front of me, her eyes blinded by fear. The next minute I was flat on my back and her considerable mass was pinning me to the dusty ground, then she was up on her feet and away, agile, almost airborne[3]. Long afterwards I remembered her marketplace smell and her unseeing eyes above mine, and the moaning, terrified sound coming continuously from her mouth, a sound she was unaware she was making.

– They are here! The soldiers are here!

They came out of the sheds and houses and passages, wielding whips and guns, occasionally firing into the air to create more chaos. A man ran out of a hut and came face to face with a soldier; he raised his hands high in surrender as, in a single motion, the soldier reversed his rifle and swung the butt at the man's head. The man fell back into the doorway and the soldier moved on to another target. I was saved from a broken jaw, or a cracked skull, because I was still on the ground trying to regain my wind[4]. Karibi and his friends, now joined by his son, stood motionless, shoulder to shoulder, watching the pandemonium[5] unfolding towards them – like a wave that had started from far away in the sea and was now unstoppably headed

1 dis (NP): this **2** stampede (v): flee in panic **3** airborne: carried by air
4 wind: (here) breath **5** pandemonium: chaos

at them on the shore, gaining strength and fury as it came. Over ten soldiers surrounded the smithy[1], facing the silent, defiant[2] men. One of the soldiers, a sergeant, stepped into the shed and pointed his rifle at Karibi.

– You, come with us.

His men rushed forward and grabbed Karibi, who didn't struggle or say a word. The other men watched, glaring at the soldiers but saying nothing. They pinned his hands behind him and dragged him away through the wide village street. In the distance a woman wailed[3] at the top of her voice, calling to God over and over: Tamuno! Tamuno!

1 smithy: workshop of a blacksmith **2** defiant (adj): refusing to obey an authority **3** wail (v): cry

2

We left before the dust had finally settled. We went to the river bank with the villagers to watch the two speedboats that had brought the soldiers fly away over the water and out of sight. Karibi sat straight between two soldiers, his hands tied behind him, his face staring into the distant horizon. His son said he'd be taken to Port Harcourt, where he'd be tried and found guilty of fraternizing[1] with the militants.

– But he's innocent. Isn't he innocent?

My question to Zaq, even I knew, was futile[2]: how was he to know who was innocent and who wasn't, after all; hadn't we both just met the man for the first time today? But I couldn't get rid of the image of Karibi, stoic and defiant in the face of the threat from the soldiers – surely only an innocent man would be so unruffled[3], so confident?

Zaq looked at me and shrugged. – Guilty of what, and innocent of what? Some of the militants actually come from villages like this, so how can you stop these people from fraternizing with them?

The old man decided to take us to his own village. It was a bit out of our way, he said, but it was the only place we could be sure of food and lodging for the night. And Zaq definitely needed some sort of medical attention, or at least a long rest.

Night had fallen by the time we finally got there. It was an entire village on stilts[4], situated by the river on a vast mudflat[5], which at that moment was under water, so the village appeared to float; narrow passages of water divided one row of huts from the next, like streets. The houses were made from weepingwillow bamboos

1 fraternize with sb.: come into friendly contact with members of a hostile group
2 futile [ˈfjuːtaɪl]: senseless, not worth the effort **3** unruffled: calm, composed
4 stilt: *Stelze, Pfahl* **5** mudflat: muddy area that is regularly flooded by the river

and raffia palms and bits of zinc and plywood[1] and cloth and it seemed anything else the builders were able to lay their hands on. The whole scarecrow settlement looked as if the next strong wind or wave would blow it away. Dugout[2] canoes rested beneath the house floors; secured by jute ropes to the stilts, they tugged[3] at the restraints like horses. We floated silently between the houses, as figures in doorways and windows waved down to us; occasionally we caught the sound of laughter over the silence, and sometimes the sound of a radio, its static[4] strange and elemental in the desolate village. Finally, we came to a stop before one of the houses, which was larger than the others. A wooden ladder dangling[5] over the water led up to its front door.

– Wait here small. I dey come.

The old man left us and climbed up the ladder to the door. The boy remained with us in the boat, wordless, looking tired and sleepy. We didn't wait long before the old man reappeared. With him was a big man who waved down to us and called out in a loud friendly voice:

– Come in, come in.

We climbed the shaky ladder, placing each foot carefully, ready to grab at whatever was nearby to save ourselves if the steps gave out from under us. I went first and then dragged Zaq after me, his weight like a sack of sand behind me. The living room was surprisingly spacious, made more so by the absence of furniture and one large open window. The floor was covered with old straw mats on which we sank as if they were cushions of the softest down. The big man sat in the only chair in the room, an armchair by the window facing the veranda and the river outside.

– You are welcome to our village.

The old man stood between us and the man in the chair, making introductions.

1 plywood: *Sperrholz* **2** dugout (adj): (here) made by hollowing out a tree-trunk
3 tug sth. (v): pull sth. **4** static (n): *Rauschen* **5** dangle: hang loosely

– My brother, Chief Ibiram, de welcome[1] you. Na him be[2] the chief of this whole village. Na my brother for the same mother.

These na[3] my friends, dem be journalist. Na good people, das why[4] I bring dem here.

– You are welcome to our village.

Clearly the Chief wasn't a man of many words, but he appeared happy to be hosting us. I looked from the old man to his brother, trying to see a resemblance: there wasn't any. Our guide was grey, wiry and gnomish, whereas his brother was an impressive figure of a man, over six feet tall, and even seated he dominated the whole room, making everything else appear on a smaller scale. The introductions over, the old man sat down beside his brother. A radio, tuned to a station speaking a language I could not identify, played softly on a side table next to Chief Ibiram.

A door opened and a young girl came in with a lamp, which she set in the middle of the floor; only then did I notice that it had grown totally dark outside. She was about ten, and as she bent down to place the lamp she glanced at us furtively[5], and in the quick, shivering light I saw her surprisingly delicate features, her smooth ebony skin, the white of her eyes, the long black lashes – and then she was gone. Later, she returned with food on a tray: boiled cassava and fish with palm oil and ground pepper. The Chief came down from his chair and we ate together on the floor. I was sure it was the best food I had ever eaten; I kept staring at the door through which the girl had appeared and disappeared, hoping she'd return bearing more food.

Zaq did not eat. He sat away from us, his back propped up against the wall, and in the lamp light I could see the sweat on his forehead. But he did not complain. He sat, still and full of whisky, his back against the flimsy[6] straw wall, and soon he was snoring. Afterwards, the old man joined the Chief by the radio and they sat listening intently. All night long they listened. I'd wake up suddenly

1 de welcome (NP): he welcomes **2** Na him be (NP): he is **3** na (NP): are
4 das why (NP): that's why **5** furtive: secretive **6** flimsy: thin, unstable

and see them seated in the same position, listening as if the message coming out of the tiny world-receiver[1] was a matter of life and death. They talked – perhaps commenting on what was coming from the radio – in a mixture of pidgin English[2] and their language. I couldn't understand their words, but I imagined they were speaking of the dwindling[3] stocks[4] of fish in the river, the rising toxicity of the water, and how soon they might have to move to a place where the fishing was still fairly good. I listened in and out of sleep and I dreamed of the little girl with the burnished[5] skin.

*

It is dark. We are on the beach catching crabs to sell to the market women in the morning. We have done this every night, she and I, but tonight the sea is harsh, frothing and spitting, and overhead the skies open up as if in sympathy. We begin to run. Boma is five years older than me, and so faster and surer on her feet, and now I slip, and it is to save me that she jumps into the waves and pushes me onto the beach to safety. I am alone on the beach in the miraculous[6], malevolent[7] storm and my sister is in the dark, dark water, arms flailing[8], and I see only the white of her rough homespun dress rising and falling, and then she is gone and I am never ever going to see her again, and now I am in the river, trying to outrun its tumultuous rise and fall, to reach her and save her and say sorry for making her fall into the water. I leave the bucket of crabs overturned and the crabs scatter all over the place, seeking their holes beneath the rising and rising water. The waves, the waves, vicious, implacable, and they have taken my sister away. And for some reason she is not sad or

1 world-receiver: radio that receives stations from all over the world **2** pidgin English: language that developed from a mixture of a simplified form of English and a local language and is used as a lingua franca by people who do not speak each other's languages **3** dwindle: diminish, get less **4** stock: amount of animals in a certain area **5** burnished: having a golden-brown colour **6** miraculous: like a miracle, unexpected and extraordinary **7** malevolent [məˈlevələnt]: evil, (here) heavy **8** flail: move in an uncontrolled way

angry; she is just calm and she keeps repeating the same thing: you lucky, lucky boy. Always lucky from the day you were born. Nothing will ever harm you. Slow down, say father and mother, we can't understand a word you're saying. I keep repeating her name, Boma, Boma. She is gone. The waves have her. The whole village comes out with lamps, and the men go out in boats when the storm subsides. We find her the next day, on an outcrop[1] in the middle of the sea, the now all calm and demure[2] and wouldn't-drown-a-fly sea. She is beached on this square of dry land in the middle of the sea and she is asleep or unconscious, and the men put her in the boat and take her home and for a whole week she does nothing but sleep and spit out sea water.

*

I woke up, half asleep, and Zaq was standing over me. He looked rested: his eyes were clear and there was a smile on his lips.

– You were having a bad dream.

– Are we leaving? Where's the old man, and the boy? – They went fishing or catching crabs or whatever it is they do around here.

He sat down in Chief Ibiram's chair and fiddled with the radio controls, then looked at me and smiled. – Did you ever think that one day you'd visit a place like this when you became a reporter?

There was a jauntiness[3] to his voice, and a glitter to his smile, and he looked almost happy. Suddenly I recalled the first time I met him, almost five years ago, when he came to deliver the annual graduation lecture at the Ikeja[4] School of Journalism in Lagos. Having graduated at the top of my class, I had been chosen, with two others, to go to dinner with Zaq afterwards. The others were Linda, the prettiest girl in my set, and Tolu, the brainiest[5]. Tolu, like me, was a big fan of the great journalist, and I was sure somewhere in

1 outcrop: small higher area not covered by the water **2** demure (adj): reserved, shy, (here) calm **3** jauntiness: cheerfulness **4** Ikeja: city in the south of Nigeria **5** brainy: intelligent

her bag was a recorder and a little notebook with a long list of questions she wanted to ask him: questions about life after journalism school, about things to expect in the newsroom, about the best papers to send applications to, and, finally, whether he would mind being one of her referees[1], or perhaps doing a letter of introduction to one of the editors ... Besides being the brainiest student in my class, she was also the most aggressive, the most annoying and the least pretty, with sickly yellow eyes that had a disconcerting[2] way of looking at you without blinking.

We were in the back room of a Chinese restaurant in Ikeja; the girls were seated on both sides of Zaq. Linda giggled as she poured more red wine into his glass, contriving[3] to thrust her remarkable chest into his face as she did so. I was across the table, and on my left were my two lecturers, Ms Ronke and Mr Malik. Their hands, I could see clearly, were in each other's crotches under the table. And the night was just starting. A light in a red lampshade hung above the aisle to our left, throwing a funereal[4] glow onto our table. We were all desperately trying to engage Zaq in conversation, but at the moment he seemed more focused on getting wasted[5]. We had been there less than an hour, and while we waited for our order he had finished a bottle of Shiraz[6] by himself; a second bottle, which he had started with the food, stood half empty before him. His Kungpao chicken, beside the bottle of wine, was still untouched. Tolu, all the time glaring[7] at the flirty Linda, cleared her throat.

– Don't you like the food, Mr Zaq?

– Zaq is my first name, actually.

– Oh, so sorry, Mr ...

– It's also my last name. I've had only one name since I became a journalist. And that was a long time ago.

1 referee: (here) sb. who endorses a job application **2** disconcerting: confusing, making people feel uneasy **3** contrive to do sth.: make an effort to do sth.
4 funereal [fjuˈnɪəriəl] (adj): suitable for a funeral **5** wasted (infml): drunk
6 Shiraz: red wine **7** glare at sb.: stare at sb. with a hostile look

Tolu fell back. As the evening wore on and her frustration mounted, I began to feel sorry for her. Zaq raised his full glass, waving it as he leaned forward and sideways towards Ms Ronke, turning his back on Tolu.

– Here's a riddle. A mad man escapes from an institution. He crosses a river and comes across some washerwomen, he rapes them, well, not all of them, as that mightn't really be possible ...

Ms Ronke winked at him, pushing aside a lick of hair from her wig – Surely that'd depend on how ... talented he was?

Ms Ronke had worked with Zaq on one of the Lagos newspapers a long time ago. She had practised journalism for more than ten years before turning to lecturing and she could hold her own with any man in anything, bawdy jokes included. Linda giggled. Tolu glared at her and cleared her throat.

– Surely, Zaq ... sir, the subject of rape is a sensitive one, most women wouldn't see the joke in ... I mean ...

Zaq nodded. – I agree with you, but remember, as a reporter you'll come across worse things out there. Now, as I was saying, this well-equipped and talented lunatic rapes all the washer women and runs away. Now, here's the question. Say you were a journalist covering the rape; your story is written, and you want a headline. And there's no sub-editor to help you out on this one. The headline has to be witty, truthful, intriguing[1], compelling[2] and with some literary appeal. What would it be? Tolu stabbed her food with her fork, not looking up. I sipped my drink and went first.

– 'Beware: Dangerous lunatic on the loose[3]'.

Zaq inclined his head. – Scary, not witty enough. Next. Ronke, give it a try.

– How about: 'Mad rapist coming your way'.

Malik raised his hand in surrender, laughing. – I'll pass. Zaq, why don't you tell us?

1 intriguing: fascinating **2** compelling: captivating **3** on the loose (infml): escaped, on the run

But Linda jumped in eagerly, putting a hand on Zaq's arm, batting her eyes at him.

– Wait. Me, me. I'll try: 'Dangerous escaped lunatic and rapist on the loose. Beware'.

– Too long. Too repetitive. And where's the aesthetic, where's the wit? By the way, Folu, this is a real story. It actually happened.

– Tolu.

– Right. Tolu. Want a go[1]?

Tolu sipped her drink and refused to speak. Linda giggled and leaned heavily against Zaq. She had had only a single glass of wine and already her eyes were dim and her words were becoming indistinct. Zaq placed both elbows on the table and clutched his glass in one hand, his voice falling low like that of a coach giving a pep talk[2].

– First of all, you couldn't get the answer because the perfect headline is never thought up; it's given to you. An inspiration. A revelation. You can make up a great headline by trying, but not a perfect one. The perfect one always comes to you after you've already published your story. Always too late. Now this guy was lucky: it came to him when he needed it.

– Come on, Zaq. Tell us.

– 'Loose nut[3] screws[4] washers and bolts[5]!' Ha ha! How about that?

*

Now, sitting in Chief Ibiram's front room, far away from Ikeja and Chinese restaurants, I wondered where Tolu was. She had been voted most likely to be famous by our classmates, and one day, I was sure, I'd turn on the TV and see her breaking some major news story, or I'd come across her byline[6] in one of the Lagos newspapers under the most interesting story of the year. Five years had passed,

1 go (n, infml): try **2** pep talk (infml): encouraging speech before a play **3** nut (n, derog): crazy person; (also) *Mutter (zu einer Schraube)* **4** screw sb. (sl): have sex with sb.; (also n) *Schraube* **5** bolt (v, infml): flee, run away; (also n) *Riegel* **6** byline: line that indicates the author of a newspaper article

and in those five years I had followed Zaq's progress in the papers, but I hadn't seen him again, not until now, not until this assignment.

*

I clearly saw images from that evening rise up before me as if popping out of the flooded and barren mudflats outside. I saw the oversized plastic bracelet on Ms Ronke's venous wrist, the gaudy playing-card patterns on Mr Malik's tie, the hair-fringed mole on the pale cheek of the Chinese restaurateur as he bent over our table and whispered solicitously[1], You lika food? More wine, yes? Halfway through the meal Zaq slumped[2] forward and passed out[3], his face missing his plate by inches but knocking down the empty wineglass. Mr Malik and I lifted him up under the arms, and while the girls got their things we took him out and sat him on a bench by the roadside, hoping the air would revive him, but after the air-conditioned restaurant the atmosphere outside was heavy and humid, plastering a thin sheen[4] of sweat on our skin. Mr Malik took off his jacket and waved it back and forth over Zaq's snoring face, his garish[5] tie swinging from his neck with each movement.

– Now, how do we get him back to his hotel room?

None of us had a car.

A Molue bus[6] stopped by the kerb[7] and the passengers got off it like somnambulists[8], their steps leaden, their heads bowed, their faces dull and expressionless. They bumped into each other as they milled about confusedly for a while, and then they began to veer off singly into the dark side streets, the glow from an *akara*[9] woman's fire throwing their shadows in front of them, long and blurred and ominous. Linda looked a bit sullen[10], perhaps unhappy at losing the

1 solicitous: anxious, worried **2** slump (v): fall **3** pass out (infml): become unconscious **4** sheen (n): shimmer **5** garish (adj): very colourful, drawing attention **6** Molue bus: big yellow bus used for public transport in Lagos **7** kerb (BE, AE: curb): *Bordstein* **8** somnambulist: sleepwalker **9** akara: Nigerian dish made from beans usu. eaten for breaktfast **10** sullen: in a bad mood

chance to share the great Zaq's bed. Tolu yawned and looked at her watch, holding her bag tightly to her flat chest, eager to leave. But for me the night was just about to begin, as I foolishly volunteered to take Zaq back to his hotel room. He vomited all over the back seat of the taxi, and the angry driver threw us out after taking his money. We stood by the roadside and watched the taxi's red back light screaming its anger at us. Then we walked for what seemed like hours through dark and narrow alleyways, Zaq's arm on my shoulder, his weight resting on my side, and it was all I could do to walk without falling. We staggered[1] from one side of a nameless backstreet to another, often unable to avoid stepping into the open gutters[2] that overflowed with the city's filth; we passed half-lit doorways where ageing prostitutes called out to us in hoarse[3] voices that lacked all persuasiveness; we passed a group of idle[4] young men who stared long and hard at us, then followed us for about a block before finally deciding we weren't worth robbing. When I couldn't bear Zaq's weight any longer, I let him slide like a sack off my shoulder. He sank to the ground in slow motion and sat hunched over[5], his face buried in his knees, his back curved. And we remained like that for a long time, side by side on the kerb, the night around us like a blanket, only lifting when an occasional bus full of passengers roared past. Then, when I thought Zaq had fallen asleep, he spoke, his voice coming to me clearly.

– Bar Beach[6].

– What?

– We're at Bar Beach. Right behind us. You can smell the water.

I stood up and turned, and there behind the rudimentary fence running beside the road was the white sand glowing in the dark, and the foamy water washing over the sand. For a while the fresh sea air had been blowing right at us, but I had been too tired to notice. Once more I put his arm over my shoulder and we staggered to the

1 stagger: move unsteadily **2** gutter: *Rinnstein* **3** hoarse: sounding rough **4** idle: with nothing to do **5** hunch over: bend over **6** Bar Beach: popular beach on Lagos' Victoria Island

noisy, crowded beach. I paid the predatory youths at the improvised gate and we went in. I spread Zaq out on the sand where the water would not reach us and, laying side by side, we immediately fell asleep. In the morning he woke me up and pointed eastwards to the huge red sun emerging out of the blue water.

– Beautiful.

– Yes, beautiful.

All around us were people sprawled out on the beach: drunks slowly waking up to their hangovers; vagabonds and lunatics exhausted from their motiveless prowling[1]; lovers who couldn't afford a hotel room for the night. I was twenty. Yesterday I had graduated from the School of Journalism, and, instead of heading off home to Port Harcourt, I had stayed to listen to Zaq's lecture, seeking inspiration. The truth was that I had no plans, no job waiting for me. My ultimate ambition was of course to become like Zaq someday: to be respected all over the country for my strong liberal views, and to write editorials[2] that would be read with awe. But hanging out with him last night had brought no enlightenment as to how to realize my ambition. He gave me his number before we parted, and in that I had at least achieved more than Tolu. I thanked him and turned to go.

– What's your name?

– Rufus.

– Rufus, you have the patience to make a great reporter someday.

I watched him head for one of the makeshift[3] bars, where a few early clients were trying the hair-of-the-dog cure[4]. Or they may have been clients from the previous night finishing up their last orders. He sat down and beckoned[5] to the barman.

1 prowl (v): walk around aimlessly **2** editorial: *Leitartikel* **3** makeshift: built from assorted materials for temporary use **4** hair-of-the-dog cure (infml): drinking more alcohol to fight a hangover **5** beckon to sb.: make a sign to sb. by nodding or waving

*

To kill time I updated my reporter's notebook, as I had done without fail every morning since the day we started on the white woman's trail. I sat against the wall, and while Zaq fiddled absently with Chief Ibiram's radio I wrote down all that I had witnessed since we left Irikefe yesterday: the abandoned villages, the hopeless landscape, the gas flares that always burned in the distance. I re-created with as much detail as I could the brutal taking of Karibi, and, as I wrote, his son's words came back to me: *He'll be taken to Port Harcourt, where he'll be tried and found guilty of fraternizing with the militants.*

Zaq fell asleep in the chair. I was hungry and, since it didn't look like anyone was coming soon to offer us food, I decided to do some scouting[1]. I got up and opened the door through which the girl had appeared yesterday with the lamp and food. I found myself on a half-exposed walkway that connected the front room to other areas of the house, presumably the kitchen and the storage rooms. From here I could see the other houses, and I could hear voices of children and women. The women were standing in an open shed around a hearth, probably smoking[2] fish. The smoke from the hearth rose through the shed's thatch roof[3] and dissipated[4] in the dull, cloudy skies. I opened the first door on my right and saw a group of children, about five of them, all about the same age, seated around an old woman. She was telling them a story. They looked up at me, and my shadow fell on the floor before them as I stood in the half-open doorway, trying to see into the dark room.

I withdrew and went to another door, and this time I was in the right place. It was the kitchen, but, apart from a few pots and pans resting on a smoke-blackened table, it was empty. In a corner was a water pot with a plastic cup hanging from a string over it. I drank, but as I turned to go the old woman entered and stood just inside the doorway, but without blocking it.

1 scout (v): *auskundschaften* **2** smoke (v): (here) preserve with smoke **3** thatch roof: *Strohdach* **4** dissipate: disappear slowly

– Hello, I'm looking for the old man ... and the boy. We came together yesterday. And ... food ...

She kept nodding as I spoke, a friendly smile on her lined[1] face, and as she nodded she repeated the same word, yes. She probably couldn't understand me, and because I didn't speak the local language I simply mimed eating – putting my right hand to my mouth.

– Food, please.

She laughed, nodding her understanding.

– Yes, yes.

She brought me a bowl full of rice porridge – it was warm and sickly sweet and filling. She stood by the door and watched me eat, nodding and smiling all the time. Through the open door behind her came the voices of the children in the back. When I asked her when the men would be back, she said nothing but kept smiling and bowing and moving backwards until she was out of the door. Afterwards, I walked out into the mudflats. I spent the next hour walking in an ankle-high flood, my trousers rolled up to my knees, taking pictures of the houses. Most of the houses were empty, the men out fishing and the women smoking fish in the shed I'd seen earlier. I went to the shed last. The older women stared into the camera lens silently, their tired, lined faces neither acknowledging nor forbidding my action; the younger women giggled self-consciously, hastily wiping the ash and sweat from their faces with the edges of their wrappers[2]; the children ran forward and posed with hands on their waists, pushing each other out of the way.

While I was on my way back to Chief Ibiram's front room, the men returned. I passed them hauling[3] their canoes out of the shallow water and tying them to the house stilts; others carried the day's catch in plastic buckets and wicker[4] baskets, and, from what I could see, it wasn't bountiful[5]. The boy and the girl took from the boat a basket with a handful of thin wiggling fishes at the bottom. The kids stopped on the veranda when they saw me, waiting for me to speak,

1 lined: wrinkled **2** wrapper: cloth worn around the waist and legs **3** haul (v): pull **4** wicker: *Korbgeflecht* **5** bountiful: plenty

standing side by side with the basket on the floor between them, and behind them the sun was huge and dying, spilling orange and red and rust on the shallow river and the mangroves.

– Smile.

They smiled. I clicked. I wanted to talk to them, but I couldn't think of anything to say. I had known the boy for a couple of days now, and in that time I had never heard him say much, only answers to his father's questions or commands, and mostly they never talked at all; each seemed to have an instinctive understanding of what the other wanted.

– When I was a boy, me and my sister, we used to catch crabs. They looked at each other. – No crabs here now. The water is not good.

The girl, whose name was Alali, was more willing to talk. The boy only nodded with his head lowered, a fixed smile on his lips. I wanted to tell them about my childhood in a village not too far away from here. I realized how very much like theirs my childhood must have been. Barefoot and underfed we may have been, but yet the sea was just outside our door, constantly bringing surprises, suggesting a certain possibility to our lives. Boma and I used to spend the whole night by the water, catching crabs, armed with sticks and basket, our hands covered in old rags to protect our fingers from the scissor-sharp claws. We usually sold our catch to the market women, but sometimes, to make more money, we took the ferry to Port Harcourt to sell to the restaurants by the seafront. That was how we paid our school fees when our father lost his job.

*

Zaq was trying hard to hide his annoyance, and he wasn't succeeding.

– You should have told us you were going to be out all day. We've wasted a whole day now. I thought your job was to be our guide, we hired you.

We were in the veranda; Chief Ibiram was inside somewhere, taking a bath. Technically, we hadn't hired the old man; he had simply appeared out of the night and become our guide, he and his son. But I understood Zaq's anger, because I felt it too. But mine wasn't directed at the old man; rather, it came from a feeling of frustration and general irritability at the way things had been going since we started on the trail of the kidnapped woman. Events were always a step ahead of us, as if Eshu the trickster[1] god was out to play with us. Zaq's anger was intensified by his strange fever, and the continuous ache from his swelling legs. The booze[2] had helped to dull the pain, but now that the booze was finished, the pain kept him constantly on edge. The old man looked close to tears; he glanced towards me helplessly, waving his hands.

– You no well sir, tha's why. I think say you go stop here rest small before we go. Tha's why ...

But Zaq's anger disappeared as suddenly as it had appeared. He lowered his voice and turned to go into the house. – We really must set out early tomorrow. First thing in the morning.

– Yes. Yes, sir. Early morning, tomorrow.

That night I listened to Zaq turning and moaning and cursing on the mat beside me, all night long battling his pain and his demons.

1 trickster: person who deceives people and plays tricks on them **2** booze [bu:z] (infml) : alcohol, liquor

3

Towards morning, sitting side by side, both of us having given up on sleep, I asked Zaq how he ended up on this assignment.

– They came to my office. It was just another dull day at work, and, believe me, setting out on an expedition after some kidnapped woman was the furthest thing from my mind.

His editor, Beke Johnson, who was also the *Daily Star*'s owner, walked into his office, his face nervous with excitement, and told him two men wanted to see him. Two white men.

Zaq recognized the husband immediately. He had seen his face alongside his wife's in the papers and on TV for the past few days. Oil-company worker, British, petrol engineer; his wife had gone out by herself and she never came back, believed to have been kidnapped by the militants. The kidnapping was of some interest to Zaq because only the day before he had written an editorial on another kidnapping, that of a seventy-year-old woman and a three-year-old girl. They'd been kidnapped for ransom[1] by militants. He titled the editorial 'Gangsters or Freedom Fighters?'

– I'm an avid[2] reader of your column.

The man stepped forward and offered Zaq his hand. Zaq looked at the hand as though unsure what to do with it, his eyes blinking in the strong light coming in through the open windows, then he stuck out his own pudgy[3] hand and shook it. He was badly hung-over[4] and his breath left his corpulent frame[5] in a heaving, gasping motion. Beke Johnson hovered[6] behind his desk, urging the visitors to please sit down, please sit down. His rumpled suit and tie, the wolfish smile

1 ransom: money paid to kidnappers in exchange for releasing the hostage(s)
2 avid: (here) enthusiastic **3** pudgy: a bit fat **4** be hung-over: have a hangover
5 frame (n): (here) body **6** hover: (here) wait without moving

on his fat face, added to Zaq's headache and he felt like reaching out and covering the smile with his hand.

The other visitor remained standing, looking out through the open window, as if to avoid a bad smell in the narrow room. Zaq took in[1] the black nondescript[2] suit, the blue shirt, the black-and-white striped tie, the well-polished black shoes: diplomatic service, most likely security section. He must have been the handler, there to make sure the husband didn't betray the famous stiff-upper-lip tradition[3].

– You want to see me?

Zaq stood with his hands clasped before him, trying not to scratch at his stubbled chin. His eyes were red and teary from gazing all day into the computer screen, his lips were parched[4], cracked.

– I am –

– I know who you are. You're in the news. What can I do for you?

The husband sighed. His eyes went to the other man, who nodded and spoke directly to Zaq.

– Well, you already know about the kidnapping, so we won't go into all that. James here is a great admirer of your writing, and it was his idea that we come to you and ask you to go with a few other journalists to confirm that his wife is still alive. We need to know that before commencing[5] with the ransom negotiation.

Zaq turned to James, waiting for him to assent. James's eyes were baggy and red, his white shirt rumpled; he had the look of a desperate man, ready to try anything in the hope of getting his wife back.

– What good will that do? There's nothing I can bring back the other reporters can't.

– I know, but I think you understand more than the others what's at stake here. Please. Listen, I feel I can trust you, though

1 take in sth.: (here) perceive sth. **2** nondescript (AE): without any special qualities **3** stiff-upper-lip tradition: traditional British attitude which consists in keeping calm and not showing one's feelings in a difficult situation
4 parched: very dry **5** commence with sth. (fml): start (with) sth.

we've never met before. I went to Leeds University, same as you ... I hope that means something to you ...

– I'm just a desk journalist. I haven't done anything like this in a long time. I'm sorry. I'm sorry for your situation, but I can't help ... I'm sure she's safe. She'll be returned safely to you. They won't harm her, they never do ...

Black Suit gave James a look that urged him towards the door, indicating that their presence here had been a bad idea in the first place and that it was time to go. But James continued speaking, his eyes on Zaq. – I wish I could go myself, and I would, but my people think it's a bad idea, I'd only end up providing them with a second hostage.

– Well, Zaq, what do you say?

Beke came and laid a fat hand on Zaq's shoulder. Zaq was looking at the dirty carpet. It had patterns of green and red interlocking squares on it, but the squares were now faded, ground into loose ribbons and threads by countless washings, and footsteps, and something else, a kind of despair, a lack of the energy needed for holding on, for persevering. The chairs and tables and filing cabinets[1] had the same look, as did the faces and shoulders of his fellow reporters when they came in off the crowded buses and the merciless streets early in the morning. He had seen it on faces coming off the buses in Lagos and Abuja[2] and Kano[3] and Ibadan[4]: a drugged, let-me-just-get-through-the-day look. He continued to stare at the carpet, for what was the point of meeting the visitors' eyes if he couldn't be of help?

Now Black Suit and James were at the door. Black Suit pulled it open.

– Gentlemen, thanks for your time. This visit must remain between us ...

1 filing cabinet: piece of furniture used to store documents **2** Abuja: capital of Nigeria **3** Kano: capital of Kano State in North West Nigeria **4** Ibadan: capital of Oyo State in West Nigeria

Zaq said it was the tone of the man's voice that made him look up. The voice was dismissive[1], almost derisive[2]. And he felt what he hadn't felt in a long time: pride, vanity – two things he had always tried to avoid because they had no place in a reporter's life.

– I'll go. I'll do it.

The men stopped at the door. James shook off his companion's hand, turned back and took Zaq's hand. He brought out a photograph from his pocket. She was a pretty woman, her hair a unique mixture of red and brunette, and in the picture she looked young, carefree, smiling confidently into the camera. Zaq guessed it must have been taken when she was younger, perhaps at university.

– How old is your wife?

– Thirty-nine. Her name is Isabel. She also went to Leeds.

Zaq nodded, staring at the picture. He saw no point in telling James that he had only gone to Leeds for a six-month journalism certificate course. He had never gone to university – he was an autodidact[3], everything he knew he had learned in the newsroom and on the streets and from books, but what he knew he knew well. He could quote from Aristotle[4] and Plato[5] and Tolstoy[6] and Shakespeare and Soyinka[7] and Fanon[8] and Mandela[9] and Gandhi[10] and Dante[11] in a conversation, casually, perfectly.

– So far we've had over a dozen ransom demands by different groups: the Black Belts of Justice, the Free Delta Army, and the –

– The AK-47 Freedom Fighters.[12]

– It's all so confusing. This is a chance to make contact with the real kidnappers. We'll negotiate, as long as she's alive, we'll pay ...

1 dismissive: disrespectful **2** derisive: mocking **3** autodidact: self-taught person **4** Aristotle (384–322 BC): ancient Greek philosopher **5** Plato (428/427 or 424/423–348/347 BC): ancient Greek philosopher **6** Leo Tolstoy (1828–1910): Russian writer **7** Wole Soyinka (born 1934): Nigerian playwright, poet and essayist **8** Frantz Fanon (1925–1961): Martiniquais-French psychiatrist and political philosopher **9** Nelson Mandela (1918–2013): South African political leader **10** Mahatma Gandhi (1869–1948): Indian political activist **11** Dante (1265–1321): Italian poet and philosopher **12** Black Belts of Justice, Free Delta Army, AK-47 Freedom Fighters: militant groups active in the Niger Delta

– How do you know this group is the real one? Do they have a name?

– No name. Here's their letter: no signature. In the letter was some of her hair: I know her hair, it's really distinctive. There's a request for five million dollars. They want us to send five reporters to confirm she is alive and well.

– Very professional.

– There's something more.

– Yes?

– Her driver, Salomon: we believe he's had a hand in this. He hasn't been to work since the day she disappeared.

– Did they go out together?

– No. But we can't find him.

Black Suit, at last wiping the surprise off his ruddy[1] face, stepped forward.

– Your job is simple. Just confirm she's alive, take pictures, etc., and we'll take it from there. It should be easy. You leave in two days, early, and by sundown you're back. Of course we're willing to remunerate[2] you quite decently for your trouble. And remember, make them understand that nothing must happen to her. She's a British citizen –

Zaq interrupted him, not raising his gaze from the picture.

– So, does that make her more important than if she were, say, Nepalese, or Guyanese, or Greek?

The man made to open his mouth, but the husband spoke first. – Simon, old chap, let me handle this.

After the men left, Beke went over to Zaq and shook his hand, patting him on the back at the same time.

– This is it, Zaq. Our big opportunity. Don't forget to take our subscription[3] form when next you meet them.

– Come on, Beke. The man's wife has been kidnapped.

1 ruddy: red **2** remunerate sb. (fml): pay sb. **3** subscription: *Abonnement*

– But, still, an opportunity is an opportunity. How often does the oil company come knocking on your door, asking for a favour? We're talking petro-dollars[1] here, and a major scoop[2]! Come on. I can imagine the headlines already. This will be the making[3] of us. Our circulation[4] will hit the roof –

– But first I have to survive the little trip to the kidnappers' den, wherever it may be.

– Well, yes. Everything will go well. God willing. They don't harm reporters.

– What about those two reporters, shot in the back on a similar assignment just weeks ago? You have a short memory. Or would you like to go in my place?

You can handle it, Zaq. You've been in worse spots.

– I'm already regretting this decision.

Beke led Zaq back to his tiny windowless office and stood at the door watching as Zaq cleared his table and picked up his jacket.

– You're not going home, are you? The day's still young. Who's going to write the editorial, the Metro column, the book review?

Zaq brushed past him. – Why don't you write them yourself, just for a change?

And that, he said, was how he was recruited.

*

Early next morning, before we left Chief Ibiram's house, I took the old man to one side and asked him if we needed to pay his brother for our board[5]. The money would come out of our expense account anyway, and the Chief had been a perfect host.

He hesitated, then he shook his round, hairless head.

– No, no pay. Na my brother, Chief Ibiram.

1 petro-dollars: money made in the oil industry **2** scoop (n, infml): important news story published before any other newspaper has access to it **3** be the making of sb.: be sb.'s breakthrough to success **4** circulation: number of sold copies of a newspaper **5** board: (here) accommodation

Last night, when we urged him to ask his brother if he had heard anything of the missing woman, or if he knew where we could make contact with the militants, he had shaken his head and said 'no' without the usual diffidence[1] to his voice. I guess he didn't want to get his family involved in our quest for the militants, and if what happened to Karibi was an indication of what also happened to informers, then I respected his decision. Communities like this had borne the brunt[2] of the oil wars, caught between the militants and the military, and the only way they could avoid being crushed out of existence was to pretend to be deaf and dumb and blind.

We got Zaq into the boat with the help of the Chief and we drifted almost aimlessly on the opaque, misty water. The water took on a million different forms as we glided on it. Sometimes it was a snake, twisting and fast and slippery, poisonous. Sometimes it was an old jute rope, frayed[3] and wobbly[4] and breaking into jagged, feathery ends, the fresh water abruptly replaced by a thick marshy[5] tract[6] of mangroves standing over still, brackish[7] water that lapped at the adventitious[8] roots. Then we'd have to push the boat, or carry its dead weight on our shoulders till we found the rope again. Sometimes it was an arrow, straight and unerring[9], taking us on its tip for miles and miles, the foul smell of the swamps replaced by the musky[10], energizing river smell, and at such times we'd become aware of the clear sky above as if for the first time. But the swamps and the mist always returned, and strange objects would float past us: a piece of cloth, a rolling log[11], a dead fowl[12], a bloated[13] dog belly up with black birds perching[14] on it, their expressionless eyes blinking rapidly, their sharp beaks savagely[15] cutting into the soft decaying flesh. Once we saw a human arm severed at the elbow bobbing away from us, its fingers opening and closing, beckoning. In my dreams

1 diffidence: modesty, humility **2** bear the brunt of sth.: be most impacted by sth. **3** frayed: shredded at the ends **4** wobbly: shaky, unsteady **5** marshy: swampy **6** tract: (here) area **7** brackish: dirty, muddy **8** adventitious: (here) growing out of the ground **9** unerring: sticking to its course **10** musky: smelling of musk (*Moschus*) **11** log: bulky piece of wood **12** fowl: chicken **13** bloated: *aufgedunsen* **14** perch: sit **15** savage: wild, violent

I still see that lone arm, floating away, sometimes with its middle finger extended derisively, before disappearing into the dark mist.

About an hour after we set out our engine spluttered, spewed out a thick clump of black smoke and went quiet. The old man and his son fiddled with the engine and attempted to restart it, but finally they gave up and we took turns rowing with oars. We rested by the river bank whenever we could, and by the time we got to the next village the sun was going down and we left the boat on the deserted beach and went to look for shelter for the night.

It turned out this wasn't a village at all. It looked like a setting for a sci-fi movie: the meagre[1] landscape was covered in pipelines flying in all directions, sprouting from the evil-smelling, oil-fecund[2] earth. The pipes criss-crossed[3] and interconnected endlessly all over the eerie[4] field. We walked inland, ducking under or hopping over the giant pipes, our shoes and trousers turning black with oil. The old man took me to the edge of the field and pointed into the distance. Zaq joined us.

– Oil rigs.

– So why haven't the militants bombed the pipelines here?

– Because the oil companies pay them not to do so.

– Or perhaps the oil companies pay the soldiers to keep the militants away.

– Or that. Yes.

We spent the night by the water, fighting off insects, unable to fall asleep till early morning, when the bright sun chased them away. When I opened my eyes the old man was talking to Zaq. They were standing near the water's edge. The boy was seated in the wet sand, idly picking up pebbles[5] and throwing them at the boat, listening to the dull wooden sound as they hit, pausing once in a while to glance back at his father. I stood up and stretched. The old man shouted

1 meagre: (here) without much vegetation **2** oil-fecund: (here) soaked with oil **3** criss-cross (v): be arranged like lines repeatedly crossing each other **4** eerie: mysterious, frightening **5** pebble: small stone

something at the boy, apparently telling him not to throw stones at the boat, for he ceased[1] immediately, lowering his head, but a moment later, like a sleepwalker, he picked up another pebble and weakly threw it, but this time into the water, where it landed with a tiny plop. I wondered what the old man was telling Zaq. He wasn't looking into Zaq's eyes but at the ground, rooting in the sand with his bare, gnarled toe, waving his hand occasionally to expatiate[2] on a point, and once he pointed at me. Zaq was not speaking; he was gazing at the boy, a sort of doubtful, surprised look on his face. I turned away from them. If they wanted me involved in whatever it was they were discussing, Zaq would let me know. But, even as I turned away, Zaq called out:

– Rufus, you'd better come and hear this.

He didn't sound worried, but he didn't sound cheerful either. Whatever it was it couldn't be worse than this barren landscape, or our aimless search, which was becoming as murky[3] as the convoluted[4] water over which our tiny vessel bobbed[5] and shook, as if impatient to be gone from here.

– He wants us to take the boy with us.

I looked at Zaq. – What do you mean, take the boy?

The old man nodded at every word we uttered, as if by doing so his meaning would become clearer to me.

– He wants us to take the boy with us when we go back to Port Harcourt. You better tell him yourself, old man.

– Yes. He no get good future here. Na good boy, very sharp[6]. He go help you and your wife with any work, any work at all, and you too you go send am go school.

– But neither of us is married. We can't take him to Port Harcourt just like that.

1 cease (v): stop **2** expatiate on sth.: talk about sth. at length **3** murky: difficult to see through **4** convoluted: (here) stirred up, swirled up **5** bob (v): move up and down **6** sharp: smart

– But see, wetin he go[1] do here? Nothing. No fish for river, nothing. I fear say soon him go join the militants, and I no wan that. Na good boy. I swear, you go like am. Intelligent. Im fit learn trade[2], or driver. Anything. Na intelligent boy, im fit read and write already even though him school don close down[3], but im still remember how to read and write. Come here!

The boy stood up and ran to us, looking at his father expectantly. He knew what was being discussed. His father must have primed[4] him for this, and now it was his turn to join the pitch[5].

– Write your name.

The boy fell to his knees and quickly cleared away the twigs and dead grass from the brown scorched[6] earth at our feet, then he wrote out the letters of his name: m-i-c-h-a-e-l. Seeing the proud smile on his face as he looked up at his father, expecting a word of approval for having done his part, I realized that all this while I hadn't even known the boy's name, or his father's. They were just the old man and his son, guiding us in these waters that they depended upon for their livelihood, daily throwing in a line[7] and hoping, always hoping, that something would bite. I felt ashamed. The look on Zaq's face mirrored mine. He patted the boy on the head.

– Hello, Michael. My name is Zaq.

– And I'm Rufus.

I shook the old man's hand. There was a smile on his face, similar to the boy's as he had finished writing.

– My name na Tamuno, but people call me Papa Michael.

Zaq took me to one side. – What do we do?

– We say no, of course. Unless you want to take him with you.

– But where, how? I live in a single room. At the end of the month I'm hardly able to pay my rent. Of course he could stay with

1 wetin he go (NP): what is he going to **2** Im fit learn trade (NP): He is fit/able to learn a trade **3** him school don close down (NP): his school has been closed down **4** prime sb. for sth.: prepare sb. for sth. **5** pitch (n, infml): speech to convince sb. to buy sth. **6** scorched: burned **7** line: (here) fishing line

Beke, my editor. But the man is a mean bastard and will only treat him as a servant. Don't you have any family?

– I have a sister, but she –

– Can't she take him?

– Well ... it's complicated. No ... she can't ...

– Well, then, clearly we can't take the boy.

I looked over at father and son. They were staring intently at us, but both immediately dropped their gaze as I turned to them. The father held the boy's hand in his, patting him gently on the shoulder with the other hand.

– We've heard your request. And you're right, your boy is a clever boy with a bright future. However, we'll discuss it some more and let you know what we decide before all this is over.

The disappointment on the man's face was unsightly[1]. Zaq put a hand on his shoulder.

– We're not saying no, you understand.

– What Zaq is saying is that this is so sudden ...

The boy began to cry. Zaq looked from the boy to me to the old man.

– Look. Okay. We'll take him. *I* will take him. I'll find a way.

– But ... are you sure ...

– No, I'm not. But I will take him. I'll find a place for him somehow. And he could be an office boy at the *Star*. Now, you, stop crying. Let's go.

At the father's urging the boy ran to Zaq and wrapped his arms around the veteran journalist's thick midsection.

– Thank you, sah.

Zaq, embarrassed, pushed him away gently.

My mind went back to our first night in Chief Ibiram's house. We had finished eating. It was too early to sleep, and the Chief and his brother had withdrawn to one side, speaking softly, listening to the radio. And the Chief had hesitated a long time when Zaq asked him,

1 unsightly: unpleasant to look at

Are you happy here? But finally, he lowered the radio volume and cleared his voice. He whispered briefly to his brother and then he turned to us.

Once upon a time they lived in paradise, he said, in a small village close to Yellow Island. They lacked for nothing, fishing and hunting and farming and watching their children growing up before them, happy. The village was close-knit[1], made up of cousins and uncles and aunts and brothers and sisters, and, though they were happily insulated[2] from the rest of the world by their creeks and rivers and forests, they were not totally unaware of the changes going on all around them: the gas flares[3] that lit up neighbouring villages all day and all night, and the cars and TVs and video players in the front rooms of their neighbours who had allowed the flares to be set up. Some of the neighbours were even bragging[4] that the oil companies had offered to send their kids to Europe and America to become engineers, so that one day they could return and work as oil executives in Port Harcourt. For the first time the close, unified community was divided – for how could they not be tempted, with the flare in the next village burning over them every night, its flame long and coiled like a snake, whispering, winking, hissing? Already the oil-company men had started visiting, accompanied by important politicians from Port Harcourt, holding long conferences with Chief Malabo, the head chief, who was also Chief Ibiram's uncle.

One day, early in the morning, Chief Malabo called the whole village to a meeting. Of course he had heard the murmurs[5] from the young people, and the suspicious whispers from the old people, all wondering what it was he had been discussing with the oil men and the politicians. Well, they had made an offer, they had offered to buy the whole village, and with the money – and yes, there was a lot of money, more money than any of them had ever imagined – and

1 close-knit (adj): (here) closely bound together **2** insulate: isolate **3** gas flare: part of oil rigs that burns the gas that comes up with the oil **4** brag (v): boast, present oneself in an overly positive way **5** murmur (n): (here) rumour

with the money they could relocate[1] elsewhere and live a rich life. But Chief Malabo had said no, on behalf of the whole village he had said no. This was their ancestral land, this was where their fathers and their fathers' fathers were buried. They'd been born here, they'd grown up here, they were happy here, and though they may not be rich, the land had been good to them, they never lacked for anything. What kind of custodians[2] of the land would they be if they sold it off? And just look at the other villages that had taken the oil money: already the cars had broken down, and the cheap television and DVD players were all gone, and where was the rest of the money? Thrown away in Port Harcourt bar rooms, or on second wives and funeral parties, and now they were worse off than before. Their rivers were already polluted and useless for fishing, and the land grew only gas flares and pipelines. But the snake, the snake in the garden wouldn't rest, it kept on hissing and the apple only grew larger and more alluring[3] each day. And already far off in the surrounding waters the oil-company boats were patrolling, sometimes openly sending their men to the village to take samples of soil and water. The village decided to keep them away by sending out their own patrols over the surrounding rivers, in canoes, all armed with bows and arrows and clubs[4] and a few guns. But daily Chief Malabo was feeling the pressure. As a chief he had no control over the families' decision about what to do with their land, but as a chief his word carried weight, especially among the elders. But what of the young men who were still grumbling, and looking enviously across the water at the other villages? The canoe patrol was something of a desperate measure, and this soon became very clear. It turned out to be the excuse the oil companies and the politicians who worked for them needed to make their next move. One day the patrol came upon two oil workers piling soil samples[5] into a speedboat. There

1 relocate: move **2** custodian: person responsible for protecting sb./sth.
3 alluring (adj): tempting, attractive **4** club: (here) *Schlagstock* **5** soil sample: *Bodenprobe*

was a brief skirmish[1], nothing too serious – one of the oil workers escaped with a swollen jaw, the other with a broken arm – but the next day the soldiers came. Chief Malabo was arrested, his hands tied behind his back as if he were a petty[2] criminal, on charges of supporting the militants and plotting against[3] the federal government and threatening to kidnap foreign oil workers. The list was long – but, the lawyer said, if the elders would consent to the oil company's demands, sell the land ... A politician, who introduced himself as their senator, came all the way from Abuja and assured them that their situation was receiving national attention, it was in the papers, and he was going to fight for them to see that their chief was returned safe and sound. With him were two white men, oil executives. The villagers chased them away. Others came, but they were all liars, all working for the oil companies, trying one way or another to break the villagers' resolve. But the villagers remained firm. Chief Malabo, whenever they went to see him, told them not to give in, not to worry about him – but they could see how he was deteriorating every day. And then they went to see him one day and were told he was dead.

Here Chief Ibiram paused in his story, his voice breaking. They were given his body, which was wrapped in a raffia mat and a white cloth, and told to take him away. Just like that. The following week, even before Chief Malabo had been buried, the oil companies moved in. They came with a whole army, waving guns and looking like they meant business. They had a contract, they said, Chief Malabo had signed it in prison before he died, selling them all of his family land, and that was where they'd start drilling, and whoever wanted to join him and sell his land would be paid handsomely, but the longer the people held out, the more the value of their land would fall.

Zaq shifted. – So what happened?

– They sold. One by one. The rigs went up, and the gas flares, and the workers came and set up camp in our midst, we saw our vil-

1 skirmish: short fight **2** petty (adj): minor, not very important **3** plot against sb. (v): take part in a conspiracy against sb.

lage change, right before our eyes. And that was why we decided to leave, ten families. We didn't take their money. The money would be our curse on them, for taking our land, and for killing our chief. We left, we headed northwards, we've lived in five different places now, but always we've had to move. We are looking for a place where we can live in peace. But it is hard. So your question, are we happy here? I say how can we be happy when we are mere wanderers without a home?

4

Tamuno saw the helicopter first. I couldn't see anything from where I stood, but I could hear the roar. The fog rose off the water and the mangrove leaves like smoke from wet kindling, blanketing the air and the sky for miles around. Then suddenly the helicopter appeared overhead, shrouded[1] in its engine's riotous[2] noise, the air pressure from its wings parting the fog. It banked and cycled and hovered, its weight seemingly borne by the white fog, and I saw the huge oil-company logo on its side. From an open window a guard leaned down, his eyes covered in huge goggles[3], his machine gun poking through the open window.

– We go. Quick, we go now, please, please.

Tamuno didn't wait for us; he turned and ran for the boat, his knobbly knees knocking against each other. We followed him, awkwardly diving into the boat. I knocked my knee against the wood and for a few minutes my left leg was totally paralysed[4]. I held my knee with one hand and with the other I clung to the side of the boat as the boy tried to bring the engine alive. When it didn't work, he took the oar[5] and pushed frantically[6], launching us into the shallow, choppy[7] water. The helicopter followed us, a disinterested bee, watching from a distance. I expected the gunman to start shooting, but nothing happened. The helicopter stayed with us for a few minutes as we progressed[8] slowly towards the distant mangrove cluster on the horizon, then it left. But before our sigh of relief had properly escaped our lips, two speedboats appeared from behind the very mangrove bush we were making for, their massive bows bearing

1 shrouded: wrapped, enveloped **2** riotous (adj): (here) very loud **3** goggles (n, pl): pair of glasses to protect the eyes **4** paralysed: unable to move **5** oar: *Ruder* **6** frantic: furious, wild **7** choppy: rough with small waves **8** progress (v): move on

down on us. In one of the boats a man in a green oilskin jacket raised a loud hailer[1] to his mouth:

– Stop and throw away your oars and weapons. Do it now!

Tamuno quickly and tremulously raised his hands to show he had no weapons. We did the same. The boy threw the oar into the water and crouched[2] on the wet floor between me and Zaq, making himself invisible, peering over the side at the fast-approaching boats. They circled us, guns trained on us. Now we could see the men clearly: they were soldiers, three in each boat, all armed. The names of the boats were printed on their sides in blue cursive characters over a dull white background: one was *Mami Wata 1*, the other *Mami Wata 2*. They kept circling slowly, coming close enough to peer into our boat. The man with the loud hailer spoke again, his metallic voice sounding so impersonal, so threatening, in the suddenly cold air:

– You will do as I tell you. If you attempt to escape, or disobey in any way, you will be shot. Leave your boat and swim over to our boats. If you can't swim, take the rope being lowered and we'll pull you over. Don't take anything from your boat.

I went first, plunging[3] into the cold water and grasping blindly for the rope; then the old man, then the boy, and then it was Zaq's turn. As he leaned heavily on the side of the heaving boat, I saw that he was reaching too soon for the rope, and with nothing to counterbalance Zaq's weight our boat simply keeled over. Zaq went under. I watched helplessly as my tote bag[4] containing my camera and my notebook and all my personal belongings floated briefly on the water before sinking out of sight. I stood up, reaching out, but a gun in my side forced me to sit down again. No one went in to save Zaq. After an eternity he surfaced, spitting out water, holding onto the overturned boat, and somehow he found the rope and was dragged aboard by two soldiers. One of them leaned over and casually shot a round at the overturned boat. We watched as it slowly sank out

1 hailer (infml): megaphone **2** crouch (v): *in die Hocke gehen* **3** plunge (v): jump, dive **4** tote bag [təʊt bæg]: large bag made of cloth

of sight. I turned away from the horror on the old man's face as he watched his boat sink beneath a sea of bubbles, and though he opened his mouth to speak, raising his hand like a boy in a classroom, nothing came out of his mouth. He slumped back when the boat finally disappeared. I was in the same boat as Tamuno, while Zaq and Michael were in the other boat. We were seated on a bench side by side, facing the soldiers, who stared back at us through their dark glasses, all except the man with the loud hailer. He had a sergeant's stripes on his sleeves and he was standing a bit in front of the others, looking calmly at us, his eyes waiting for an explanation.

– We're reporters.

I was sure Zaq, if he could speak at all after that fall into the water, was telling them the same thing in the other boat.

– You can explain yourself to the Major.

After about an hour we saw stunted[1] palm trees on the horizon. They seemed to be jetting out of the water, and behind them the land appeared a few seconds later. A sudden and unexpected place, with the water circling it like a moat[2], and you didn't see it till you were practically on top of it. A thin trail of mangroves and palm trees on marshy ground led away from the water to more solid ground and a footpath inland. More soldiers appeared behind trees and out of dugouts[3] and behind sandbags, guns raised, eyes fixed on us as our escorts bound our hands behind our backs before leading us off the boats. We were taken down a path that meandered[4] between the trees, and disappeared beneath thick grass; as we walked I often had to lean against Zaq to stop him from falling to the muddy ground. When I tried to explain to a sergeant that Zaq was not feeling well, he raised his gun at me.

– Keep walking.

At last we arrived at a camp: a few sheds and huts arranged in a square formation around a central clearing where three low and leafy trees grew. We sat under the trees and watched the Sergeant

1 stunted: (here) dying, in bad condition **2** moat: *Wasser-/Burggraben*
3 dugout (n): shelter dug in the ground **4** meander (v): follow a winding course

make a call on his radio[1], not saying much, occasionally grunting a 'yes' and a 'no', then finally 'over'. He put down his gun and waved impatiently to one of the men, who stepped forward and untied us.

– So, you are the journalists. We have been expecting you.

Zaq started to stand up, then sank back to the ground, falling flat on his face. I rushed forward and tried to help him up, but he slumped back again.

– What's wrong with him?

– He needs to see a doctor.

The soldier looked at Zaq, then at me.

– Well, the Major said to treat you well till he comes. You're lucky we have a medic here. Just don't try to escape. If you do, you'll be shot.

I looked at him, trying to determine if he was joking. Escape how, to where? But his red eyes showed no trace of merriment[2].

– We can't escape without our boat.

He motioned to one of the soldiers. – Take them to the doctor. No, just you two.

– The old man and the boy work for us. They're our guides ...

– They will be fine. Go.

He was wearing military fatigues[3], so I asked him if he was also a soldier. He laughed.

– A soldier? No, no, just a doctor. A bloody civilian like you.

His voice was thin and slow and precise.

– Dr Dagogo-Mark. Call me 'Doctor'; everybody does.

His shed was a little removed from the other huts; its large doors and windows made it airy and cool; in a corner was a table carrying a few tins of medicine, carefully labelled. Near the table was an open wooden chest[4] in which I could see a jumble[5] of medicine bottles and syringes and various containers. On another table behind the

1 radio: (here) *Funkgerät* **2** merriment: joy **3** military fatigues (pl): army uniform **4** chest: large wooden storage box **5** jumble (n): untidy mix

chest was what looked like a titration stand[1] with tubes[2] hanging from it, while under it was a burner connected to a gas cylinder. An old and dirty white laboratory jacket covered the Doctor's fatigues; the jacket was a size too small for him and stretched tightly across the shoulders. Occasionally a foul stench from the faraway swamps blew in through the open window on the back of a sporadic and wispy[3] wind. Zaq lay on his back on a cot[4] on the floor, knocked out by an injection the Doctor had given him. Beside him were two other cots with soldiers sprawled out on them, still dressed in their camouflage uniforms and boots, their eyes dulled by fever. The Doctor had looked at Zaq and asked me how long he had been ill.

– Well, on and off for about twelve days now.

He had taken blood and urine samples and said he'd work on them and let us know what was wrong by tomorrow. And then he had knocked Zaq out with the injection. I was seated in a wooden chair close to Zaq, and it was all I could do to keep my eyes open. I wanted to ask the Doctor about this place, about the Major who seemed to be the man in charge, but my mouth remained heavy and stiff, so I let my mind wander. It wandered all the way back to the day, at the office, when I raised my hand and volunteered to come on this assignment.

*

The invitation – written in black ink on a ten-inch-square handbill – to interested and experienced reporters to go to interview the kidnapped British woman had hung unanswered for two days on the notice board next to my editor's office, and now he was going to take it down, but first he wanted to make a speech. The editor, Dan Itega, a man in his fifties who for some reason disliked me on sight, loved making speeches.

1 titration stand: instrument usu. used in laboratories to analyse substances
2 tube: (here) test tube, small glass tube used for chemical tests **3** wispy: weak
4 cot: camp bed

The Reporter was the third-largest paper in Port Harcourt, with lots of experienced reporters, and ordinarily such an important assignment wouldn't have come my way: I was a mere cub reporter[1], and technically not even that any more because the editor had unceremoniously transferred me to the photography department. But fate had started its work in my favour two weeks earlier when two reporters, Max Tekena and Peter Olisah, were killed after answering a similar invitation. Olisah worked for a Port Harcourt evening paper called *The Voice* – I had never met him, but Tekena was my colleague. He was a star.

It is my first week in Port Harcourt after graduating and I am about to be interviewed for a job. I am standing in front of the gates at *The Reporter*. I am wearing a jacket, my only jacket, and underneath my shirt is properly tucked in; flanking me on each side is another applicant. We have survived a rigorous pruning[2] process from a list of over fifty and now our fate is in the hands of the proprietor, known by all his employees as the Chairman. Only one of us will make it. Now we are in the Chairman's anteroom, and we have been seated here for hours, looking up hopefully whenever the door to the office opens. This is our third day of waiting. Sub-editors sit with us waiting to go in to consult with him over the next day's edition. A young secretary sits behind a typewriter, a cravat[3] fashionably tied around his collar, his face fresh and alert. Ah, how accomplished he must be to work directly for the Chairman. He must be the best among the best. Max Tekena sits to my right: he is a talkative boy of about my age and loves to reel off his CV[4] – he has been an apprentice on three papers, one of them a Lagos paper, and he is sure this one will be a shoo-in[5] for him. He is tall and lanky[6], his eyes are alert and restless, he has a way of licking his lips as he speaks, a born preda-

1 cub reporter (infml): young reporter who is trained on the job **2** pruning: cutting back of plants, (here) selection **3** cravat [krəˈvæt]: piece of cloth loosely worn around the neck **4** CV: curriculum vitae, *Lebenslauf* **5** shoo-in (n, infml): sure win **6** lanky: *schlacksig*

tor. The other applicant is a girl: she is quiet, but apparently more accomplished than me. She has her own blog and can talk about complex trends in fashion and knows who is sleeping with whom in Nollywood[1] and Hollywood. Her list of sources and contacts and informants is endless, and she is the prettiest thing I have ever seen. How can the Chairman resist her? We all clutch our portfolios in our sweaty hands. Mine contains the few pieces I did at journalism school, and my single claim to fame: my online article about the oil fire that consumed[2] my little town, killing and maiming[3] a quarter of the population, including my sister and my best friend's father. My heart is beating fast and for some reason I am sure I will never get the job, but I am willing to stick it out with the others. To wait them out. We have been coming to the office for three days without seeing him and it seems he is testing us to see who will give up first. Patience, after all, is a foremost virtue in journalism – Zaq told me that at Bar Beach in Lagos.

And then he steps out of his office with an entourage of three behind him and he looks at us and turns to his secretary with the blue-and-white cravat and says, Who are they, what are they doing here in my anteroom?

It is the first time I've seen him in the flesh.

The Chairman tells us, Go and write an essay each on today's top headlines. And we, What exactly should we write? And he, It doesn't matter, just remember this: keep to the point, stay close to home. The further from home you wander, the closer you get to Siberia. Always remember that.

The girl is the first to drop out. She says she has an offer elsewhere, a fashion magazine, and really she can't waste her days sitting in some anteroom trying to figure out silly riddles about Siberia. Before she goes, she calls me outside and says, You're wasting your time. The boy is from the same village as the editor. He'll get the job. It's all arranged. I thank her and return to the anteroom,

1 Nollywood: Nigerian film industry **2** consume sth.: (here) destroy sth. completely **3** maim sb. (v): mutilate sb., permanently injure sb.

where Tekena and I continue to sit, not next to each other as before, united, but facing across from each other, adversarially[1], and when I get tired of his cocky[2], knowing smile I stand up, go to the toilet and call the number Zaq gave me at Bar Beach. And he answers.

– I need your help, Mr Zaq.

In the end both Max and I are hired. But from the beginning it is clear that I'm not in the same league as Max Tekena. He is a natural[3], and before the end of our probation period[4] he has a front-page story. The editor walks him round the newsroom, from table to table, the cover in his hand, praising him, and at my corner he stops and says, Young man, you will accompany Max here on local assignments, but as a photographer. Your CV, if it is all true, says you have done some photography. Well, work with him, and you might learn a few things.

I didn't hate Max Tekena. He turned out to be my only friend in the newsroom; at lunch we always sat together and talked about girls and football and movies. I'd have hated him if he were just the editor's kinsman[5], but he was also talented. He had it, that instinct only a real journalist has, the ability to almost effortlessly predict what story is going to grow, and to follow it relentlessly to its logical conclusion. Maybe that was why he died early. He had gone with six other reporters deep into the forest to interview five foreign hostages taken from their offices, in broad daylight, by masked gunmen. The kidnappers, eager for publicity, would usually invite a select team of reporters to their hideout to confirm that the hostages were alive and unharmed, after which they would make long speeches about the environment and their reasons for taking up arms against the oil companies and the government, and finally they'd send a ransom demand through one of the reporters. After a week or so, depending on how quickly negotiations went, the oil companies paid up, and the hostages were set free, unharmed, each with his bag full of anecdotes. But this time things didn't work out quite so smoothly. One of

1 adversarial: positioned opposite each other like opponents **2** cocky: arrogant
3 natural (n): *Naturtalent* **4** probation period: *Probezeit* **5** kinsman: relative

the hostages, a desperate Filipino contractor[1], perhaps doubtful of ever regaining freedom, had suddenly bolted and attempted to get away in one of the speedboats waiting to take the reporters back to Port Harcourt, but he didn't get far. The militants, in black overalls, their faces covered in masks made of green leaves, fired wildly, and afterwards three men lay dead on the pebbly[2] beach. One was the Filipino; the other two were the reporters Max Tekena and Peter Olisah.

*

And so, understandably, this time the invitation to interview a hostage hung unanswered in front of the editor's office. The editor took down the notice, shaking his head regretfully.

– I don't blame you guys for holding back, but I hate to see other papers out-scoop[3] us. The event is tomorrow, and already three reporters have signed up, from the *Globe*, *The Voice* and the *Daily Star*.

He laughed. His voice grew derisive. – Guess who from the *Star*? Zaq.

I was standing with the other reporters in the little passage between the editor's office and the newsroom, listening, avoiding the editor's eyes, but when I heard Zaq's name I stepped forward.

– I'll go.

The editor opened his mouth to laugh, but when he saw I was serious, the laugh turned to a sneer.

– Well, well, the little photographer wants to be a real reporter, eh? Well, come into my office and tell me what you have in mind.

1 contractor: *Auftragsunternehmer* **2** pebbly (adj): covered with pebbles
3 out-scoop sb. (infml): publish a sensational news story before sb.

The editor sat facing me, his paunch[1] overflowing onto the desktop, his expression switching between contempt[2] and a frown[3]. On his left sat the news editor; on his right, the deputy editor.

– Well, talk.

I stammered. I hesitated. I mumbled[4]. I told them I'd write it not as a kidnapping story only, but I'd try to find out what kind of woman the hostage was: if she had children, if she regretted coming to Nigeria, if she had any message for her husband. Things like that. The three men waited to hear more, but I remained quiet.

– Is that all?

I could see the editor was trying hard not to snigger[5].

– Well, sir, there is also the effect on the international price of oil.

– Aren't you afraid of the danger? You could get killed.

– I see it as a great opportunity to show what I can do, sir.

I didn't tell them that, though I wasn't sure exactly what to look for, I was confident that with Zaq there everything would work out fine. He'd be my guide, my teacher. Once, when he was drunk and helpless, I had looked after him; now it was his turn to look after me. Fate, it seemed, had brought us together.

1 paunch: belly **2** contempt (n): disrespect, attitude of looking down on sb.
3 frown (n): wrinkling of the brows that indicates scepticsm or displeasure
4 mumble (v): talk incomprehensibly **5** snigger (v): quietly laugh in a mocking way

5

The Major sat on a field stool, the type made by unfolding the top of a swagger stick[1], his rifle on the muddy ground by his foot, talking into a radio. Seven men knelt facing him under the trees in the central clearing[2], their hands tied behind them, all wearing the same abject[3] expression on their faces. They looked dirty, their skin was flaky[4] and reptilian, chalk-white, as if they had been dragged through an acreage[5] of ash. Behind the seven, but not very far away from them, were Tamuno and Michael, squatting on their haunches[6], looking perplexed and anxious.

The Major stood up and pointed at the kneeling men with his swagger stick, shaking his head to show his disappointment in them. He hadn't looked in my direction yet. The boy started crying and held his father tight when the Major went over to them and stared down at them for a long time without saying a word. Then he came over to me.

– So, you are the journalist. Where's the other one?

He turned to his men when he asked the question, not waiting for my answer. Two of them stood behind me, their guns vaguely pointed at me. A soldier had found me in the Doctor's shed in a chair next to Zaq's narrow cot, my eyes closed, my ears waiting for the slightest sound from Zaq. He had kicked me in the shin to wake me up, and even in the gloom of the shed I could see his glare.

– You, come! Both of you. Now. The Major wan see you. Now. Oya[7].

1 swagger stick: stick carried by a military person as a sign of authority
2 clearing (n): open area surrounded by trees **3** abject (adj): humble, submissive
4 flaky: raw, cracked **5** acreage [ˈeɪkərɪdʒ]: area **6** haunches (pl): *Gesäß*
7 Oya (NP): Let's get it on.

I stood up and almost fell down again. I wasn't aware of how tired and disoriented I was. I swayed[1] like a height-drunk alpinist, half-way through his climb, unsure if he was ever going to get to the top, and not really sure if he cared any more.

– He can't come. He's sick.

– Well, you come.

The Doctor was seated behind his desk, writing on a piece of paper. He didn't look up as the man led me out into the dying day. Now I watched the Major walk up and down in front of us, his tall legs stretching out fully beneath his oddly foreshortened[2] torso, as if measuring the ground, and finally he stopped in front of me and looked me full in the face.

– Do you know what danger you run, two journalists, an old fisherman and his son, running about in these waters? How old is the boy?

The boy, seeing the Major staring at him, and now walking towards him, took his father's arm again, burying his face in the old man's shoulder. The old man looked up at the Major, a rictus[3]-like smile on his face.

– Sorry, sir, no be him fault. Na small pikin[4], sir.

The old man bowed down his head when he had finished speaking, ready to take on himself whatever blow was meant for his son. For a moment the soldier looked as if he would reach out and drag the boy out of his father's arms and force him to answer the question, but then he turned away from the two and faced his men.

– Put them with the others!

The soldiers grabbed the old man and his son and led them to the seven kneeling men. I noticed how puffy[5] and sleep-deprived the eyes of the seven men looked. I stepped forward to protest to the Major but a hand on my wrist pulled me back. I shook off the hand, thinking it was one of the soldiers, but it wasn't. It was the Doctor.

– Wait. This is not a good time to talk to him.

1 sway (v): *schwanken* **2** foreshortened: appearing shorter than it actually is
3 rictus (fml): unnaturally twisted smile **4** pikin (NP): child **5** puffy: swollen

The Doctor looked tired. We watched as the Major berated[1] the men in a loud, but surprisingly passionless, voice.

– You call yourselves freedom fighters? To me you are just crooks[2] and I will keep hunting you down and shooting you like mad dogs. This country is tired of people like you. Sergeant, bring the watering can!

The Sergeant was standing with five other soldiers under a tree, close to the kneeling men, and at the Major's order he picked up a rusty iron watering can from the ground and took it to the Major. I sensed a hush[3] descend on the men. The soldiers seemed to have forgotten to raise their guns and point them threateningly at the kneeling men. The Doctor shifted on his foot and I heard his sharp intake of breath as the Major raised the can and started to pour the water on the head of the man on the outer right. Then the unmistakable acrid[4] smell reached me.

– Is he pouring petrol on them?

The Doctor nodded. I pulled away from him and in a few steps I was standing beside the Major, and when he turned and glared at me my courage faltered[5] and for a moment all I could do was shake my head and point at the boy and the old man.

– Major. We are really sorry if we broke the law by coming into these waters. But we were invited by the kidnappers ... and this man and this boy, they work for us. They're innocent. Let them go. Please. We just want to find the kidnapped woman and to interview the militants, that's all.

The Major turned and stared at me for a while before speaking, and then with each word he poked[6] a finger into my chest.

– Listen, here I decide who is a criminal and who is not. I say who is a good egg and who is bad. Don't dare to tell me what my job is. Remember, you could easily be there on your knees with them. You are still not free of suspicion. Don't forget that.

1 berate sb.: scold sb., rebuke sb., severely critize sb. **2** crook (n, infml): criminal **3** hush (n): silence **4** acrid (adj): biting **5** falter (v): give way **6** poke (v): (here) touch with the tip of one's finger

He turned away, stretched out his hand and commenced dripping oil on the bowed heads. I returned to the Doctor, shaken. I turned away so as not to watch the shock and pain and frustration on the bowed faces as the precious, corrosive[1] liquid touched their skins. The Doctor also looked away towards the water, lost in some detail of the ruined, decomposing landscape. But I couldn't turn my face away for long. I was a journalist: my job was to observe, and to write about it later. To be a witness for posterity[2]. I witnessed the stoic and anticipatory[3] posture of the kneeling men. I witnessed the brutal anointing[4] in silence, smelled the reek[5] of petrol hanging in the air, pungent[6], acrid, and I wondered how the men could stand it. Already I felt sick and dizzy[7] from the fumes. I had never liked the smell – it brought up memories in me, memories I would rather have kept down.

– This isn't the first time this has happened, is it?

– No. It's not.

The Doctor sounded agitated[8], but his eyes remained fixed on the Major, who was moving up the line, systematically dousing[9] the bowed, cringing[10] heads.

– Look at the soldiers, look at their eyes, all feverish with excitement and expectation.

– Expectation of what?

– Of the day when the Major will strike a match and throw it at the bowed, petrol-soaked heads. One day it will happen – see how the Major's hands shake with the temptation.

The Major's loud mocking voice cut the air.

– What, you can't stand the smell of oil? Isn't it what you fight for, kill for? Go on, enjoy. By the time I'm through with you, you'll hate the smell of it, you won't take money that comes from oil, you

1 corrosive: harmful **2** posterity: future generations **3** anticipatory: expectant
4 anointing (n): act of rubbing oil on sb./sth. **5** reek (n): unpleasant smell
6 pungent: *stechend* **7** dizzy: *schwindlig* **8** agitated: nervous **9** douse sb./sth.: pour liquid on sb./sth. **10** cringe (v): shrink back in fear

won't get in a car because it runs on petrol. You'll hate the very name petrol.

– They say he became like this after his daughter was raped. She was only eighteen. A student at the university. She was the brightest in her class, she was studying to become a doctor ...

– You want resource control[1]? Well, control this. How does it feel? This will teach you to kidnap innocent children. This will teach you to terrorize innocent villages.

– One day she's walking to the hostel from the library, it's late at night, she has an exam the next day and she's been reading and doesn't know it's so late. Then a car pulls up beside her and she's offered a lift. She recognizes one of the faces, a classmate. She gets in.

– Sergeant! Get me more oil. These people are so thirsty. They drank it all up. Would you believe that? Hurry up.

– But the car doesn't take her to her room. They head for the city. She begins to scream when her pleading[2] to be taken back to the hostel meets with only drunken laughter. They take her to a strange room in some run-down hotel and lock her up in the wardrobe after sealing her mouth with duct tape[3]. They leave her there all night. That boy that she recognized, he is about to be initiated into a campus fraternity, and part of his initiation ceremony requires rape, and he has to supply the girl ...

One of the men returned with the watering can and handed it to the Sergeant, who handed it to the Major.

– So, where were we, who is next?

– She only happens to be in the wrong place at the wrong time. The next day, they take her to a graveyard and rape her repeatedly, then they let her go. The frat boys didn't think she'd give up their names; besides, one of the boys was some minister's son. But she did. Nothing happened to him of course; he was only suspended from university for a term. The Major here, he took it calmly, sur-

1 resource control: control of a country's natural resources **2** pleading (n): begging **3** duct tape: strong adhesive tape

prisingly. Many thought he'd lose his head and maybe shoot the boy, and in anticipation of this the boy's father sent his son away to a university in London. Well, the Major is a patient man. He waited. A year later the boy came home for Christmas. The Major heard about it and one night he got two of his men and went to the boy's favourite nightclub and abducted[1] him right in front of everyone. They took him to the graveyard and shot him in the groin[2] after breaking his four limbs[3]. He didn't die. They made sure of that. He phoned his father, who came and got him and flew him overseas for treatment. The Major was arrested, and court-martialled[4]. The army sent him away to this place as punishment, and he's been here three years now. He's still angry, volatile[5], unpredictable, and one day he's going to light that match. Even his men know it. Just a matter of time.

– What happened to his daughter?

– They said she transferred to another university in the north, Zaria or Maiduguri, and completed her studies.

The boy, Michael, was last in line. The Major was as conscientious[6] with him as he was with the others, making sure the oil found every exposed surface on the boy's face. I witnessed the boy desperately spitting out the oil as it ran down his face, wiping his eyes and nostrils with the sleeve of his homespun shirt, but the friction from the wiping only chafed[7] his skin, inflaming it, making the corrosive oil sting[8] harder. I promised myself that if I got out of here I'd write about this, every detail, every oil trickle, every howl of pain. Now I knew what Zaq meant when he said so long ago in that lecture that this job would sometimes break your heart. He said journalism shows you first-hand how nations are built, how great men achieve their greatness. And then he had quoted the proverb[9] about how elephants achieve their great size: they simply eat up everything that stands in their path, trees and ants and plants and dirt, every-

1 abduct sb.: kidnap sb. **2** groin: area of the genitals **3** limbs (pl): arms and legs **4** court-martial sb.: put sb. on trial in a military court **5** volatile: (here) suffering from mood swings **6** conscientious: meticulous, careful **7** chafe sth.: rub off the uppermost layer of sth. **8** sting (v): inflict a burning pain **9** proverb (n): short popular saying containing a lesson

thing. I lowered my head to control the rage. I felt impotent, helpless, like a man running in his sleep with his legs crossed. At last the Major flung away the empty watering can. He strode over to us, his face contorted[1] by some obscure rage. He was breathing hard.

– Journalist, you want to interview the rebels, well, here they are. There will be time for that.

I looked at the kneeling men. One of them, the eldest, with grey hair, the one in the middle, looked like he was finding it hard to focus, wiping his face and swaying, intoxicated[2] by the oil fumes; then he pitched forward and puked into the muddy brown grass in front of him.

– Take them away, and make sure you bring them out here tomorrow morning for their morning shower.

– When can I interview them?

I was following the Major into his shed, the command shed. He turned and stared at me for a long time, thinking, then the anger left his face to be replaced by a malevolent smirk. He put a hand on my shoulder.

– You – how can I be sure you are who you claim to be?

– But, we are –

– Do you have any ID? Nothing? Not even a recorder, a pen, a notebook? What kind of reporters are you?

– We lost our things when your men sank our boat.

– Hmm. So far I have treated you like gentlemen. I am a gentleman, an officer and a gentleman. Ask my men. They love me because I am a fair man. But I have one question only for you: how can I know you are who you claim to be? That is all. Answer me that question and you are free.

He smelled of sweat and the marshes, and oil. The oil had left stains on his trouser legs and on his boots.

– We're looking for the English woman, for the story. That is all.

– I'm looking for the woman too, everyone is looking for her. You think you can find her if we can't? Still, I don't trust you. I can't

1 contorted: twisted **2** intoxicated: *beraucht, benebelt*

trust you, you see my dilemma? You have till tomorrow to think of something. Talk to the other guy. Tomorrow, I want proof. Answers. Otherwise I'll have to lock you up with the rebels, and treat you the same way.

– What of the old man and his child? They're innocent, nothing to do with all these –

– Go. I have work to do.

– I must insist, Major.

– Insist? Did you say insist? Do you know what's going on out there? There's a war going on! People are being shot. In Port Harcourt oil companies are being bombed, police stations are being overrun, the world oil price is shooting through the roof. You insist! I can shoot you right now and throw you into the swamp and that's it. Now, get out.

6

– What can we do to help the old man and his son, Zaq?

– Nothing, my young friend. I wish it were that easy to intervene and change the course of things. It isn't. We'll observe, and then we'll write about it when we can.

We lay side by side. The Doctor had given me one of the cots vacated by a sick soldier who had been moved to one of the huts for the night. Zaq and I were alone in the infirmary[1]. Half of the structure was open to the elements, and not far away in the swamps we could hear the bullfrogs bellowing[2], we could see the glow of the gas flares like distant malfunctioning[3] stars. Though it was humid and airless, our blankets were pulled to our necks – they were our only protection from the mosquitoes. The Doctor had apologized for the accommodation; the only alternative to the infirmary was the lock-up[4], where the militants were being held under heavy guard, and, as much as we wanted to interview them, spending the night cooped up[5] in a tight hut with them didn't appeal. Zaq was sleepless, restless, and though his voice was weak and raspy, he kept talking, keeping me from nodding off.

– You don't regret being here, do you?

– I don't know, Zaq. I'd have given a lot not to have witnessed the boy and his father being drenched[6] by the Major.

– I've seen children snatched away from their mothers, never to be reunited. I've seen husbands taken from their wives and kids and sent away to prison. I've seen grown men flogged[7] by soldiers

1 infirmary: room/building where sick people are treated **2** bellow: make a loud noise with one's voice **3** malfunction (v): not work properly **4** lock-up (n, infml): prison **5** cooped up: locked up **6** drench sb./sth.: pour a large amount of liquid on sb./sth **7** flog sb.: hit sb. with a whip

in front of their kids. That's how history is made, and it's our job to witness it.

– And is it always like this?

– No, not always. I've also witnessed ordinary bystanders pull passengers from burning cars, I've seen judges sentence generals and politicians to hard labour, without fear. I've seen students stand up to soldiers and policemen, protesting against injustice. If you're patient, you'll see those moments too, and you'll write about them.

We watched the flares shake in the wind, wavering[1] and dimming, but always regrouping to shine on again; we listened to what sounded like singing far away in the distance. Across the water a dog, or a hyena, howled and was answered by other howls. Then for a moment there was silence.

– Tell me, Rufus, why did you become a journalist?

*

I have turned fifteen and my father is standing over me, gently shaking me. Outside the night is turning to day in a pageant[2] of orange and pink colours. In the open doorway is my mother, and in her hand is a little wrap. I packed my bag the night before; now I pick it up and my father leads me past the living room, past the kitchen, past my sister still asleep on her little mat in the corridor between my parents' bedroom and the kitchen, to the waiting motorbike outside. My mother rushes forward and hugs me. As the *okada*[3] flies through the early morning towards the station where I'll take the ferry to the next village, and then the bus to Port Harcourt and my new life as an apprentice photographer, it is Boma I miss, and it is to her I make a promise: that I'll return safe and sound, and our life will continue, happy and free. The plan is my father's; he has lost his job, just like half the town. They all worked for the ABZ oil company,

1 waver (v): become weaker **2** pageant [ˈpædʒənt]: *Festzug* **3** okada (NP): motorcycle taxi

and now the town, once awash[1] in oil money, watches in astonishment as the streets daily fill up with fleeing families, some returning to their hometowns and villages, some going on to Port Harcourt in the hope of picking up something in the big city. Many years later I'll suddenly run into an old classmate, a half-forgotten neighbour, destitute[2] on the backstreets of Port Harcourt. Get a trade, my father said, get something you can do with your hands, and this will never happen to you. Cast thy bread upon the waters.[3] Recently he has turned religious. He wakes us up at 6 a.m. daily to seek God's intervention in our affairs. He has been contemplating going back to his old profession of teaching and has asked God to show him if this is the right thing to do, but God still hasn't replied, and every day his doubt increases. I don't know how or when he met Udoh Fotos, how or when they arranged for me to go to Port Harcourt and live with Udoh Fotos as an apprentice and learn the trade – all I know is that the day I turn fifteen my father sends me off to Port Harcourt to learn photography. In my first year I do not learn much about light and darkness, or the many lenses packed in the back room of Udoh Fotos's studio, or the difference between a Leica and a Canon and a Kodak, but I learn from Mrs Fotos how to cook rice and *garri* and how to sweep the junk-filled three-bedroom house and how to bathe the four rude shin-kicking children every evening and how to wake up at 6 a.m. to go to the public tap seven times to fetch water to fill the plastic drum in the kitchen. I grow thin. I develop a weary, tense, animal-like demeanour[4]. In those early months I would happily have run away if I'd had the money, and if I'd known how to negotiate[5] the myriad side streets and alleyways of the shabbiest[6] section of Diobu[7], Port Harcourt. And later, when I am able to run away, I am checked by the question of what I will tell my father. For I have realized that he has sent me here to become a man, so that I

1 awash in sth.: full of sth. **2** destitute: poor **3** Cast thy bread upon the waters: quotation from the *Old Testament* (*Book of Ecclesiastes* 11) saying that people will ultimately benefit from their good deeds **4** demeanour [dɪˈmiːnəʳ] (AE): behaviour **5** negotiate sth.: (here) find one's way through sth. **6** shabby: in bad condition **7** Diobu: densely populated neighbourhood of Port Harcourt

can see how harsh and unfair and difficult life is – and if I can stand it, I might have a chance. Three years later, at the end of my apprenticeship, when Udoh Fotos hands me a flimsy[1] certificate with my name scrawled[2] across it and his spidery signature at the bottom, I understand why apprentices like me at the end of their training, or servitude[3], throw what they call a Freedom Party. In those three years my father comes only twice to visit me, and I go to visit home only once.

*

I paused when I heard Zaq snoring. He had asked me the question that had started me on this memory rummaging, and he hadn't waited to hear the answer. But I was happy to see him sleeping. I was a bit nervous about what the test results would be tomorrow. I turned and faced the open window of the shed, gazing at the sky, unable to sleep. The memories were like floodgates, easier to open than to close.

*

Here I was with my certificate, going back home, leaving Port Harcourt for good, I hoped. But when I at last located my family, it was not where I had left them, in the town where I was born and raised. I found out that after moving to a succession of smaller houses, they had finally moved to a town called Junction, whose economy rode on the back of the two asphalt roads that neatly divided the town into four equal parts. My mother looked thinner, tired, and she didn't talk very much. She had appeared briefly excited at my return, hugging me and asking me questions about my time in Port Harcourt; then, as if that display of emotion had drained her of her little reserve of energy, she retreated to the kitchen, not to cook but

1 flimsy: thin, of low quality **2** scrawl (v): write in an untidy way **3** servitude: condition of being unfree and forced to work for sb.

to stare into the flames in the hearth. My father, on the other hand, was full of energy, almost fidgety[1] with it, unable to sit still.

– Come.

He took me to a large barn at the back of the house. Even before he opened the door I could smell the petrol, and when he turned on the light I saw more than ten drums, most of them empty. We sat on two wooden stools in a clear space between two drums.

– Now that you have your certificate, what are your plans?

He hadn't even touched the certificate. He had only glanced at it and nodded distractedly.

– I don't know. I'll look around and maybe open a photoshop –

– No, not in this town. There's nothing here.

He pointed at the empty oil drums.

– This is the only business booming in this town. I buy from little children. I buy cheap and I sell cheap to the cars that come here at night. Emmanuel, John's father, is my partner. You remember your friend John? Well, Emmanuel has proved himself to be a true friend. He's the only one of my former colleagues whom I can still call a friend. He came up with this plan. We started the whole thing with his savings. It's not a bad business, really. We get by, we give the police a little something to look the other way, but sooner or later they'll get greedy. They'll arrest us, or take over the whole business themselves. I don't want you to be here when that happens. There's nothing for you here. Go back to Port Harcourt. You're smart. Talk to your master. You'll find something. And when you do, don't forget us. Don't forget your mother, and especially your sister.

All I could ask, after he had finished speaking, was, Where do the children get the petrol you buy from them?

They come to me with their little gallons[2] and I don't ask them where they get it.

In the two days I spent at home before returning to Port Harcourt, I saw how much my father had changed. He had turned his

1 fidgety: restless, nervous **2** gallon: unit for measuring volume (3.79 liters in the USA; 4.55 liters in GB), (here) small container for liquids

back on religion, and now smoked and drank *ogogoro*[1] almost non-stop. He left home early in the morning in a pick-up truck to go to the bush, where he and his partner bought the petrol from the kids, and he returned home only after midnight, often drunk. The house stank of petrol and cigarettes. He said he smoked just to kill the petrol smell.

I fell into journalism out of necessity, not because I had proven talent like Max Tekena, or vision, or any ambition to be the next Zaq. I just walked into a newspaper office in Port Harcourt and presented my photography certificate. I returned to Port Harcourt, but I did not take my father's advice. I did not go back to Udoh Fotos of Creek Street, Diobu; instead I went to the offices of *Whispers Magazine*. It was a small monthly magazine whose photography editor had sometimes bought pictures of street scenes and the waterfront from my master to fill up empty pages, and I'd been the one who took the pictures in a brown envelope to his office. Now he listened to me and when I was through he shook his head.

– How old are you?

– I'm eighteen.

– I'll give you a job, but on a temporary basis. Have you ever thought of becoming a journalist? Not just a photographer, but a real reporter. You could go to school in Lagos. I have a form here: fill it out and post it. They give scholarships. Give it a try.

I gave it a try, and for six months, as I waited to hear back from the Ikeja School of Journalism, I did odd jobs at *Whispers*, cleaning the office in the morning, washing the managing editor's car once a week, running errands[2], and taking pictures of hawkers[3] and fishermen and market women for the 'Pictures from the Streets' page. In return I was paid a thousand naira[4] a month, and was allowed to sleep in the office. That was how I became a journalist.

1 ogogoro: West African alcoholic drink distilled from palm tree juice **2** run an errand: perform a small task for sb. by going somewhere **3** hawker: sb. who sells things on the streets **4** naira: Nigeria's currency

Zaq snored on. I wanted to ask him how he became a journalist. What inspired him. If he enjoyed being one, and if there were moments when he felt like giving up. He had looked close to giving up when I met him that day at the waterfront, the day we set out on this assignment.

*

We left the oil-company jetty[1] early that day, six of us, five reporters including Zaq and myself. The kidnapped woman's husband, James Floode, and two other white men were there to see us off. Floode looked distracted and after a brief address to us, in which nothing new was said apart from an exhortation[2] to be careful, and during which he kept turning to whisper to one of the men, he said nothing more. Our guide wore a gun on his waist and his green shirt and blue trousers and calf-length[3] boots had the semblance of a military uniform. Although he looked physically intimidating, over six feet tall with a clean-shaven pate[4], my hope was that he was good with that gun. There were men wearing similar uniforms all over the oil-company premises, some with machine guns that they kept shifting from hand to hand, as if itching to use them.

I tried to cover my nervousness at this open show of firepower, but I could see I was not the only one feeling nervous. The other reporters kept glancing at our guide's gun as well. The oil company had decided to replace two Port Harcourt reporters with two from Lagos, and I felt surprised and pleased that I wasn't one of the two dropped. Perhaps they wanted someone young, with a fresh perspective, or perhaps my photographer's credentials had secured me a place, but it didn't matter. The Lagos reporters were dressed in suits and ties and soft city shoes, as if they were going for a press briefing in a conference room in Ikoyi[5]. They were sitting on the

1 jetty: landing platform for boats **2** exhortation: strong advice **3** calf-length: reaching up to below the knee **4** pate (infml): skull, head **5** Ikoyi: rich neighbourhood of Lagos

front bench, right next to our guide, who was hunched over the wheel. They hadn't introduced themselves, so I had no idea what paper they worked for. One of them was trying to make notes in the open, windy boat, pressing down his notebook with one hand; the other was shouting into his mobile phone, battling against the engine's roar and the increasingly poor service.

I sat next to Zaq and introduced myself, shouting over the loud noise of the boat engine.

– Rufus, from *The Reporter.*

– A good paper.

After that he went quiet, his arms tucked under his orange life-jacket, his red, teary eyes focused on the vast blue water leaping towards us. Clearly he didn't remember me. I hid my disappointment, and reminded myself it had been five years since that day at Bar Beach, and five years since I made my phone call to him. I wanted to compare views with Zaq, to see if he thought we were in any danger from the kidnappers, but he kept his eyes on the water, appearing at times to be sleeping, his face lowered into his bulky life-jacket. He looked queasy[1], already sea-sick. Looking at him – the curled grey tufts[2] in his hair, the thick midsection resting in his lap, a testament to his love affair with the bottle – I found it hard to believe that this was once the most famous reporter in Lagos, and probably in all of Nigeria.

We headed south. I turned and looked back at the receding[3] waterfront, and the swath[4] of white foamy furrow[5] following in the boat's wake, curving when we curved, a soothing[6] and mesmerizing[7] sight that for a moment took my mind off whatever awaited us at our rendezvous. Soon we were out of the open water and into the narrow channels that were like valleys bordered on both sides by dense palm plants or sometimes by unexpected cliff faces. Here the going became slow, and after a few hours the city lay far away

1 queasy: sick, nauseous **2** tuft: cluster of hairs **3** recede: (here) become more and more distant **4** swath: *Schneise* **5** furrow: *Furche* **6** soothe: calm **7** mesmerize: hypnotize

behind us. There were no people or houses to be seen on either bank, only birds jumping out of the tall thin trees and flying away in a flutter of wings and leaves as we approached. Even the Lagos journalists had stopped their loud, self-important whisperings and were listening to the increasingly desperate attempt by our guide to make radio contact with the kidnappers. When we asked him what was going on, he admitted he had no idea where we were going; he had been instructed to head for a general direction and at a certain point to call a particular frequency on his radio to be guided in. Now we seemed to be going about in circles, and we could hear the rising frustration in his voice as he screamed into the radio while manoeuvring the wheel with one hand. No one was responding on the other end.

– I am here now, I need a contact. Over!

– What's going on?

Nkem, the reporter from the *Globe*, stood up and went closer to the guide, shouting his question into the wind and water spray. The guide waved the radio over his head, as if aiming to throw it into the water, or at Nkem. The channel had become narrower and by now I wasn't sure if he knew exactly where he was. I knew the general geography of this area, and I knew how confusing and indistinguishable from one another the interconnected rivers and creeks could be, which was why, I was sure, the militants had chosen it for this meeting. The waters were inconstant, and could change from the clearest, friendliest blue to a turbid[1], unknowable grey in a minute; every tree on the banks and every turning looked like the one before it. We had been circling for about half an hour now and still we had not made contact. We made a turn and suddenly we were in the open water again. I could see the relief on the journalists' faces: better to be here, where we could see for miles ahead, and away from the hot, claustrophobic mangroves and the ominous[2] swamps that had seemed to be closing in, bearing down on the boat. We went

1 turbid (adj): impossible to see through **2** ominous: frigthening, indicating that sth. bad will happen

fast and straight for about thirty minutes and suddenly we could see a chain of islands in the distance ahead of us: the tall oil palm trees were like flags waving us in. We passed the first island and as we approached the second one we saw a fire burning on the beach, right by the water. At first we took it for some kind of beacon[1] signal meant for us, but, as we got nearer and could see past the trees, more fires appeared, and they were random and out of control. The whole island was aflame. The journalists stood up one after the other, holding the sides of the boat for balance, trying to look beyond the trees on the beach.

A wooden boat was responsible for the fire on the beach; it was broken to bits, probably from a direct hit by a rocket. Inland, the smoke rose like a tornado into the sky, high over the savaged, seared[2] trees. Our guide circled round the burning boat, the sweat running down his egg-clean head and into his shirt, and he looked uncertain as to what to do next.

– This doesn't look good.

He turned to us, his expression half apologetic, half puzzled[3], uncomprehending. He shouted again into his ineffectual radio, but only static, then silence, greeted his effort.

– Can we go down? We must take some pictures.

Nkem was already clicking away. The others also took out their cameras and started jumping into the knee-high water. I was impressed when I saw the Lagos reporters jump into the water, suits, ties, soft shoes and all. I hopped into the water and waited for Zaq, who was elaborately[4] folding up his trousers before getting down. He took no pictures; instead he made notes in a tattered[5] notebook as he walked around, raising his legs high over the wet undergrowth, sweating, breathing hard through his mouth. I stayed close to him, observing him as I took pictures.

– You don't have a camera.

He shrugged and said nothing.

1 beacon: light for guiding vehicles (usu. boats) **2** seared: burned **3** puzzled (adj): confused **4** elaborate: with great care **5** tattered (adj): damaged, torn

– So what do you think happened?

– This thing is so uncomfortable.

He took off his cumbersome[1] life-jacket, which we had all been advised to wear but which only Zaq had actually worn, pulling at the straps impatiently, turning a full circle like a dog chasing its tail, all the while cursing. When I repeated my question he turned his puffy, bloodshot eyes to me and shrugged again.

– An ambush[2], obviously. Someone must have informed the soldiers about this meeting.

– You mean, someone in the kidnappers' camp?

– Maybe. But certainly someone who knew where and when.

The island looked like a midway stop where traders met to buy and sell, and travellers picked up supplies, rather than an actual village. Now it was deserted: the people, with their chickens and goats and pots and pans, must have escaped rippleless[3] down the river in their dugout canoes after the first shot was fired. We moved inwards gradually, pushing aside wet leaves and slimy tendrils[4], looking at the signs of carnage[5]. Trees lay on the ground, cut in half, dripping vital sap[6]. The smell of burning hung in the air. In the centre of a compound a hut had been hit square on its conical[7] roof, causing the thatch to cave in, and now the grass and the rafters[8] all lay in a big pile of ash in the middle of the hut. Zaq was kneeling in the bush behind a hut, talking to the guide, pointing at something in his hand, and when I joined them I saw that he held a spent cartridge[9].

– What kind of gun would you say?

The guide took the cartridge from Zaq and tossed it up in the air and caught it again. He seemed happy to find something he could be authoritative about.

– This is a 7.62 mm x 39 mm shell, fired from an AK-47, most likely. The militants use it a lot.

1 cumbersome: difficult to handle, bothersome **2** ambush: *Hinterhalt*
3 rippleless: (here) without making any waves **4** tendril: curling stem of a climbing plant **5** carnage: massacre, bloodbath **6** sap (n): juice of trees
7 conical (adj): having the form of a cone (*Kegel*) **8** rafter: wooden beam that supports a roof **9** spent cartridge: cartridge that has been fired from a gun

– So there was definitely a gun fight?

– Not much of a fight, obviously. They didn't know what hit them. They were taken by surprise by a gun helicopter, or more likely a gunboat. The boat on the beach was the first to go, and then the huts.

One of the men gave a shout from behind a tree, and when we went to him we found the journalists in an excited huddle, cameras flashing. A body in a torn blue shirt. It was half covered by bamboo leaves so that the torn stomach was only partially visible, but even that was too much. Undigested[1] food mixed with blood covered the grass around the corpse, flies hovered and descended, oblivious to the clicking cameras and the sound of retching[2] going on all around. The face was squeezed in a grimace of pain, the mouth open in a voiceless howl; he must have seen the gun raised and pointed at him just before the bullet ripped into him. He looked young, not more than twenty. There was a trail of blood that started from the body and disappeared into the grass, indicating how he must have dragged himself after being hit, only to collapse where he now lay. Not far from him, two more bodies lay in a bush, bloody, broken and twisted. I moved away from the group and faced the smooth rippling surface of the water visible in the distance; I took a deep breath. Zaq was bent over in a bush not far from me, retching his guts out. He finished and stood up, his face wet with sweat, wiping the vomit from his mouth with a white handkerchief. He saw me looking at him and managed a weary smile. He lifted his hand weakly and pointed towards the boat.

1 undigested: not yet processed by the stomach **2** retching (n): vomitting

7

– I used to know your editor, Dan. We were reporters together in Lagos, a long time ago.

Zaq was facing me in the boat, raising a hand to protect his puffy face against the wind that would suddenly surge[1], then subside[2], over the water. From behind the trees we could hear the excited voices of the reporters as they took more pictures. I could imagine them jostling[3] each other, changing positions, trying to get a better and an even better shot of the dead bodies. Zaq was sitting on the same seat he had arrived in, but this time he was leaning weakly against the side of the boat, taking deep gulps of air, still recovering from his retching fit. He had taken out a whisky flask[4] from his pocket and was sipping from it. I sat facing him, draining the water from my shoes. Zaq had grown suddenly talkative, perhaps a nervous reaction to the gruesome[5] spectacle we had just witnessed. The waves gently raised and lowered the boat, the motion calming my frayed nerves. He lit a cigarette and offered me one. I didn't smoke, but I took one anyway. He blew smoke into the air.

– You may not remember me, but we have met before. Five years ago, in Lagos. I was a student at the School of Journalism, and you had come to give a lecture.

– I've given many lectures in my life. At one time I was giving almost two every week.

– And you helped me get my present job. You gave me your number and I called you. I still have the number ...

He looked a bit uncomfortable, turning away partially from me, but I went on, hoping he might remember if I jogged his memory hard enough.

1 surge: increase, get stronger **2** subside: die down **3** jostle sb.: push sb.
4 flask: small bottle (usu. for alcoholic drinks) **5** gruesome: terrible, shocking

– In that lecture you talked about journalists as conservationists … that we scribble[1] for posterity … and you said though most of what we write may be ephemeral[2], a note here about a car accident, a column there about a market fire, a suicide, a divorce, yet once in a while, maybe once in a lifetime, comes a transcendental moment, a great story only the true journalist can do justice to –

– I see. Well, your memory is better than mine. It was a long time ago. I was giving a lot of lectures at that time.

I saw no point in going on, though I wanted desperately to ask him if he thought we were pursuing just such a great story, and what it would take to do justice to it. In his lecture he said that the mark of a great journalist is the ability to know a great story when it comes, and to be ready for it, with the words and the talent and the daring to go after it. Nothing must be allowed to stand in the way. Now, he looked as if the only thing he wanted to do was go back home. I wasn't sure he still believed in what he taught.

– So, where do you think she might be?

He was staring at the scum[3] on the surface of the water as it washed against the boat, leaving a bubbly[4] film of oil on the wood. He shrugged.

– She wasn't here, that's for sure. My guess is that the bodies out there were going to be our escorts to wherever she's being held. It can't be far from here.

– What of the soldiers?

– Somewhere in these waters, still patrolling, trying to find the hideout. And I think we should be heading away from here as soon as we can. We don't want to be caught in a crossfire between the soldiers and the kidnappers …

Zaq suddenly stopped speaking and stared past me at the path leading to the island; the men's voices, I realized, had gone quiet.

1 scribble (infml): write **2** ephemeral [ɪˈfemərəl]: lasting only for a short period of time **3** scum: foam **4** bubbly: with many bubbles

Then, just before I turned to see what he found so arresting, I heard the command:

– Oya, move faster!

The reporters were walking in a single file, their hands raised above their heads, and flanking them were figures in black wearing masks, their guns pointed at the men. There were about five of them, and one saw us and quickly came to the boat. He waved one hand at us impatiently.

– You two, come down. Now!

We raised our hands and joined the others by the water. We watched the incoming tide deposit bits of wood and grass and bird feathers at our feet. Still holding the gun on us, the men climbed into our boat one by one and moved off. Not until the boat had long disappeared into the distance did we slowly lower our hands.

– Where did they come from?

Zaq's question met with a confused babble[1] as everyone regained speech at the same time.

– They won't send it back.

– They will, they promised.

– They will.

– How can you trust them?

– Well, they didn't shoot us.

– I knew I shouldn't have come on this assignment.

– Remember what happened to Tekena and the other one, what's his name ...

– Olisah. They were shot, in the back.

– We're all lucky to be alive.

– They will send back the boat.

Zaq's confident comment amidst the growing hysteria made us all look to him to see if he knew something we didn't, but he had already turned away and was facing the water. We turned back and continued arguing.

1 babble (n, infml): incomprehensible talk

The militants must have been hiding in the bushes after escaping the unexpected attack by the soldiers, and all the while they had observed us, waiting for the right moment to come out. They had held us hostage for not more than ten minutes, appearing more interested in getting off the island than in doing us harm. Only one of them had spoken to us. He was the shortest and thickest, with what looked like a gunshot wound on his arm.

– Journalists, we go send your boat back. Just wait here small[1].

When Nkem stepped forward to ask him a question, he made a dissuasive[2] gesture with his gun, making Nkem jump back immediately.

– We're journalists, and we're on your side. We want to report the truth, how your men were brutally slaughtered today for no reason. We just want to ask you a few questions.

– No questions. Just wait for your boat.

– But ...

– You, which paper you work for?

– I work for the *Globe* ...

– You too talk.

– We just want to find out about the hostage ...

The men in the boat conferred[3] briefly, and then the short man, who seemed to be their spokesman, turned to us.

– The woman dey fine.

And then they left with our boat.

Zaq unscrewed the cap on his hip flask, raised it to his mouth and drained it. He turned to the guide. – Use the radio. Call for another boat.

The man looked sheepish[4]. He wiped the sweat from his face.

– I ... I can't. They took away my radio, and my gun.

He looked diminished[5], jumpy and ready to go with the first suggestion from the reporters. We sat on wet mossy logs and watched the waves rise and fall. It was almost 5 p.m. and darkness was rap-

1 small (NP): for a short while **2** dissuasive (adj): (here) indicating not to do sth.
3 confer: discuss **4** sheepish: *unbeholfen* **5** diminished: (here) insecure

idly setting in, and as we waited we argued in our minds whether or not the boat would return.

When I got tired of watching the Lagos journalists try over and over again to make calls on their unresponsive[1] mobile phones, I decided to take a walk on the beach. It was almost 7 p.m., and already some of the men, resigned to the fact that we might be spending the night here, had moved inland to look for some kind of shelter. I remained by the water, not because I was convinced the boat would return for us, but because I knew the midges[2] and mosquitoes were fewer here with the sea breeze to chase them away, but even then one needed more than two hands to fight them. They found every exposed spot on the arms, the neck and especially the face.

– Are there bigger islands nearby?

Zaq was leaning against a palm tree, his empty whisky flask in his hand. His voice was slow, tired. He belched[3].

– Yes. Lots of them. There are fishing communities all over the islands, and by morning these waters will be busy with boat traffic.

– So, all we have to do is survive the night.

– Right.

I left him leaning on the tree, staring into the water after he had thrown the empty flask into it. I walked with the frogs and crickets[4] and crabs. Over the sound of the water the night birds took turns singing the world a lullaby[5]. I walked, feeling the water wash up my trousers and the crabs scurrying[6] out of my way with their surprisingly fast sideways pace, always keeping me in view. I walked to suppress my hunger and the pain in my legs and the rising cold biting at my skin, and when I got tired of walking I turned back. The men, back from their futile search for shelter, had started a fire; its flame glowed weakly, wavering in the humid wind coming off the water, briefly illuminating their anxious faces. I joined them and we

1 unresponsive: (here) not working **2** midge: tiny fly that bites **3** belch: *rülpsen* **4** cricket: *Grille* **5** lullaby: song sung to children to get them to sleep **6** scurry: move quickly

stood there, solemn, not talking, staring into the half-hearted fire, listening to the waves and noting how the sound they made oddly resembled the rumblings in our stomach, waiting and hoping, but not expecting, that the boat would return.

But towards midnight it came, silently gliding over the dark water, its presence betrayed only by the soft slicing of the boatman's oar.

– It's here!

The moon was out by now, its silver light murky and mobile on the water. It was a canoe, and in the transforming light of the moon it looked longer than it really was, almost endless, its rear end merging with the water.

– It's not our boat!

We stared, standing close together like skittish colts[1], as a man came out of the canoe and pulled it onto the beach. Then he approached us with the oar still in his hands, partly raised across his chest like a shield. There was a second figure in the boat, holding a hurricane lamp, its dim, almost invisible flare bobbing up and down with the waves. In the poor light only the man's broad outline was visible: he looked thin and wispy, like a spirit of the forest. The oar came up to his shoulder, his shirt was whitish and even in the dark I could tell it was the sort of rough and shapeless homespun worn by the fishing folk in this area. He advanced slowly, perhaps unsure what manner of reception to expect, but it was clear that he wasn't here by accident, that he was here for us.

– Who are you?

Our guide stepped forward challengingly, towering over the tiny man, seeking to reassert his lost authority.

– I come carry you go Irikefe. Them send me.

– Who sent you?

A redundant[2] question. It was clear the militants had kept our boat and had convinced this terrified boatman – with money but more probably with terror – to take us to wherever we could get

1 colt: young horse **2** redundant: superfluous, unnecessary

lodging[1] for the night. Keeping our new and spacious boat was not a surprising thing for the militants to do, but sending the boatman back for us was definitely unexpected. They weren't inhuman, after all. I was glad we weren't spending the night on this spooky[2], cold and ravaged[3] island. Somehow the eight of us all fitted into the dugout canoe with its two plank-like crossbenches. I sat on the wet floor, my back against somebody's knees, my knees pulled up to my chin, and as we pulled away from the beach I lowered my head and listened to the rhythmic sound of the oar slicing[4] the water and the occasional anxious question being thrown at the reticent[5] boatman. He had the same answer to all our questions.

– Yes, sah. Irikefe Island. No far, but e far small. Soon we go get there.

His companion was a small boy of about ten, his son perhaps, who said nothing throughout the trip. No one in the boat had heard of Irikefe, so with our imaginations we built various versions of what awaited. I saw a hotel, with clean water, and a clean bed, and a huge meal; I saw a long restful sleep and an early departure tomorrow; I saw us reaching Port Harcourt before noon to a hero's reception from our colleagues and editors; I saw my story on the front pages; and, finally, I saw myself being restored to my rightful place as a reporter. In the weeks to come we'd get drunk for free in our various press clubrooms as we added yet another detail to the already overwrought tale of our daring adventure. I had a draft of my story in my head, and trapped for posterity in my point-and-shoot Sony digital camera were images of the gutted[6] bodies half hidden in the bushes, the thatchless, burned-down huts, the bullet-broken palm trees, and the spectacular fire throwing up a cloud of smoke over the tall trees. I must have been lulled to sleep by the movement of the boat, for I came awake suddenly when the boat lurched up, then down, and then stopped. We were on shore. I got to my knees and

1 lodging (n): accomodation **2** spooky: eerie, frightening **3** ravage sth.: devastate sth., destroy sth. **4** slice sth.: cut through sth. **5** reticent: quiet, unwilling to communicate **6** gutted: with the inner organs torn out

looked to land. Trees, and far away what seemed to be dim flickers of light from houses or cars. The others were already jumping out of the boat. I joined them, but as we got set to go, we were stopped by the boatman's voice.

– Wait small for Oga[1] here. E be like say e no[2] too well.

It was Zaq. He was hanging over the edge of the boat, retching into the water, and then he collapsed back inside it. We all rushed over to see him lying in a pool of water at the bottom, his sweaty face illuminated by the boatman's lantern, his unfocused eyes staring up at us, breathing with difficulty through his mouth. I reached down and tried to pull him up, but it took three of us to get him out. We staggered to dry ground, where we sat him down and stood over him, unsure what to do next. The Lagos reporters stood to one side, looking at their watches, impatient to be off, not attempting to assist in any way. I knelt beside the boatman, who was trying to communicate with the bowed Zaq. As I touched his arm, which was hot and dripping with sweat, he looked up at me, licking his dry lips.

– If I can get a drink, I'll be fine. I'm just tired. All I need is a drink. Just a little bit.

His voice in my ear was hoarse, whispery. I felt sad and disappointed by this once great reporter, whose success and dedication had to some extent inspired my own career and doubtless that of many others. I turned away from the beseeching[3], pitiful grin on his sweaty face, and suddenly I felt angry. It was a helpless, directionless anger, and it disappeared almost as soon as it came.

– If we can get to a hotel you can have something, I'm sure. But we have to go now. It's late already.

I moved away from him. He lurched to his feet, and the boatman went to him and held his left arm.

– Is … is there a hotel nearby?

– Hotel? No hotel. We go shrine.

– Shrine?

1 oga (NP): boss, master **2** E be like say e no (NP): It seems that he is not
3 beseeching: pleading, imploring

– Yes. You get food at shrine.

– Did you hear what he said? Do you know where you're going?

My shout reached the others, who had already put a good distance between themselves and us, drawn to the faraway lights, like camels scenting[1] water, and they stopped and waited for us.

– Aren't we going to a hotel? There must be a hotel here somewhere.

– The man said we're going to a shrine ...

– Shrine? What shrine?

I had no answer for them, so I urged the boatman and his boy to keep walking. The man seemed harmless enough, and if he said we should go to some shrine, I was willing to follow him, especially if there was food to be had.

We went slowly, supporting the weak, dead-weight Zaq between us. Twice we had to stop as he slipped gasping onto the muddy ground. Then we dragged him up and started again. It was an arduous[2], back-breaking progress, worsened by the humidity in the airless, tree-bordered path, and I was soaked in sweat by the time we got to the shrine, about a quarter of a kilometre from the water. The thick vegetation suddenly disappeared and we were in an open yard where still, silent shapes couched in darkness were watching our approach. Our steps faltered, finally coming to a stop in instinctive response to the menacing[3] air of the immobile figures ahead of us. At first I thought: the kidnappers, waiting in ambush. But why were they so still? The boatman lifted his lamp so the light fell on the figures.

– Na statue. Many statue. For the shrine.

We passed the statues warily[4], once more packed together like skittish[5] colts, our heads swivelling[6] wildly to keep the figures in view, half expecting them suddenly to jump on us. At the edge of the yard we could see an open doorway in which a lamp glowed

1 scent sth.: smell sth. **2** arduous [ˈɑːdʒuəs]: difficult, exhausting
3 menacing: threatening **4** wary: cautious **5** skittish: nervous
6 swivel (v): turn

brightly. The boatman disappeared into the hut and we waited outside, straining to hear the exchange coming faintly from within, but we didn't have to wait long. He soon came out, followed by a man leaning on a stick, a blanket flowing down from his shoulders.

– We have been expecting you.

He spoke in English, his words slow and distinct, and he looked from face to face as he spoke.

Nkem stood boldly, almost challengingly, before the man, his arms akimbo[1]. – You were expecting us?

– Yes. I am Naman, assistant to the head priest. Apologies, the head priest is not well and cannot be here to receive you. We've been instructed to take care of you for the night. Tomorrow you can catch the ferry back to the city.

The man's voice carried easily over our heads and into the open yard behind us, a voice accustomed to addressing congregations[2]. There was confidence in the way he raised his hand as he spoke, and in the way he threw his chest forward when he moved, and yet the voice remained even, clear, polite.

– Come inside.

He stepped aside and waved us forward, smiling. The hut was surprisingly roomy, and would easily accommodate all six of us. It was bare of furniture except for mats strewn over the mud floor. We took off our shoes and sat, gladly, on the hard floor, our backs against the curving wall.

– This will be your quarters[3] for the night. We apologize for any discomfort, but this is all we can provide at such short notice. And before we could ask him any more questions he left us, stepping out into the night as soon as he uttered his last word. We left the door and the single window open to trap whatever passing breeze we could, but, despite the stifling[4] heat in the room, Zaq, seated next to me, was shaking violently, his arms wrapped around him, trying to

1 arms akimbo: arms bent at the elbows with the hands on the hips **2** congregation: gathering of people (usu. in church) **3** quarters (pl): accomodation **4** stifling: *stickig*

keep warm. He was lying on his side, his head almost touching the floor. I hoped he'd simply fall asleep and wake up tomorrow when it was time to go. I felt as if I was being made solely responsible for him, and I wanted to say to the others, Don't you know who Zaq is? Surely they knew about him, especially the Lagos reporters. After all he had once been one of them. But these haughty[1] faces looked young, ignorant – one looked even younger than me – and I saw how their puzzled eyes travelled round the room, landing on face after face, trying to gauge[2] if we were in real trouble, or if this was a brief discomfort that would disappear with the coming of day. No, they'd be too young to know Zaq.

Zaq's Lagos days ended almost five years ago, and in this business that was a whole generation. A generation of papers, his generation, had died out, its place taken by another generation, my generation. Broader, glossier[3], racier[4], cockier.

Not long after the priest had gone a woman came in carrying a large bowl of water and placed it by the door. Then smilingly she invited us to wash our hands, and as we washed two more smiling matrons[5] came in, one with a bowl filled with steaming bean porridge, the other with a tray bearing chunks of lumpy home-baked bread. Not a three-course gourmet meal, but at this moment it tasted like the best meal I'd ever had. The priest, Naman, did not return; only the women did, to remove the dishes. We drank water from a plastic pitcher[6] and before long we were all drowsy[7]. Some of us were already sprawled out and snoring, having arranged our limbs around each other's as best we could. All night I kept an eye on Zaq, who had a rough time of it, burning with fever and sweating till early morning, when his temperature dropped and he fell asleep.

I was the first to wake up, or maybe I hadn't slept at all, and when I opened my eyes it was dark in the room, and outside I could hear

1 haughty: arrogant **2** gauge: estimate, determine **3** glossy: (here) shiny, attractive **4** racy: exciting, sexy **5** matron: older woman who usu. is also a mother **6** pitcher: *Karaffe* **7** drowsy: sleepy

the faraway call of roosters[1] accompanied by insects ushering in the day. It was 6 a. m. It'd be at least another hour before the others woke up. I carefully made my way past the sprawled-out, intertwined[2] limbs and emerged outside to sea air and birdsong. Nostalgia settled on my shoulders like the arm of a long-lost friend, urging me to look back and listen; it had been years since I heard such morning sounds, such silence. I walked for a while in the sculpture garden, studying the decaying clay figures, then I climbed a hillock[3] overlooking the water and stared at its rippling, glittering surface. I saw a flock of morning birds emerge from a leafy cove[4] on the opposite bank, and then I returned to the hut. All the men were outside already, except for Zaq, who was lying on his back on the mud floor, his eyes fixed to the concave[5] thatch roof. When I stood over him I saw his forehead covered in sweat, his lips parched and bleeding. He tried a smile, but couldn't make it.

I helped him outside and sat him on a log under a tree. A man in a long white robe came and told us a pick-up truck would be here any minute to take us to the pier, where we'd get the ferry back to Port Harcourt. Some of the men stood under the leafy gardenias and acacias that grew all over the yard; some walked in the sculpture garden taking pictures of the statues, asking the tall priest questions. In the daylight the still figures didn't look as menacing as they had last night. All their faces were carefully aligned to face east or west. The ones facing east had a happy, ecstatic, worshipful expression, their clumpy, broken-fingered hands open, raised as though to receive the morning sun, while the figures facing west had their heads bowed, their lips turned down. There was a contorted and tortuous quality to the figures that made them appear grotesquely life-like, naturalistic, like seedlings that had just now sprouted from the earth, still learning how to stand straight. There were dozens of them, some old and decaying, some looking newer.

1 rooster: male chicken **2** intertwined: entangled, twisted together **3** hillock: small hill **4** cove: small bay **5** concave (adj): rounded inwards

– We believe the sun rising brings a renewal. All of creation is born anew with the new day. Whatever goes wrong in the night has a chance for redemption[1] after a cycle.

– Who made the figures?

– The worshippers[2], that's what we call ourselves. Some of these figures go back almost a hundred years to the founding of the shrine. The sculpture garden is the shrine to which this whole island is dedicated.

The priest stood a little detached from the journalists, maintaining his smile, his hands clasped behind him; the blanket from yesterday was gone and in its place was a white cotton robe that shook and sparkled in the morning breeze. He turned when he heard the truck approaching.

– Ah, here's your transportation to the ferry.

I turned to Zaq, who was seated with his back against the tree; his head was bowed, and his eyes when he raised them looked dull.

– The truck is here, Zaq.

– I can see that.

– Time to go.

– I can't stand up.

– I'll help you, come on. Take my hand.

– I think I'll stay here.

– What? But you can't stay here.

I looked around, trying to involve the others in our exchange, but most of them were scrambling for the truck.

– We have to get you to a doctor.

– I'll stay another day, if they'll have me.

– Well ... that is no problem.

The urbane[3] priest was just behind me, a smile on his infinitely kind face.

– Are you sure? He needs a doctor.

1 redemption: *Erlösung* **2** worshipper: sb. who takes part in a religious ceremony **3** urbane: polite and confident in social situations

– We have a nurse here and she will attend to you. But perhaps you won't need her. The air alone will heal you. I have seen it happen. But I must warn you that it will be several days before the ferry is back this way.

– I don't mind.

– Listen, Zaq ... Are you sure?

He slumped, all the effort leaving his shoulders.

– Will you take a message for me, Rufus? It's for my editor, Beke Johnson. Here's his card. Call him and tell him I'll be back in a few days.

I took the card. For the first time since I saw him yesterday, he had a smile on his face. He motioned for me to come closer, and when I leaned forward I could smell stale[1] drink on his breath and see clearly into his watery and red and yellow eyes.

– I like the air here. It's pure. Who knows, I might even get some sort of religion.

I nodded, unsure if he was serious or joking. The truck honked[2] twice and the journalists waved impatiently for me to hurry up.

– Have a safe trip.

The priest walked me to the truck.

– Your friend will be fine with us. Don't worry.

I gave him my office number, and Zaq's editor's number, just in case Zaq became seriously ill.

– But we don't have phones here.

– Just keep it. In case of emergency.

As the truck bumped its way through the dew-soaked morning vegetation towards the pier at the other end of the island, my mind kept returning to Zaq. I had an image of him in that hut, alone, sweating, pining for a drink, haunted by whatever memories were pursuing him. As we got to the village centre the landscape changed: the huts disappeared, and grey brick houses with rusty zinc roofs lined the single dirt road. The houses were grouped into compounds by walls of mud and straw, and behind every compound was a little

1 stale (adj): no longer fresh **2** honk (v): sound a vehicle's horn

field of vegetables and cassava, their climbers circling over each other, aspiring upwards, using slender[1] sticks stuck into the earth as crutches[2]. Children came out, wiping the sleep from their eyes, and women with long-handled brooms cleaned the house fronts. Here, time seemed suspended and inconsequential[3], and for a moment I felt Zaq had chosen the better option by remaining and not hurrying to return to Port Harcourt.

1 slender: thin **2** crutch: *Krücke* **3** inconsequential: unimportant

Part Two

8

– Your friend, I am sorry to say, is dying.

The Doctor was an overweight cherub[1] and when he breathed he did so with painful effort through his mouth; the wheezing[2] and spluttering[3] sound accompanying it was loud and unpleasant. He was dressed in the same military fatigues and boots, but this time without the grubby[4] white jacket, and whenever he leaned forward the shirt buttons across his fraught midsection threatened to pop[5]. The shirt was wet under the armpits. He smoked incessantly, and as he spoke his words came out shrouded in cigarette smoke. How did he manage, in the midst of such aridity[6] and want and barrenness[7], to look so fat, so gross[8]? But as he spoke, and as I listened, I soon forgot his physical appearance. He was intelligent and sympathetic, philosophical almost, his tiny eyes seeming to probe deep into his listener's soul, searching for whatever ailment[9] was plaguing him.

Out of a vague sense of decorum[10] he had led me out to break the news, away from the feverish eyes of the soldiers, and from the sleeping Zaq. He offered me a cigarette and when I shook my head he nodded approvingly. Now we were walking back and forth on the edge of the water, and we kept swatting[11] at the midges and flies that flew out of the grass at our feet.

– What exactly is wrong with him, Doctor?

– Have you ever heard of dengue fever[12]?

I hadn't.

1 cherub (derog): corpulent person **2** wheeze: breathe with difficulty **3** splutter: make a sound similar to coughing or spitting **4** grubby: dirty **5** pop (v): burst open **6** aridity: severe dryness **7** barrenness: lifelessness, infertility **8** gross: *widerlich* **9** ailment: chronic desease **10** decorum: proper behaviour in a given situation **11** swat at sb./sth.: (try to) hit sb./sth. with a flat hand **12** dengue ['deŋgi] fever: dangerous and contagious tropical disease that causes high fever

– It's a haemorrhagic[1] fever, very dangerous. It kills very quickly if not treated immediately.

– Is that what he has?

– No. It's a similar strain[2], quite new, still nameless. I've come across it only two or three times before in this area. Bugs and the water, you know, and if that combination doesn't kill you, the violence does.

– You mean he won't live?

He avoided my perplexed gaze and waved his hand round, embracing the whole visible universe in his gesture.

– Somewhere in these godforsaken[3] waters, that's where he must have picked it up. There're plenty of bugs flourishing here. And he was in pretty bad shape to begin with. I suspect his liver is gone already.

He wiped his sweaty forehead, giving me another full view of the armpit. I felt an irrational hatred for him and nothing would have given me greater pleasure than to puncture[4] his overfed middle and calmly watch whatever stuffing[5] was inside pour out.

– Well, you have to do something about it.

– I'm afraid I can't. Not with the tools I have here. You'll have to take him back to Port Harcourt, to a proper hospital.

– I'll talk to the Major. We need transportation immediately.

– You could try, but I doubt he'll help you in any way. He's not a very obliging[6] kind of person, I'm sorry to say. Do you know, I saved his life, that's how I ended up here as the doctor, and yet even I can't be sure of him at any time. Mercurial[7], that's what he is. Unpredictable. It's the oil and the fighting. It affects everyone in a strange way. I'm going to write a book on that someday. I've been in these waters five years now and I tell you this place is a dead place, a place for dying.

1 haemorrhagic (adj): causing bleeding **2** strain: (here) variety of a disease **3** godforsaken: given up by God **4** puncture sth.: (here) stab sth. **5** stuffing (n): filling **6** obliging: kind, willing to respond to people's requests **7** mercurial: unpredictable

He pointed at the faraway orange sky. – Those damned flares. There weren't that many of them when I first came here. Sometimes I feel like I've been here all my life.

– Well, then, what are you saying, what should I do? My friend is dying. Tell me what to do.

– Ah, it is not easy ...

Happy to find a listening ear, he grew talkative. I could imagine how he must have spent his days here, hunched over his beakers[1] and blood samples, his speculative, philosophical observations met by the groans and whimpers[2] of soldiers.

A leaner, more idealistic man, he had been posted to a village not far from here five years ago, fresh from medical school. The old doctor, who was about to retire, met him at the boat and had boys take his bags to his new quarters, a spacious hut near the dispensary[3]. The next day the old man showed him around the village and the two-room dispensary. The village consisted of not more than twenty families, and each family's ailments had been neatly recorded and filed in the old doctor's shaky but neat handwriting and stored in alphabetical order in files kept in two formidable-looking iron filing cabinets in the back room.

– It was a small village. At first I was lonely, and daily I thought of nothing but how to work my way out of that posting, but I soon grew fond of the place and the people. Anyway, the old doctor, before he finally bowed out[4], took me from door to door, and to the neighbouring communities, introducing me to the people. I set up mobile clinics in my boat, I held educational classes in churches and schools, talking to teachers and pastors and community leaders. But I soon discovered that the village's chief discontent was not over their health; they were a remarkably[5] healthy people, actually. One day an elder looked me in the face and said, I am not ill. I am

1 beaker: (here) cup for medical samples **2** whimper (n): weak, unhappy sound **3** dispensary: (here) place where sick people are treated **4** bow out: retire, stop working **5** remarkable: extraordinary

just poor. Can you give me medicine for that? We want that fire that burns day and night. He told me that, plainly, pugnaciously[1].

– Well, as if in answer to his request, two years after my arrival in the village, oil was discovered. Be careful what you wish for, they say. Yes, just on the edge of the village, by the water, there was oil in commercial quantities. The villagers feasted for weeks. They got their orange fire, planted firmly over the water at the edge of the village. Night and day it burned, and now the villagers had no need for candles or lamps, all they had to do at night was to throw open their doors and windows and just like that, everything was illuminated. That light soon became the village square. At night men and women would stand facing it, lost in wonder, for hours, simply staring till their eyes watered and their heads grew dizzy. Village meetings, which used to take place early in the mornings on Saturdays in one of the school classrooms, now took place at night under the orange fire: the elders, in their wrappers and holding their walking sticks, would arrange their chairs in a semicircle and hold forth[2]. A night market developed around that glow, and every evening women brought their wares. Some came from the neighbouring villages, they bought and sold, they set up portable iron hearths[3] and fried *akara* and fish which they sold to happy children under that fire. And when Brother Jonah came back from the city, or, as he described it, from the belly of the big whale, after being away for three years, it was under the orange glow that his congregation met every Sunday night. They'd dance, their faces raised up to that undying glow, singing their thanks and joy, their voices carrying for miles over the water. They called it the Fire of Pentecost[4]. I don't know what that means exactly, but it made them very happy. They said it was a sign, the fulfilment of some covenant[5] with God.

– Well, I did my duty as their doctor. I told them of the dangers that accompany that quenchless flare, but they wouldn't lis-

1 pugnacious: aggressive, ready to participate in an argument or a fight **2** hold forth: talk at length **3** hearth: *Herd* **4** Pentecost: *Pfingsten* **5** covenant: alliance, agreement

ten. And then a year later, when the livestock began to die, and the plants began to wither on their stalks, I took samples of the drinking water and in my lab I measured the level of toxins in it: it was rising, steadily. In one year it had grown to almost twice the safe level. Of course the people didn't listen, they were still in thrall[1] to the orange glare. When I confronted the oil workers, they offered me money, and a job. The manager, an Italian guy, wrote me a cheque and said I was now on their payroll. He told me to continue doing what I was doing, but this time I was to come to him only with my results. I thought they'd do something with my results, but they didn't. So, when people started dying, I took blood samples and recorded the toxins in them, and this time I sent my results to the government. They thanked me and dumped the results in some filing cabinet. More people died and I sent my results to NGOs[2] and international organizations, which published them in international journals and urged the government to do something about the flares, but nothing happened. More people fell sick, a lot died. I watched the night market fold up, and the council meetings cease. The church also folded when Brother Jonah got a job as a clerk with the oil company. Almost overnight I watched the whole village disappear, just like that. I feel angry at the oil company, and I also feel angry at myself. I was their doctor, I should have done more than I did. Well, since then I've become something of an itinerant[3] doctor. I go from community to community and I try to create awareness of the dangers lurking[4] in the wells and in the air above. They all share the same story, the same diseases. I do what good I can. I watched his lips as he spoke, watched his cigarette burn and the smoke rise in loops[5] high over his head, adding more pollutants to the polluted air, but all the time my mind was trying to make sense of what he had said about Zaq.

1 in thrall to sth./sb.: fascinated by sth./sb., captivated by sth./sb. **2** NGO: non-governmental organization **3** itinerant (adj): moving from place to place **4** lurk (v): hide **5** loop (n): ring

He put a hand on my shoulder. – I'm sorry about your friend. I'll talk to the Major. I'll try to persuade him to let you go, but, I warn you, don't expect a quick response. Take your friend to another doctor. Get a second opinion, but that won't really help much, I'm afraid. I've seen this happen many times in this area. A man suddenly comes down with[1] a mild headache, becomes feverish, then develops rashes[2], and suddenly a vital[3] organ shuts down. And those whom the disease doesn't kill, the violence does. Sometimes I wonder what I'm doing here; I tell you there's more need for gravediggers than for a doctor.

I wanted to ask the Doctor if he thought the fighting would end soon, who was right, who was wrong, if he knew where the Professor was, if he had heard about the kidnapped woman, but instead I turned and looked towards the shed where Zaq lay, breathing away his life.

– Thank you, Doctor. I have to go to my friend now.

– By all means. Let's go together.

He led the way, belching smoke, his fat arms horizontally suspended from his sides, his fat bottom almost popping out of his trousers, and I could hear his wheezing, phlegmy[4] breathing, and I wanted to shout after him, Doctor, heal thyself[5]!

1 come down with sth.: catch sth. (a disease) **2** rash (n): *Ausschlag* **3** vital (adj): necessary for survival **4** phlegmy: slimy **5** thyself (arch): yourself

9

– The Major will speak with you. I told him about your need to be gone from here as soon as possible. He's waiting for us in the command hut. Let's not keep him waiting.

The Doctor led the way, and Zaq and I followed. Soldiers bearing rifles came and went, some nodding briefly to the Doctor as they passed us. The command hut was situated at the edge of the camp, right by the path we took coming in from the boat. The Major met us in front of the hut, waved us in, a smile on his face.

– Hope you had a good night, hope the mosquitoes didn't bother you.

He was in a good mood today, almost conciliatory[1], making a joke about the rock-hard bread he gave us and the black sugarless tea in dented[2] aluminium cups. Zaq and I sat on a long hardwood bench that faced the command table, with the Major on the other side of it. The Doctor sat apart, by a square window looking out on the trees by the waterfront. I ate the hard dry bread and sipped the cold tea, but Zaq didn't even look at the bread, and the tea he downed in a single gulp, more from thirst than from an enjoyment of the bitter, inky[3] taste. He didn't look like a dying man – he looked rested and alert. The Doctor said it would be like this, good days alternating with bad ones. I hadn't told Zaq all that the Doctor had said, only that his condition was serious, and he needed to be in a hospital as soon as possible. He had nodded and failed to inquire any further.

I decided to take advantage of the Major's good mood immediately.

– The old man and the boy … when can we talk to them?

1 conciliatory: willing to end an argument by being friendly **2** dented: *verbeult*
3 inky (adj): tasting like ink (*Tinte*)

– Tell me, what do you know about them?

– They're simple peasants, trying to make a living. We've been together this past week, believe me, they're not rebels.

– I know these people more than you do. You know the problem with you reporters? You believe everything you read in the papers.

The Doctor laughed, the Major waited for us to laugh, and when we didn't he went on.

– Let me give you an example. The Doctor here told me that one of your plans on this trip is to interview the Professor, yes? Well, what do you know about him? I'll tell you what you know: he used to work for an oil company, and one day he grew disgusted with the environmental abuse and he became a militant to fight for change. That's what the papers say. Well, that isn't true.

Zaq lifted his empty tea cup and put it down again.

– Well, Major, what is true?

– The Doctor can tell you about the deserted villages around here. They used to be well populated, you know, thriving[1]. Now the people have all packed their things and left, because of the violence. People like the Professor are responsible for that, they call themselves freedom fighters, but they are rebels, terrorists, kidnappers. Do you keep up with the news? Ah, yes, you write the news. Well, just now, on that radio, it was announced, they just kidnapped a three-year-old girl in Port Harcourt, and you know what, her family is not connected to the oil industry. A three-year-old girl. They don't care if they're caught, or shot. Their life is so miserable to begin with, and they dream of becoming instant millionaires. It's my job to pursue them to their swamp hideouts. I capture them, and most times it's easier to shoot them than to capture them. Saves time, saves the government money.

– Now, let's come back to this so-called Professor. We have a big file on him, on all of them. His name is Ani Wilson. A secondary-

1 thrive (v): grow, be prosperous

school dropout[1], a backstreet thug[2] and bully[3] who went to jail for the first time at fifteen. When he came out at twenty he became a party thug in the pay of his local government chairman, who was up for re-election. He was convicted of murder at the age of twenty-two and sent to prison for life. He broke out of jail at thirty, by which time he had realized there was no future in being a petty thug and hired gun[4]. Luckily for him, his politician godfather had reinvented himself as a pro-environmentalist and won a seat in the senate. But they parted ways when Ani was bought by a rival politician, who paid him to kill his erstwhile[5] godfather[6]; the assassination attempt was foiled[7], and his godfather called the police on him, and that was when he moved into the swamps and joined a rebel group that specialized in kidnapping foreigners for ransom. You know who the leader of that group was?

– Who?

– He was known as the Professor – only he wasn't a real professor. It was just his gang name.

– And so –

– And so Ani killed him in a power struggle and took over not only the leadership but the title of 'Professor' as well. The myth of the Professor lives on.

– I see.

– I'm glad you see. I know these people. I'm the one who can handle them, the only one. They understand only one language: force. That's all.

The Major brought down his fist on the flimsy table, making the cups and pens jump.

– And what of your prisoners here? Are you going to try[8] them?

1 dropout (n, infml): sb. who leaves school/university without finishing her/his education **2** thug (infml, derog): criminal **3** bully (n, infml): person who intimidates/threatens other people **4** hired gun (infml): paid killer
5 erstwhile (adj): former **6** godfather: *Pate* **7** foil sth. (v): prevent sth. from happening **8** try sb.: put sb. to trial

– You journalists, with your fancy[1] ideas about human rights and justice ... all nonsense. There are no human rights for people like them. You jail them and in a year they'll be out on the streets. The best thing is to line them up and shoot them. But, you people ...

The Major made a dismissive[2] gesture with his hand and stood up. He went to the window and looked out towards the river.

– We want to interview them, your prisoners. We want to hear their side of the story.

The Major turned to Zaq, his head tilted, considering the unexpected request.

– You, I thought you were sick and wanted a doctor immediately, even though the Doctor here is the best in the whole world. It is true. He saved my life.

The Doctor sipped his tea and continued to look out through the window.

– I'm feeling better, thank you. Let us interview them.

– Well, why not. I'll bring them over here right away and you will listen to them and afterwards you tell me what you think.

– No. Don't bring them here. If they think you ordered the interview, they'll be guarded, they won't open up. Tonight, lock us up with them, let them think we're also under suspicion.

– Are you sure you want to be locked up with them?

The Major looked from Zaq to the Doctor to me. Zaq nodded. I nodded, even though this was not something Zaq had informed me about earlier.

– Well, then, you'd better do it as soon as you can, tonight. Tomorrow we leave for Irikefe – that is actually the main reason I called you. We just heard the island has been attacked by your friends, the rebels. There is serious fighting going on at the moment and they need reinforcements[3]. We leave early tomorrow. You can

1 fancy (adj): extravagant **2** dismissive (adj): (here) signalling that sb. can leave
3 reinforcements (pl): (here) extra soldiers sent to make up for lost forces and/or make an army more powerful

come with me, or you can stay with the rebels till I come back. You decide.

– We'll come.

– Good. That's settled. Now, I want to know more about you two. I'm curious about people and their motives. Why did you come here, to a war zone? You could get killed. Are you looking for fame? Is that it? Tell me how you came here.

It was a long time before nightfall, when we'd interview the militants. There was a lot of time to kill. So I told him how I received the assignment to interview the English woman, and about the burning island, and how we all ended up on Irikefe. I told him almost everything, but I did not tell him about Boma, and how I found her waiting for me that day when I returned to Port Harcourt.

*

She was alone, and I could tell she had been crying, when I got home in the evening. I had gone straight to the office to write my piece for the next day's paper as soon as I arrived in Port Harcourt in the afternoon; my legs were still wobbly from standing for almost the entire length of the journey. The ferry had made so many stops on the way till I began to think we were never going to reach Port Harcourt that day. We had picked up women carrying chickens in baskets and crabs in buckets and squealing[1] goats led by ropes around their necks on their way to the market. The air in the ferry's central lounge soon grew foul, forcing me to abandon my seat next to a fat, laughing, gesticulating woman and her two children to stand outside by the rail, my eyes focused on the receding coastline, my mind contemplating what awaited me in Port Harcourt.

Boma was seated on my wicker armchair, facing the TV, but in such a way that her profile showed the undamaged side of her face, and even when she looked up at my entrance she still managed to keep the burned, badly healed side of her face hidden. She did it

1 squeal (v): make a shrill noise

unconsciously, but the scar always dictated how she stood, how she sat. It made me sad when she did that, especially with me. How could I tell her that she really needn't do that with me? Only with John, her husband, was she ever able to sit without regard to where the light fell, but two months ago John had left her, and now she had taken to stopping by more often, even when I wasn't around. She'd wash the dishes and cook and sweep the room, but sometimes, though I had never caught her at it, she just sat and cried.

Today her bags and crockery[1] and TV and other household things were heaped in a corner of my tiny living room.

– The landlord[2] kicked me out.

She lived in a tenement house[3] similar to mine, in a room-and-parlour[4], owned by the same hard-faced, unsmiling landlord. The landlord had started hanging around outside their door soon after John, who worked for a courier company as a mail sorter, lost his job six months ago. Since Boma was only a trainee typist and didn't get paid, I had shared my monthly pay with them, knowing that they had only me to turn to, as I had only them.

I went to the bathroom to urinate and to wash my face, and when I came back she stood up, went to the cooker in the corner and dished out some rice for me.

– You must be hungry.

– Thank you.

When the silence grew too heavy, even with the TV on, I told her of the kidnapping, and the devastated island. When I got to the dead bodies, she burst into tears.

– The poor people, they could be anyone, just anyone. I knew she was thinking of John. He had become very political, hanging out in backstreet bar rooms with other unemployed youths to play cards and drink all day, always complaining about the government.

1 crockery: items such as plates and cups to serve food and drinks **2** landlord: sb. who rents out a house or an apartment **3** tenement house: apartment building that often only meets minimum standards of sanitation and comfort **4** room-and-parlour: small apartment without bathroom

He had been full of anger before he left, the kind of anger that often pushed one to blaspheme, or to rob a bank, or to join the militants. I had seen that kind of anger before in many of my friends, people I went to school with; some of them were now in the forests with the fighters, some of them had made millions from ransom money, but a lot of them were dead.

– Boma, John has more sense than that.

John had married her when others had cringed and recoiled at the sight of her red, constantly watery eyes and curdled[1] cheek.

We had grown up together, the three of us; fought the bullies together in primary and secondary school, parting only when I left home, the first time to become a photographer's apprentice in Port Harcourt, the second time when I went to journalism school in Lagos. At first I thought John had stuck to Boma out of pity, and I resented[2] him for it; I really truly believed only when I saw the exchange of rings, and the joy on my sister's damaged face.

She slept on the bed and I spread a blanket on my old and tattered carpet in the living room after moving some of her things into the bedroom. Boma went to sleep immediately, but I couldn't sleep, and when I got sore from endlessly tossing and turning, I switched on the TV and watched a science fiction movie about a submerged[3] world. The polar ice cap has melted and land has sunk under water and is now talked about only in legends. The star, Kevin Costner, is a hated mutant, with gills[4] and webbed feet[5], and he is clever with contraptions[6] and devices. In one scene he takes the heroine under water in a bell jar and shows her an inundated[7] city. This is it, he tells her; there is no dry land, so quit hoping. There is only water. There are long and beautiful shots of endless ocean, with only Kevin Costner's frail boat on it, dwarfed[8] by the liquid blue vastness. I fell

1 curdled: *geronnen*, (here) hardened and disfigured from the burning **2** resent sb.: dislike sb., hate sb. **3** submerged: completely covered by water **4** gill [gɪl]: organ with which fishes breathe under water **5** webbed feet: feet with toes connected by skin **6** contraption: small machine or piece of equipment **7** inundate sth.: flood sth. with water **8** dwarf sth.: make sth. look small by comparison

asleep with the movie still playing, thinking there was something sad about a people who were born and lived and died on water, on rusty ships and boats and fantastic balloons, their days and nights filled with the hope of someday finding dry earth, their wars and industries and relationships and culture all driven by the myth of dry land.

10

The Reporter was a moderate, middle-brow[1] daily occupying the two bottom floors in a five-floor building in central Port Harcourt. Across the street from our offices was a private elementary school that came awake at 8 a.m. and remained awake till 4 p.m.; next to it was a nightclub that came awake at 8 p.m. and remained awake till 4 a.m.; and further down the street in a row were a mechanic's garage, a restaurant and a car wash. *The Reporter* had been in existence for more than seven years now, and in that time the staff strength had grown from twenty to two hundred, and the print run[2] from one thousand to over ten thousand. It was owned by Godwin Amaechi, 'the Chairman' to his employees, a seventy-year-old veteran journalist who still came to the office earlier than everyone else, and stayed till 10 p.m. after the next day's issue had been put to bed. He controlled every aspect of the paper, from its accounts to its editorials, with a dictator's hand, albeit[3] a benevolent one. I had seen colleagues who were currently out of favour duck into a doorway at his approach; I had seen sub-editors make a sign of the cross before going into his office for a meeting. At midday, every day, except Sundays when he stayed home, he'd carry out what we privately called the 'ceremonial inspection of the guards', starting from the long, rectangular[4] newsroom, where he'd chastise[5] a poor reporter or praise a deserving one, and ending up at the dining room on the ground floor an hour later. For the next hour he'd sit at the head of the table, surrounded by editors and other senior staff, each doing his best to outshine[6] the other in suggesting ingenious[7] story ideas.

1 middle-brow (adj): not overly sophisticated, not very difficult to unterstand
2 print run: number of copies printed **3** albeit: although **4** rectangular (adj): *rechteckig* **5** chastise sb.: rebuke sb., scold sb., severly critize sb. **6** outshine sb.: make a better impression than sb. **7** ingenious (adj): creative, smart

The day's favourite reporter usually sat to the Chairman's right at those grim lunches – an honour that was as painful as torture, said those who had experienced it.

Today I was experiencing it. For over an hour I answered the Chairman's questions, giving as much detail as I could, hardly blinking, hardly breathing, mostly swallowing without chewing, gulping down mouthfuls of water to stop myself from choking on my pounded yam[1]. Now I understood why some colleagues called these lunches 'The Last Supper'.

– You've done a great job. Good pictures.

– Thank you, sir.

– Have some banana.

– Thanks.

– And tell me about Zaq. I understand you were there with him?

He waved the morning paper which carried my article.

– Yes. He was very helpful. He's still out there, on Irikefe Island. He said he needed the break.

– I knew him, once. We used to work for the same paper. But that was a long time ago.

The kidnapping, which had receded to the inside pages the past couple of days, had inched[2] back to the front page once again, mainly because of the violent gun battle on the island. Some of the men, like Nkem at *The Globe*, speculated in their reports that Mrs Floode might be dead, using garish pictures of dead bodies and burning huts to support this. My story, which my paper brought out in a special edition, had captured more attention than the other reports, perhaps because I had referenced and quoted Zaq a lot in my piece, and also because, due to my training, I knew how to use pictures more effectively than the other reporters. My close-ups[3] conveyed the shrill urgency and tragedy, which my text tactfully refrained from mentioning, with twice the impact. This morning two Reuters[4]

1 yam: edible potato-like root of a tropical plant **2** inch (v): move slowly
3 close-up (n): photo taken from a very short distance **4** Reuters: important international news agency

reporters, after reading my story, had come to the newsroom to chat with me. After the meal, which I could still feel suspended in a hard lump between my chest and my stomach, I sat in the deserted newsroom to recover from my ordeal[1]. Most of the reporters were out on their beats[2] and would start to trickle in only in the late afternoon, when they wrote their pieces for the next day. When I felt the strength return to my legs, I stood up and crossed over to the editor's office. I found him seated behind his desk, the fan in the corner focused directly at his face, a toothpick stuck between his lips, his tie loosened, exposing his lumpy neck.

– Ah, here comes our star reporter. When are you going to see the husband?

– Right now. He's expecting me. I just came in to let you know –

– Go, go. Make sure you get a good interview.

– Well, he said no interviews, till after everything is over.

– Once it's over, it's over, isn't it? Anyway, go get whatever you can out of him, then take the rest of the day off. And take the day after that. We'll find a nice exciting assignment for you when you come back.

He stood up and shook my hand. His behaviour towards me had dramatically changed since I returned from Irikefe.

– The Chairman is really pleased with you. He thinks you'll make a good reporter. We shall see.

The Floodes' house was one of the many colonial-style buildings on the Port Harcourt waterfront, where most of the wealthy expatriate[3] oil workers lived. It was hidden behind a tall, barbed-wire[4]-topped wall, and I passed through two gates and about half a dozen security men talking to each other on radios.

I was led in by a uniformed guard. We crossed a huge lawn to the front door, which the guard pushed open without pressing the bell.

1 ordeal: torture, martyrdom, (here) difficult situation **2** beat (n): (here) area covered by a reporter **3** expatriate (n): sb. who lives abroad (usu. for work and only a limited period of time) **4** barbed wire (n): *Stacheldraht*

I followed him into a spacious living room dimly lit by shaded wall lights; an ornamental[1] fan turned slowly in the centre of the ceiling. We went out through a back door that led to the patio[2], where Floode was waiting, seated on a wicker chair, a cocktail on a glass table in front of him. He waved the guard away, then he stood up and took my hand.

– Thank you for coming, Mr ...

– Rufus.

– That's a good name. Is that a common name around here?

– I know a few.

He waved me to sit.

– I haven't been here long, you know. This is my second year in the country and I'm still trying to understand the place and the people. I think Nigerians are very nice and hospitable.

– You still think so, even after the kidnapping?

James Floode looked momentarily surprised at my directness, but I wanted to get to the point as quickly as possible. I wasn't used to talking to people like him, and I was nervous. He sighed and his eyes turned dark as he reached forward and picked up his drink. He must have had a few before my arrival: his movements were slow and deliberate[3], just like his speech. So far he had refused to talk to the media, including his country's media, apart from a few prepared comments about missing his wife and his hopes that the kidnappers would release her soon. I'd be the first reporter he had agreed to speak to – I was aware how important this moment was, even though I was here by default[4].

– Tell me, are you married, Mr Rufus?

– No. Please call me Rufus: it's also my first name. No, Mr Floode. I'm not married. I'm only twenty-five.

1 ornamental (adj): serving as decoration **2** patio [ˈpætiəʊ]: terrace **3** deliberate: (here) careful **4** by default: automatically (as a direct consequence of sth.)

– Call me James. Well, a lot of you chaps[1] do marry rather early, isn't that so? A few of the workers I know, very young, but they always talk about their families. Children and all.

– Yes, there are a lot who marry early.

He sighed again and went quiet, as if he had lost interest in that thread of talk. He stood up.

– Let's go inside. I'll show you something.

Drink in hand, he led the way into the living room. He picked up the remote and flicked on the TV and there, on the BBC channel, they were talking about the kidnapping. Isabel Floode, a British woman, had been kidnapped by rebels in the Nigerian Delta, an attempt to make contact was spoiled[2] by an unplanned military intervention, and now it was doubtful if Isabel was still alive. Some oil companies had already stopped sending expatriate workers to the region, and were even thinking of shutting down their operations because the cost was becoming higher than they could bear, and this possibility was already causing a tension in the oil market, with prices expected to rise in response.

He turned off the TV.

– It's like a circus. I can't go out, not even to the office, reporters stalk me everywhere, and the funny thing is I don't even know what to tell them, I don't know what's happened to her. That's why I wanted Zaq to go in there and find out. And now you say he's not well. What's wrong with him? Is it serious?

– He needs rest. The air out there is good for him.

James scratched his stubbled[3] chin, again looking at me strangely, waiting for me to say more, but I returned his look and kept quiet.

– But we had a deal, he agreed to go out there and be my eyes and ears.

– Mr Floode –

– Call me James.

– James, there really isn't anything to report.

1 chap (infml): guy **2** spoil sth.: ruin sth. **3** stubbled: covered with a very short beard

– But what did you see? What do you think? Is she alive or not? You said you have some pictures for me. Did Zaq give you any message for me?

I showed him the pictures, the ones that hadn't been published in the papers: the burning boat, the houses, the sculptures on Irikefe, and finally a picture of myself with Zaq under a tree. Zaq had suggested the last just for proof. Floode put them back into the envelope and placed them beside his drink on the table.

– Let's get you a drink.

He picked up a bell from a side table and rang it loudly. Then, as if unable to keep away from the news, he turned on the TV again. The screen was filled by a blown-up[1] photo of a smiling Isabel, and behind her was a crowded street, a bridge, and far in the distance the iconic Big Ben clock tower. Next, there was a shot of picketing[2] youths holding placards in front of an oil-company building in Port Harcourt. This segment was accompanied by a long, rote-like[3] voiceover about poverty in Nigeria, and how corruption sustained that poverty, and how oil was the main source of revenue, and how because the country was so corrupt, only a few had access to that wealth.

Floode turned off the TV and turned to me. – Such great potential. You people could easily become the Japan of Africa, the USA of Africa, but the corruption is incredible.

I said nothing, looking to the door to see if the maid was coming in answer to Floode's ring. He warmed to this topic, scratching his chin vigorously as he spoke.

– Our pipelines are vandalized daily, losing us millions ... and millions for the country as well. The people don't understand what they do to themselves ...

– But they do understand.

– What?

– Have you ever heard of a town called Junction?

1 blow up sth.: (here) enlarge sth. **2** picket (v): take part in a protest
3 rote-like: sounding as though learned by heart

– No. I don't think so ...

– I'm from there. Almost five years ago I came home from Lagos after graduating from journalism school and found half the town burned down. The newspapers said the villagers brought it upon themselves by drilling into the pipelines to steal oil ...

– Yes, I have heard of that, isn't that a place called Jesse?

– That is a different place. There are countless villages going up in smoke daily. Well, this place, Junction, went up in smoke because of an accident associated with this vandalism, as you call it. But I don't blame them for wanting to vandalize the pipelines that have brought nothing but suffering to their lives, leaking into the rivers and wells, killing the fish and poisoning the farmlands. And all they are told by the oil companies and the government is that the pipelines are there for their own good, that they hold great potential for their country, their future. These people endure the worst conditions of any oil-producing community on earth, the government knows it but doesn't have the will to stop it, the oil companies know it, but because the government doesn't care, they also don't care. And you think the people are corrupt? No. They are just hungry, and tired.

– Hmm, well, I've read about it before. A tragedy. But it does illustrate my point –

– No, actually, it illustrates my point.

– Ha ha! You argue rather well, I must give you that ... Now, where's that ...

He picked up the bell and rang it again, impatiently. After a while the door to the patio opened and a maid entered. She was dressed in a blue uniform that reached just below her knees, with a white apron[1] around her waist. She stood next to the TV and stared at Floode, her head inclined, not saying a word.

– Get my guest here a drink, Koko. What can she get you?

– A beer will do ... Star.

– And a refill for me.

1 apron: *Schürze*

She turned and disappeared into the kitchen. I watched the movement of her full waist beneath the close-fitting uniform. She returned a moment later with a tray bearing my bottle of Star and a glass of whatever Floode was drinking. She set the bottle on the side table next to me. She was young and plump, not fat, but very heavy around the hips, and she looked more like a student than a maid, and though she was not conventionally pretty there was a compelling sexuality about her. I was sitting across from Floode, watching her as she bent forward to place his drink next to him, and I saw his left hand almost absently but gently brush against her thigh, and if she hadn't turned and flashed him a quick smile I would have dismissed the gesture as an innocent accident.

– Thanks, Koko. That will be all.

He saw me staring at him and he shifted his gaze to his drink. I cleared my throat.

– Mr Floode, Zaq said I should ask if everything was okay between you and Mrs Floode? Was there a fight, or ... He looked long at me, sipping his drink. I stared back at him. I loved the way his face turned meat-red, and the way he used his glass to cover his mouth, which had suddenly tightened, I loved the debate in his eyes: to kick out this nosy[1] African or to tolerate him. He smiled.

– I should tell you to go tell him it's none of his business.

– He just wants to know as much as possible about the circumstances of the kidnapping ...

– Aw, what the hell. Things were far from well between us. We had agreed on a divorce, then the kidnapping happened ... She shouldn't have come to Nigeria.

– Why?

– She came hoping to save our marriage, but we had drifted apart long ago. We met at university, you know. But then, after the marriage, I got this job. I was posted to all sorts of places and I guess she must have got tired of the constant change. Some people like it, some don't. We agreed that she should wait in England. And I, I was

1 nosy (adj): overly interested in other people's affairs

just beginning to discover how good I am at my job. I'm a chemical engineer, and I'm one of the best. Then the transfer to Nigeria came, I left and she remained in Newcastle, and all the time we were drifting apart. Then six months ago she arrived here, but by then it was too late. There's another woman, you see ...

– Does Mrs Floode know about this woman?

– Yes.

– This woman, is she local?

– Let's just say she lives here in Port Harcourt. I want to protect her identity as much as I can. She's expecting our child.

– I see.

– Do you, young man? The irony is that Isabel thought we could save our marriage by having a child. That was her plan. The first day she arrived she said let's make a baby, and what was I to say?

I opened my mouth to ask another question but I closed it again when I saw what looked like a tear leaving the corner of his eye. Too much emotion, or too much whisky. He wiped his eyes and looked up.

– So, will Zaq be all right?

– Yes, he'll be attended to by a nurse at the shrine.

– I wonder if I can prevail upon him to seek a little further, not to hurry back? He's an excellent reporter, and I'm sure that if anyone can get to the kidnappers, he can. Might he be persuaded, do you think?

– You'll have to ask him, I guess, and his editor.

– As you can see, my mobility is a bit restricted. May I ask you to find out for me?

– How?

– Go back to this Irikefe place, talk to Zaq, see what he says. I'm willing to pay him, and you, of course, for your trouble. Go tomorrow: you can return that same day, so you'll lose hardly any time at all from work. I'll have a boat ready to take you there.

– I can't ...

– Why? You're a reporter: I should think you'd jump at such an opportunity.

– I ... have a few personal issues to take care of.

I was thinking of Boma in my room, her eyes still red from yesterday's tears, waiting for me to return with some sort of solution to her housing problem.

He misread my reluctance[1] for bargaining[2]. – Look, dear chap, I'll pay for your time. I know you'll need to prepare, buy equipment and so on. How about a hundred thousand naira? All you have to do is go back to the island, give Zaq my message and come back.

He was offering a lot of money, more money than I had ever seen. My mind flew in many different directions: I thought of the dead bodies covered by bamboo leaves, and I knew anything could happen to me on such a trip. I had been lucky once: I had gone and returned safely, I had published my story, I had been praised by my editor and the Chairman, why push my luck? But, on the other hand, there was the money. I needed it to pay Boma's rent, and my own rent, for that matter ...

Of course I could take the money and not go back to the island. I'd be lying if I said I didn't think of that possibility. After all he couldn't sue me, could he? I could tell him something came up and that was it. A hundred thousand was nothing to a man like him. Besides, I didn't really think much of Mr Floode. If he really cared for his wife, shouldn't he be out there in the jungle with Zaq, instead of here, drinking cocktails, watching TV, sleeping with the maid – if he was sleeping with the maid, that is? I could take his money and walk out and nothing would happen. Wasn't he in my country, polluting my environment, making millions in the process? Surely I was entitled to some reparation[3], some rent money from him? But even as I took the money, and an extra hundred thousand that he said was for Zaq, I still wasn't sure what I'd do when I walked out of his gate.

– Tell Zaq he has my permission to negotiate with the kidnappers. My embassy has warned me against paying ransom just yet,

1 reluctance: unwillingness **2** bargain (v): negotiate to get a better price
3 reparation: compensation

but there's no reason why we can't start negotiating. I just want to end this whole thing as quickly as possible. Do you understand?

I took two plain brown envelopes from him and put them in my jacket pocket, feeling the weight in my chest and shoulders.

– I will send you a receipt[1].

He shook his head and took my hands and looked into my eyes earnestly. – No need for that, Rufus. I have to trust you. You're my only hope, you and Zaq. My wife's life is in your hands. I know things aren't that good between us, but she's a good person and she doesn't deserve this.

I avoided his eyes as I left him to his cocktail, his split-unit air-conditioning, his beautiful maid, his BBC news, his stubble, his double-gated seafront house, and made my way back to the city.

I found Boma seated on a chair in front of the open door. She was staring ahead at nothing, her head bowed. She looked up and smiled when I touched her on the shoulder. I sat beside her and we watched my co-tenants[2] come in one by one, back from work, their eyes tired and vacuous[3], their shoulders bent. They waved or grunted briefly at us as they went into their rooms to take off their shirts and hang them on the nail behind the door, to be picked up again tomorrow morning on the way to work. Today we had electricity, so those with TV would flop into a chair before it and stare into the flickering surface as they ate soaked *garri* or whatever food there was to hand. Eating and watching mindlessly till they fell asleep. Those without TV, or those who simply couldn't bear the steaming heat in their rooms, would come out and sit on the veranda to catch whatever breeze was passing by.

– Hey, Rufus my countryman!

Isaac, my neighbour. He was Ibibio[4] and for some reason he thought I was from his village, and, though I told him I was not, he

1 receipt: document confirming that money was transferred or handed over
2 co-tenant: neighbour, tenant living in the same building **3** vacuous: empty
4 Ibibio: ethnic group living mostly in Abia, a state in south-eastern Nigeria

always laughed and said he recognized my features, and he was sure he knew some of my cousins. And every day he would greet me with his loud, booming call, My countryman! How life? And I had taken to answering back with as much cheer as I could muster[1] after a full day, My countryman! Life de turn man[2]. Family is worth clinging onto wherever one can find it. And now he felt easier about asking me for a loan when he ran short in the straight and narrow days just before pay day. Across the compound Madam Comfort, her husband, Mister John, and their six children were seated on stools in front of their open door, having their evening meal. All along the length of the veranda other families had similarly turned this narrow space into an extension of their living room, eating and calling across to each other or just staring into space.

– I have to go back to Irikefe tomorrow.

– You said it is very dangerous out there.

– I'll be fine. What of you, what are you going to do?

– I don't know.

She got up and disappeared into the room and then reappeared with a plate of jollof rice[3], which she handed to me.

– Thanks.

– More and more I'm thinking of moving to the village to stay with mother.

We had discussed this many times before. Mother was still unused to Boma's scarred face – it was as if she expected it to one day disappear, and with it the memory of that tragic day. Whenever they met, mother always broke down at the sight of her daughter's once pretty face, now a total scabrous[4] mess. The last time she'd run into the room and cried and cried and eventually Boma had joined her and the two had cried together till their voices went hoarse and they couldn't cry any more.

– Is that what you want?

1 muster (v): *aufbringen* **2** Life de turn man (NP): Life changes people. **3** jollof rice: rice cooked with tomatoes and spices **4** scabrous: rough to the touch

– But what is there to do? I'm beginning to get tired of waiting. Sometimes I'm not sure any more what I want to do.

I took out some money from the brown envelope and handed it to her.

– Here, use this to pay your landlord ...

– No. I'm not going back there. I'll look for another place.

– Of course you can stay here till you find somewhere suitable, I just want you to be sure about what it is you want.

I moved my chair out of the way as my next-door neighbour came out of her room to go to the kitchen.

– Hello, Rufus. Na your sister be dis?[1]

– How now, Grace. Na my sister.

Boma lowered her face, instinctively.

The Lucky One, that was Boma's name for me, Mr Lucky. Growing up, I always had a knack for[2] coming out unscathed[3] from the most scary accidents. But in this one case I wish I had been unlucky, I wish I had been there when it happened, to share in her pain, my family's pain. Instead I had been away in Lagos, and it was John who had been by her side as she was taken to the hospital screaming and shouting that she was blind, she couldn't see. When I came home, proudly clutching my journalism certificate, he pulled me aside and told me they were getting married as soon as she was out of hospital. They had had five very good years of marriage, I could vouch for that, being their neighbour, but it would have been better if he had quietly broken up with her after she had left the hospital, as soon as she was able to look in the mirror without crying, left her to create her own thick skin, her own defences.

I had never seen Boma so broken, so defeated, as on the day she told me he had gone.

– Maybe if we had children? A nice little boy to make him feel proud. It's my fault, I kept telling him to wait, wait ... I know it is this face. He used to run his hand over my face and say he didn't really

1 Na your sister be dis? (NP): So, this is your sister? **2** have a knack for sth.: have a talent for sth. **3** unscathed: unharmed

care, that as far as he was concerned, I was still the same beautiful girl he'd met when we were kids, when they moved into the house next to ours.

Now that it was dark and cooler, the neighbours got up one by one and took their chairs inside. In one of the rooms a man and his wife were fighting, their words loud and full of hate. In the background their children were crying, there was the loud sound of a slap, the crying stopped, the shouting stopped. Peace reigned.

11

Zaq was lying on a mat under an acacia tree, and though the air was hot and humid, he was covered up to his chin in a brown wool blanket. He attempted a smile when he saw me, but the smile was soon overtaken by a grimace.

– I'm cold. I'm so cold.

His face, gaunt[1] and dejected[2], turned towards the faraway still figures. In the distance I could see a few worshippers in their long white robes, standing in groups before one of the huts. I was shocked by his appearance.

– Maybe you ought to think of returning to Port Harcourt: you don't look very good.

– I don't know what you came back to do, but I'm glad to see you.

His voice was so faint I had to ask him to repeat himself.

– See, I brought you a few things.

At the waterfront in Port Harcourt, while waiting for the boat, I had impulsively stepped into one of the many stores facing the sea and grabbed two bottles of Johnnie Walker. I guess I was still haunted by the image of Zaq begging for a drink that day on the beach. He forced himself up and reached greedily for the bottle, his hands shaking. And suddenly I had misgivings.

– I'm not sure this is a good idea ...

But his hand tightened over the bottle, and I was surprised at how much strength there was in his grip. He leaned his back against the tree trunk[3] and opened the cap; his hands shook and the spirit spilled as the bottle found his mouth. He drank as if he was sucking life and health out of the bottle, but finally he stopped, gasping and coughing, and the spark gradually returned to his eyes. After that

1 gaunt [gɔːnt]: very thin **2** dejected: depressed **3** trunk: stem of a tree

greedy, focused exertion[1], he kicked off the blanket and released a long, blissful[2] sigh.

– Ahhh! You've just saved a life, Rufus.

– Has the nurse been to see you?

– Yes. She was quite nice to me.

In the distance I saw a figure in white coming towards us: it was Naman, the officious priest who had welcomed us three days ago. He knelt beside Zaq's mat and his face momentarily clouded when he saw the open whisky bottle, but he said nothing.

– Welcome back, Mr Rufus.

– Thank you.

– I see you've returned to see how your colleague is doing. Perhaps take him back with you?

– No, actually, well, yes. If he's strong enough to go.

– Nurse Gloria said you are making good progress, Mr Zaq. She said you had a rough time last night, but now that the fever has broken, you will feel better. She will be back this afternoon to take a look at you.

– Where's the nurse now?

– She has business to attend to in Port Harcourt, but while there she will buy some more medicines for you.

Zaq moaned and held his head. – I think I'm dying. I feel like a ghost already. Do you believe in ghosts, priest?

– Of course we believe in spirits, good and bad. The bad ones are the ones who have sinned against mother earth and can't find rest in her womb. They roam[3] the earth, restless, looking for redemption –

– Okay, okay. I am not interested in your theology.

I put Zaq's bad temper[4] down to the fever, his truculence[5] to the whisky. The priest stood up.

– Actually, I came to help you back to your room, but I am sure your friend here will help you. I have to go. It is time now for our evening worship.

1 exertion: effort **2** blissful: very happy **3** roam (v): wander, walk about
4 bad temper: bad/angry mood **5** truculence: defiance, aggression

He shook my hand.

– Good to see you again. Let me know if you need anything.

– A very busy man, isn't he?

Zaq stared thoughtfully after the departing priest, belching as he took another sip from the bottle.

– I wonder what he knows about the kidnapping.

Zaq allowed me to lead him back into the hut, still grumbling about ghosts. The shrine, as this section of the island was called, occupied the entire waterfront, with the hillock and the sculpture garden intervening[1] between the huts and the water. The huts were arranged as if to form two lines on a rough isosceles triangle[2], with the sculptures occupying most of the middle space and the beach forming the base line. The first hut facing the statues was a sort of reception room, which was where we had first been hosted. Now we had been moved to another hut, a smaller one, just behind the reception hut. Not too far from us was the worship room. It was bigger than all the other huts, and a single wooden statue stood like a guard before the entrance. I could see men and women in white robes crowding together near the statue, waiting to go in for the evening service. The other side of the island was the village proper, about a mile away and separated from the shrine by a large buffer area of tall leafy trees. The villagers were all connected to the shrine by religion, and the chief priest had authority over the whole community. The villagers were fishermen, mostly, making their living on the river that poured its water into the sea, leading away into a hinterland of marshes and forests and swamps.

As I led Zaq to the hut we would be sharing, we passed close to the worship hut and some of the men and women, now kneeling before the entrance, looked at us briefly as they waited their turn to go in. I wondered idly what religious ritual went on inside the hut, whether the tall impressive priest was seated on a chair before the

1 intervene between: (here) be situated between **2** isosceles triangle: triangle with two sides of equal length

shrine, handing out communion[1] wafers[2] or whatever their equivalent of those might be, or whether there were mad orgiastic[3] dances and trances – but I doubted the latter. These people didn't look like the dance-and-trance type – they appeared remarkably composed and solemn.

Our hut was as spacious inside as the first one had been, even though it looked deceptively narrow from outside. A mat was laid out for me already, and across from it was Zaq's mat, with his slippers in front of it and a worshipper's white robe hanging from a nail above. He saw me looking at the robe and shook his head.

– I had to change into something. They were kind enough to wash my things for me.

– What kind of religion is it?

– No idea. The only thing I'm interested in right now is what their connection is to the militants.

My mat had a single sheet spread over it and a pillow where my head should rest. I removed my shoes and sat down. There was nothing else in the hut except for a water pot against the wall and a lamp hanging from a hook over the pot. Zaq lay on his mat, his eyes glittering, a sheen of sweat on his forehead. The whisky bottle was down to half full.

– So, what news from the city?

I briefed him on my interview with Floode and handed him his money. He opened the envelope and let the money fall out all over his lap, then he looked at me and shook his head, laughing drunkenly.

– That is what I call good journalism.

I told him of my visit to his editor, how I got to the offices of the *Star* very late in the afternoon, confident that no editor would leave the office until the next day's paper had been put to bed. The office was

1 communion: (here) religious ceremony **2** wafer: *Oblate* **3** orgiastic: wild, uncontrolled

next to a dump site[1], and facing it across the road was a police barracks. From the office's dim and miserable interior one could hear the bugle calling the men to the parade ground, and one could smell the dump site. I found Beke Johnson eating from a lunch box on his desk; the box gave up a strong smell of burned palm oil and onions. A square red stain sat in the centre of his blue tie. The office was narrow and long, like a corridor, and his desk was at one end, near the window that faced the barracks. On the table were files spilling out papers, an old computer, a stapler and a stone paperweight, all jostling for space with the lunch box. He ate with a loud, wet sound, his mouth open. It was an unremarkable place, with two unremarkable women working in front of two computers at the other end of the corridor.

The editor looked even more unremarkable in his rumpled, oversized suit and tie; he could be an apparatchik[2] in some grey, concrete ministry building. All he wanted to know after I had introduced myself was when Zaq would be returning. When I told him Zaq was ill, he looked sceptical.

– Tell him to hurry up and get well, otherwise I'll stop his salary.

– I don't think I will be seeing Zaq till he gets back.

The editor thought about that briefly, his mouth moving mechanically like a masticating[3] ruminant's[4], his eyes looking at me unhappily.

– Well, you must have a means of communicating with him, surely? By phone?

– No, phones don't work on the island.

– Well. Did he give you his piece to bring to me? Nothing? What am I going to publish tomorrow? What kind of a reporter is that? Ah, he still thinks he is a star Lagos reporter. But he is lucky to be working for me.

1 dump site: place where garbage is dumped **2** apparatchik: blindly devoted official **3** masticate (v): chew food **4** ruminant: animal that brings up food from its stomach and chews it again (e.g. cows)

– I can send you a few things – I have some pictures, and a few paragraphs.

– Well, make sure you do that as soon as you can. I have deadlines. I'm conscious of my obligations, unlike some people.

I felt sorry for Zaq, sorry that he had to work for such a dull, sour employer, and it was at that time that I realized how colossal Zaq's fall from grace had been. When I stood up to go, he waved me back into the seat.

– Where are you going? Sit down. Let me tell you about your friend.

He pushed his lunch box aside and wiped his hands ineffectually with Kleenex. He leaned forward and once more waved me back to my seat, imperiously[1], impatiently.

– Once, he was the best.

– Yes, I know. He used –

– No. You don't know anything. Listen. Did he tell you we were rookies[2] together at the *Daily Times*? Oh, he didn't? Then did he tell you that we shared a flat in Surulere[3] for one year? I was twenty-two, he was twenty-one. Ah, I can see us now. Green, wet behind the ears. Of course there was nothing like journalism school then, you just finessed your way[4] into things. I bet you went to a journalism school, didn't you? They are useless. You learn nothing there. All you need is to open your eyes, make the right contacts, and be bold. Well, nothing like journalism school for us. You begin as a cub reporter, and if you survive, you become king of the jungle, or at least something high up on the food chain.

Beke drank from a water bottle, belched, and fished around with his tongue for strings of meat between his teeth. He wiped the sweat from his bald head.

– Well, Zaq and I were assigned to the news desk. In those days there was no specialization, no one cared if you wanted to cover

1 imperious: expecting to be obeyed **2** rookie (infml): beginner **3** Surulere: residential area of Lagos **4** finesse your way (infml): (here) find your way by trial and error

the arts, or business, or news, the editor simply sent you wherever he wanted. We were assigned to news, but Zaq wanted something different. He was full of ideas, restless. At night he never slept. He wanted to do feature stories about everyday things, ordinary lives. But this was a different age, late seventies, early eighties, things were different then. People bought papers for news only, facts, or at least that was how the editor saw it. But Zaq wasn't the kind of person to sit around waiting for things to change. He quit, just like that. Even I was taken by surprise. I remember the exact day, in 1982, it was a Monday, usually our busiest day, the newsroom was full, most of us were back from our beat and we were rushing to get our copy[1] ready for the sub-editors. The editor was there in a corner, berating one of the reporters, waving a piece of paper about, and then I saw Zaq get up from his desk and walk right up to him and call him by his name. Who dared call the editor by his name? It was unheard of, and right in front of all the junior reporters and interns[2]. He went right up to him and said, Tunde, I quit! And he walked out. Those days you didn't need a resignation letter, reporters just wandered in and out of newsrooms.

– Ah, anyway. He left. He also moved out of our flat while I was at work, with no forwarding address. Just like that. I asked around our friends, but no one knew where he had got to. I didn't see him again till a year later, and you know where he was all that while? At Bar Beach. If you knew Bar Beach in the eighties, which you didn't, ha ha. You certainly didn't. Ever heard of the Bar Beach Show? That was in the seventies. The Bar Beach Show. Armed robbers tied to sand-filled tin drums and shot by soldiers right in front of cheering crowds. That was the Bar Beach Show under the military government. In the eighties, it was beer shacks[3] and prostitutes. We had democracy, the dark days of the late sixties and seventies were over, the country was desperate to put the civil war behind it. The victims were just glad the nightmare was over, and the victors – well, what

1 copy (n): text written to be published in a newspaper **2** intern (n): *Praktikant(in)* **3** shack: hut

victors? Makeshift bar rooms and restaurants lined up along the beach, and young girls from all over the country went to Lagos looking for opportunity, most of them from respectable backgrounds, but Lagos doesn't care how respectable you were in your village. Hey, this was Lagos. They ended up as prostitutes on Bar Beach. Some ended up pregnant and homeless on the streets, and they were the lucky ones. The unlucky ones died, their bodies to be discovered in the water days later, washed up in faraway Lekki[1]. Raped. Brutalized. Strangled. Stabbed. Well, Zaq saw the story in that when the rest of us saw only prostitutes selling sex. Every day he'd be there with those prostitutes, talking to them, and who knows, perhaps sleeping with them, maybe pimping[2] for them. Ha ha. No, just kidding. Come on, young man, lighten up. Some of the girls were really pretty. Regular-looking girls, only they weren't regular, they were prostitutes. I'd go there when there was no news to chase and I'd sit with him in the shacks and drink beer, and some of the girls would come over and sit with us.

– One of them would later become famous for her involvement with him. I could tell that day, when I first saw her, I could tell there was something special between them. She was younger than the others, about eighteen. And, thinking about it, he wasn't all that much older than her. We were very young then, young and stupid and full of dreams. In Lagos you can dream, you see. There are no boundaries[3], no traditions or family to hold you back. It is that kind of place. Anyway, this girl, Anita, she sat right next to him and didn't leave us even when the others drifted off to hustle[4] men. And when she heard I was a journalist she said to me, Zaq is writing a story about us. Did you know that? She didn't speak much, but when she did she spoke well. She was pretty, perhaps the prettiest thing I've ever seen, and believe me as a journalist I've seen a lot of pretty things. It's hard to think that way about a prostitute, right? And she

1 Lekki: peninsula east of Lagos city **2** pimp for sb. (sl): be a pimp (*Zuhälter*) for sb. **3** boundary: limit **4** hustle sb. (sl): approach sb. (to get sth. from him/her)

had manners, good breeding[1]. I could tell. She had her hands on the table, and they weren't garishly painted like the other girls'. Her nails were cut short, clean, her make-up was moderate, adequate. She was like a college girl. She seemed lost in that place, out of her element. Yes, I said to her. Zaq told me. Is Anita your real name? She looked at Zaq quickly before she answered, Yes. Why do you want to know? Zaq looked at her and said, Are you sure you don't want to be going now, Anita? You can't stay here talking to us all night. He laid a hand on her shoulder as he spoke. I had never seen Zaq like that before, so gentle, so soft and mellow.

– The fool was in love. I watched Anita wrinkle her pretty nose and shake her head, No. I enjoy being with you. And she stayed with us till we left. I told Zaq, Be careful. I think she likes you. But of course I meant he should be careful not to like her too much. He laughed, confident, arrogant as usual. They're just subjects for me. That's all. I'm going to write the most in-depth, interesting feature on prostitutes in Lagos. But who wants to read about prostitutes in Lagos, I asked. That was when he told me Anita's story. He said Anita had been thrown out of her parents' house when she became pregnant at sixteen. Her boyfriend couldn't marry her because he was too young and still in school. Zaq said that in the traditional system her boyfriend would have had no option but to marry her. But now her Christian parents threw her out because she had brought shame upon them. He said that by writing about the girls he would be showing what was happening to all of us, how we were gradually changing as a people. Our values, our culture, our way of life. All changing irrevocably[2]. Think about it.

– That shows you how ahead of his time he was. Well, he wrote his story. And he got his job back, plus a promotion. You've read the piece, I'm sure, perhaps studied it in that school of journalism you went to. 'Five Women', he titled the story. Not 'Five Prostitutes', 'Five Women', you get that? Every weekend he told the story of one of

1 breeding: (here) upbringing **2** irrevocable: impossible to change back to how it was before

the five. They were all below twenty. And you know what he said? People cried as they read the intimate stories of these girls. The politicians were compelled[1] to act. Governors' wives started a scholarship scheme to send the girls back to school, they called it 'A Better Life for Fallen Women'. Speeches were given on TV, international organizations invited Zaq to talk about his experience of living with the prostitutes in order to write about them. All over the country, charities working with the police raided[2] brothels[3] to save innocent girls from their terrible life, but hey, not all of them wanted to be saved, or rehabilitated[4], they just wanted to be prostitutes! Ha ha.

– Well, our weekend paper became the biggest-selling thing in the country. Zaq's byline became a magic formula. People read whatever he wrote, and he did write great stuff. Crusading[5] kind of stuff, but always from the inside, intimate. But you know what, he told me that with all that success he missed his days at Bar Beach. He missed Anita. She went back to school and actually graduated. And I think it was to forget her that Zaq threw himself into the pro-democracy movement when the military dictators returned in the late eighties. He wrote fiery[6], fearless anti-military pieces that even our editor was hesitant to publish. Zaq left us and was immediately wooed[7] by all the prominent papers. In the end he went with *Action!* magazine in Ikeja as editor. He did some of his best work then. This was the late eighties, remember, most of us had to maintain two or three addresses just to stay a step ahead of the military goons[8]. But you've heard all this before at that school you went to, haven't you? You have, well, just humour[9] me, unless you have a wife to go back home to. Let me conclude my story, there may be a lesson in this for you. And what is that lesson? Don't fall in love with a prostitute, my friend –

1 compel sb.: force sb. **2** raid sth.: forcibly perform a search of sth. **3** brothel: house where prostitutes offer their services **4** rehabilitate sb.: return sb. to a normal life **5** crusade (v): (here) campaign/fight for a cause **6** fiery (adj): glowing, (here) passionate **7** woo sb.: make an effort to win sb. for sth. by being nice to her/him and making promises **8** goon: violent criminal paid to threaten people **9** humour sb.: give in to sb.'s wishes

– I really have to ... it's getting late –

– Just listen, I'm almost finished.

I listened, even though I knew the rest of the story. A major part of Zaq's life, because of the sheer brilliance of it, had been lived in full public view. At a certain point he stopped being the man behind the news and became the news. He reached the height of his fame during the worst years of the dictatorship – the Abacha years, from 1993 to 1998.

– After the dictatorship most people, including myself, expected him to join the new government, but he kept his distance. He went back to his former paper, *Action!*, and continued his in-depth, weekend-style features. But not with the same conviction. By then he had started drinking heavily. His editorials became increasingly critical of the new government that he and his pro-democracy pals[1] had worked so hard to bring to power, but then in 2003 he joined the government. He became an adviser to the information minister, a tough and controversial figure with many enemies in the cabinet.

– Well, it was at this point that Anita miraculously re-entered his life. Only this was not the same awkward, young girl he had written about in his famous 'Five Women' article. This was a grown woman. Poised[2]. She had been to university, she had a good job with a bank in Lagos, but of course her veneer[3] of respectability didn't stop the gutter press[4] from tagging them 'The Prostitute and the Radical'. There were pictures of them together at fancy parties, book launches, media events.

This was in 2004, the year I first met Zaq, the year he gave the lecture at my school, the year his heavy drinking began to finally take its toll on him[5].

– A wedding date was announced. Later, the papers said that he went to London against his better judgement. Anita wanted

1 pal (infml): friend **2** poised: in control of oneself **3** veneer (n): superficial outward appearance **4** gutter press: tabloid press **5** take its toll on sb.: do harm to sb.

her trousseau[1] from only the best stores on Oxford Street[2], and the minister was kind enough to offer to foot[3] the bill as his wedding present. He took the couple along with him when he went to a Commonwealth[4] ministers' conference in London. Only they never got past customs. Cocaine was discovered in Zaq's toilet bag, among his shaving things. At the trial he said he had no idea how it got there. The papers back home suddenly turned vicious on him, some implying that he'd been carrying the drugs for the minister. Others, who took the time to investigate Anita's background, discovered that while at university she'd had a series of liaisons[5] with very rich men, some of them associated with the drug world. At the trial, he said not a single word against her, his only plea being that the minister shouldn't be associated with the story. But of course the minister was sacked[6], and Zaq's Lagos career came to an end. After a year in a UK prison he was deported back to Nigeria, where he was set free after serving only a month in jail. And after his jail term, he disappeared from Lagos.

I stood up.

– Thanks, Mr Johnson, but now I –

– Okay, okay. You really have to go. But tell Zaq to get back here as soon as possible. Tell him not to try me[7], tell him not to force my hand, or else ... from tomorrow no pay. Tell him that.

– But what if –

– Just tell him.

1 trousseau [ˈtruːsəʊ]: things a bride gets for her wedding (usu. from her parents) **2** Oxford Street: famous shopping street in London **3** foot sth. (infml): pay for sth. **4** Commonwealth (of Nations): political organization of Great Britain and its former colonies **5** liaison [liˈeɪzn]: (secret) sexual relationship **6** sack sb. (infml): fire sb., dismiss sb. from a job **7** try sb.: (here) challenge sb. in order to find out whether sth. (e.g. a claim, a threat) is just a pretence or meant in earnest

12

Zaq had fallen asleep while I was talking, his whisky bottle, now three quarters empty, clutched[1] tightly in his hand. I went out and walked up the hillock, and suddenly I was facing the water over the top of the scanty[2] trees. The wind from the sea blew into my face, fresh, moist, and I was instantly filled with an unaccountable[3] exhilaration[4]. I felt free. With my back against a tree, I faced the water, and when I got tired of staring at the water I opened my book. But as I bent my head to read I noticed a white shape in the distance, many white shapes, a procession coming out of the line of trees on the path that circled the hillock, leading to the sea. They were each holding a staff[5], and towards the middle two men were bearing what looked like a body covered in a white sheet on a stretcher[6]. I thought I was about to witness some kind of sea burial, and I debated whether to dash back to the hut to get my camera. But I decided against it; I didn't want to miss anything. A low chanting[7] reached me faintly where I sat. When they got to the edge of the water, they put down the stretcher and then the corpse threw aside the white sheet, miraculously sat up and started to crawl on all fours, its robe dragging in the wet sand, till its knees and arms were in the waves, and then it sat in the water. The others gave out a loud sigh and joined the sitting figure, forming a semicircle behind it, their backs to me, facing the huge dying sun, their arms outstretched, supplicatory[8], and their sighs suddenly turned into loud wails. They went on like this for a long time, swaying rhythmically, imitating the movement

1 clutch sth.: hold sth. **2** scanty: only few **3** unaccountable: inexplicable **4** exhilaration: excitement **5** staff (n): (here) stick **6** stretcher: portable bed made of cloth with poles for a frame **7** chanting: ritual singing **8** supplicatory: pleading, begging

of the waves, and then one by one they came out of the water and headed back to the huts.

– They believe in the healing powers of the sea.

I turned, startled[1] by the voice above me. A woman, her face unclear because my eyes were still blinded by the sun, was facing me, backing the sun. She was tall and slim, wearing a long black skirt and a green blouse.

– Hello.

I stood up.

– You were watching the worshippers.

– The worshippers.

– Yes. You must be the other reporter. I'm the nurse. I've been attending to your friend. I saw you come up this way.

I pointed at her clothes. – You're not worshipping with them today?

– I'm not a worshipper. I'm just the nurse.

– Well, I see …

Now that I could see her properly, I put her age at about thirty, but she had intimations[2] of lines on her face, signs of habitual worry, or grief, and there were a few white streaks in her hair, but instead of making her appear aged the lines and grey hair made her look interesting, beautiful in an unconventional way.

– I'm Rufus.

– I'm Gloria.

We stood side by side and watched the procession disappear into the trees.

– Who's on the stretcher?

– You don't know?

– No.

– That's the head priestess. They've started the ceremonies for her death.

– Death?

1 startle sb.: surprise sb., catch sb.'s attention **2** intimation of sth.: sign of sth., hint at sth.

– She announced this week that she is dying soon. The procession you saw is part of the ceremony.

– And you, how are you involved in all this?

Before I could ask another question she looked away, and for a moment I thought she found my direct questions rather rude, but she didn't look annoyed: she was staring up at a cloud of bats that had suddenly appeared out of the trees, cackling[1] as they swarmed into the darkening sky, frolicking[2] in the last light. She turned and beckoned to me. – Come, we will be late for dinner.

I followed her down the slope[3] and into the sculpture garden.

– These islands used to be a big habitat[4] for bats; now only a few dozen remain here and there.

– Why?

She wordlessly turned and pointed at the faraway sky, towards the oil fields. – Gas flares. They kill them. Not only the bats, other flying creatures as well.

Dinner was an open-air affair, with the worshippers in white sitting in little groups under the trees on benches and logs and in the grass, eating with their fingers, laughing and calling out to each other. I felt a bit out of place in my jeans and short sleeves, but having Gloria with me saved me from being the only one not wearing a white robe.

– This is Rufus.

I shook hands all around and nodded politely as introductions were made. We had joined a group of four sitting in the grass not too far from the kitchen. Gloria told me to sit while she went to get the food, and as she turned to go I saw Naman coming over to join us. Soon an intricate[5] discussion around theology had started. He gave, I realized for my benefit, a brief history of the shrine. I ate and listened.

1 cackle (v): make a shrill sound **2** frolic (v): behave in an excited and happy way **3** slope: descending part of a hill **4** habitat: natural environment of an animal **5** intricate [ˈɪntrɪkət]: complicated

The shrine was started a long time ago after a terrible war – no one remembers what caused the war – when the blood of the dead ran in the rivers, and the water was so saturated with blood that the fishes died, and the dead bodies of warriors floated for miles on the water, until they were snagged on mangrove branches on the banks, or got stuck in the muddy swamps, half in and half out of the water. It was a terrible time. The land was so polluted that even the water in the wells turned red. That was when priests from different shrines got together and decided to build this shrine by the sea. The land needed to be cleansed of blood, and pollution.

– And what of the sculptures?

– The sculptures came later. As the priesthood grew, some became specialists in mud and wooden figures. These figures represent the ancestors watching over us. They face the east, to acknowledge the beauty of the sun rising, for without the sun there would be no life. And some face the west, to show the dying sun the way home, and to welcome the moon. And each day the worshippers go in a procession to the sea, to bathe in it, to cry to it, and to promise never to abominate[1] it ever again.

– And did that help? Did the rivers return to normal?

– Yes, and ever since we have managed to keep this island free from oil prospecting[2] and other activities that contaminate[3] the water and lead to greed and violence.

I looked at Gloria and wondered what she thought of the story, and of the worshippers in general, but she was focused on her food. She looked like a child sitting there in the grass with her long skirt around her shapely legs, a child lost, or merely playing with its toys.

– So, why aren't you a worshipper?

My voice was low so that only she could hear me. But I was not sure she had heard me, because her head was still bent over her plate. I cleared my voice to repeat myself, but she looked up and smiled.

1 abominate sth.: (here) behave in a hateful way towards sth. **2** prospecting (n): searching for natural resources **3** contaminate sth.: pollute sth.

– Well, I'm quite new here. The shrine hired me to work as a nurse. I really haven't thought much about the religious aspect of things.

I pushed my plate aside. The yam with fish stew was surprisingly tasty. The others had finished eating too and were still talking to Naman.

– How long have you been here?

– Two months this trip, but I come and go.

– And you stay here at the shrine?

– I have a place in the village. I use it whenever I'm here. I wanted to bring the conversation round to the kidnapping and the militants, but I didn't want to sound rude or pushy.

– Are you happy here? Do you feel safe?

She looked at me, her expression solemn, thoughtful. – Everything makes sense here.

– I see. Will you come to see Zaq? He was in pain when I left him.

I was reluctant to leave her. So far she had been willing to answer my questions, and perhaps if I could take her to the hut she'd be willing to answer even more direct ones. She was not a worshipper, and she had been on the island long enough to know what was going on, which made her an ideal source. And I found her very attractive.

– Yes, of course. I'll see how he's doing before he turns in. We found Zaq seated on his mat, facing a fire in a brazier[1] that had been placed near his feet. His back was propped against the wall and his face didn't change expression when he saw me enter with Gloria. He appeared lost in thought.

– The nurse is here to see you.

It took him a few minutes to look up, sighing heavily as he did so. The flames danced in the light and shadows on his face, merging with and accentuating[2] the hollows and lines on it. His eyes were shiny, and I knew that he had been at what was left of the bottle.

1 brazier: metal container used to burn material (e.g. wood or coal) **2** accentuate sth.: emphasize sth.

When the nurse knelt before him and took his wrist in her hand, she noticed it too. She also saw the bottle of whisky near his pillow. She reached forward and took it.

– You've been drinking. Your pulse is very weak, I can't allow you to drink.

And she flung the bottle at the open doorway, into the dark. To my surprise Zaq did not protest. He looked at her with a fixed gaze.

– Ah, nurse. You look great today.

– And you look drunk today, Mr Zaq.

– Rufus, isn't she very pretty?

The sternness[1] went out of her face, and for a moment she appeared uncertain – her hand went up to adjust her scarf – and then she became serious again. I went out and sat on a tree trunk by the hut door. From there I could see the sculpture garden: the frozen community watching the night, warding off[2] evil, ears cocked[3] for the night's watchword[4], whatever that might be. She came out and stood quietly beside me. I wanted to talk to her, but there was a stillness about her that I didn't want to shatter. At last she turned and looked at me.

– It's so peaceful here, isn't it?

She sat down on the log beside me, and I felt the back of her hand brush against mine briefly. We sat in silence for a long time, watching the darkness.

– It is my fault. I brought him the drink. I thought it would cheer him up.

– You didn't force him to drink it. He's old enough to know what's good for him.

– He is a good man. A great reporter.

She didn't say anything to that. At last she stood up.

– I have to go now. My place in the village is near the jetty. You must come and see the jetty if you're still here tomorrow.

1 sternness: strictness **2** ward off sth.: keep sth. at a distance so that it cannot harm you **3** cock one's ears: listen attentively **4** watchword: signal word that allows people belonging to the same group to identify each other

It's beautiful in the evening when the boats come in.

– I will.

She left, and I watched after her until her shape became one with the night, invisible.

– I think she likes you, Rufus my friend.

Zaq had come out onto the grass and felt around on hands and knees till he found his whisky bottle. Now he kept spitting out bits of grass as he took long sips at the bottle.

– No, she doesn't.

– She likes you. Trust me. I may not look it, but I do know about women. I saw the way she was looking at you. No doubt about it. She likes you. You're not married, are you?

– No. Not yet.

– Surely you must have a girlfriend back in Port Harcourt? Look at you, a very fine young man, and being a journalist the girls must be after you all the time.

– Well, not really. I'm always busy with the job.

There was Mary, whom I'd met at journalism school, but I didn't tell him about that. Mary, who wanted so badly to get married. She had made all the plans, and at night she'd go over them with me in the little room we shared not far from the campus. It was a tenement house, a face-me-I-face-you. I moved in with her a shirt, a brush, a shoe at a time. It was cheaper if we stayed together, she said. Looking back, I guess she must have started planning to marry me from the first day we met. She was that kind of girl. Forward-looking.

She was a TV journalist and her employers had sent her to the journalism school to specialize in news editing. Sometimes she'd go away for the weekend, and I knew she was away with her old boyfriend from her office. She never talked about him, and I never asked her – why would I, since I didn't really love her? She was pretty and clever and the sex was good, but I didn't see myself spending the rest of my life with her. Whenever she came back from her little trips she'd hold me all night long, tight, sometimes crying just to show how much she'd missed me.

Once, she went to Ibadan to visit her family, and when she came back she had changed. She was scared, and for two nights she didn't sleep. When I asked what was wrong, she told me about the holy man. Her father had died many years back, and her mother wanted to remarry but wasn't having any luck, and so she asked a holy man to pray for her. He moved into the guest room, and then one day Mary came home to find he'd moved into her mother's bedroom, and had impregnated not only her mother but also her seventeen-year-old sister. She went to the police, but her mother refused to back her up, and her sister was terrified and confused and didn't know who to support, and all the while the holy man was there in the background, not saying a word, clutching his Bible, taking the name of God in vain[1]. And she had left. She gave up. She held me tight, till I couldn't breathe, sobbing, I don't have a family any more, you are all I have. Promise me you'll be with me always.

But I didn't tell Zaq any of this.

– My last girlfriend wanted to get married, but I wasn't ready. We were too young. Twenty-three, both of us. She wanted us to run away to Abuja and start a life together. Alone. Away from family and friends.

– No. She was wrong, and selfish. You can't run from your family. It's not right.

The next day Zaq was a changed man: he woke me up early, in time to see the procession go for its morning dip[2].

– It's time to find out a few truths. Time to move on.

– You mean go back to Port Harcourt?

– You know, I'm not going back.

– What do you mean?

– Just what I said. All the time I was in that windowless, airless office, with my good friend Beke out there behind his editor's desk gloating over the fact that he was now actually my employer, the

1 take sb.'s name in vain: misuse sb.'s name to justify sth. **2** dip (n): (here) quick bath

great Zaq cut down to size – he had always been envious of me, you see – all that time my greatest fear was that I'd die there, unable to get out and follow a true story one more time. I knew all I had to do was stand up and walk out, but I was scared, for the first time in my life I was scared. I was scared of failing. I've failed so many times before, in my profession, and in many other things as well.

– You are talking in riddles, Zaq.

– I have plans. I can get backers[1]. Come with me to Lagos and we'll start a new paper, a real paper.

– I have to be in the office.

– Well, think about whether to take the ferry back, or to come with me into the forest in search of the woman. Perhaps you're thinking, Ah, he's still drunk, tomorrow he'll have forgotten all about this. But you don't have to answer immediately. We'll talk about it some more. But I can tell you have the makings of a real reporter. You ask the right questions, and the fact that you actually returned to this island shows you're not afraid to take chances. And I think luck is on our side: here we are, pursuing what is almost a perfect story. A British woman kidnapped by local militants who are fighting to protect their environment from greedy multinational oil companies. Perfect. A good story for any paper.

I listened in silence, though I wanted to say to him: I'm flattered that you think I'm a great reporter, potentially, but right now my sister with her scarred face and even more scarred psyche is in my room, shedding tears. I need to be there to make sure she doesn't do anything crazy. And, another minor point, if I don't get back to my office very soon, I'll lose my job.

But I only nodded.

– Think about it.

In his lecture that day in Lagos, Zaq said that the best stories are the ones we write with tears in our eyes, the ones whose stings we feel personally. After visiting my sister at the hospital, unable to sleep, haunted by the image of burned flesh and the smell of pet-

1 backer: sb. who supports sb./sth. (e.g. financially)

rol that clung to the hospital walls and corridors, I picked up pen and paper and the words had come effortlessly. I wrote about our childhood, about our days catching crabs to pay our way through secondary school, about Boma's dreams of becoming a doctor. I had posted the story on the internet, and it had been quoted and reproduced over and over on websites. And of course I had used it when applying for a job: it was a part of my CV, a part of my experience. To be a great reporter required a lot of suffering, a lot of back story, and I was finding that out for myself.

– One more thing. I do remember now that day at Bar Beach. That day with you and your lecturers at the restaurant.

– Well, good.

– I also remember your call, but I didn't get you your job.

– What do you mean?

After your call, I did mean to ring your chairman to persuade him to give you a chance, but I was busy that day and –

– And so ... I got the job all by myself ...

– I guess you did.

– I don't know whether to thank you or to curse you.

– I'm being honest with you. Now come. Let's go see the priest.

13

We found him in his hut behind the worship room, changing into a fresh robe. When he opened the door to our knock, he didn't look surprised to see us.

– Ah, Mr Zaq, I see you look better. You must be anxious to return home. We are happy to have you here as long as you like, both of you, of course, but the nurse thinks that you ought to see a doctor soon.

– Where is the British woman ... and the Professor?

Zaq stooped and entered through the low door, then he straightened up pugnaciously before the priest.

– The Professor?

– Come on, it's no secret that these islands and villages are under his protection. We're not the army, we're reporters. We want to know what he's done with the woman. We want to ask him why he has turned from being a freedom fighter to a kidnapper of women and children. We want to know if the white woman is alive.

The priest sat down on a tall stool, a tired droop[1] to his shoulders.

– I think it would be best if you just went back home.

– Not until we see the woman.

– That may not be possible.

– Why not? Don't tell me you have a hand in the kidnapping?

– No. We are a holy community, a peaceful people. Our only purpose here is to bring healing, to restore and conserve ...

– Just tell us what you know.

Naman took a deep breath and stood up.

– Come with me.

1 droop (n): downward curve

His words and movements were decisive[1]. We followed him, his fresh robe dragging in the wet, muddy grass. We passed the worshippers, some coming out of their huts, standing under trees, looking after us curiously. Gloria was in a group with three women, talking and laughing, but she stopped talking and stared at us. Zaq bowed slightly in her direction and she nodded. I slowed down, half turning to face her, but Zaq made an impatient gesture with his head and I quickened my pace. We walked on. The priest took us past the sculptures, away from the water, into the woods. Here the heat was trapped between the trees, and the dead leaves on the ground were putrid[2]. Soon we appeared at a clearing surrounded by chicken wire. It was a cemetery, with headstones[3] looking as lonely and forlorn[4] as only headstones can. He pushed open the flimsy wooden gate and waved us in, like a man inviting us into his living room. He stopped before a fresh, unmarked mound[5].

– The kidnappers brought her here about a week ago, and yes, one of them was the Professor. We try as much as possible to keep out of their way, and they leave us alone. We don't talk to them, or to the army. But they brought the white woman here. I objected[6]. But he said they only came because she was seriously ill, and they knew we had a nurse here. They said they'd be on their way in a few days. Well, after two days some of them set out in a boat. They had two boats, and they set out in one, about seven of them, including the Professor. The woman was attended to by our nurse, who diagnosed a fever and diarrhoea[7]. Well, we waited for them to leave, and when they didn't I went to their hut and asked what was going on. They said they were still waiting for the Professor to return. They looked uneasy. Well, as we were talking, the Professor came in, with only two men. The rest, he said, had been killed in the fight with the sol-

1 decisive: (here) firm, determined **2** putrid (adj): (smelling) rotten
3 headstone: gravestone **4** forlorn: lonely, sad **5** mound (n): pile **6** object (to sth.): be against sth., protest against sth. **7** diarrhoea [ˌdaɪəˈrɪə] (BE, AE: diarrhea): *Durchfall*

diers. He was wounded but he wouldn't sit. He said they had to leave at once. I left them, then ...

The priest stopped speaking and stared silently at the fresh mound of earth in front of us.

– Then what? Did she die?

– He came to me just before they left. He brought me here and said, They will come looking for her, if they do, show them her grave. This is for the men they killed. Maybe this will teach them not to mess with[1] us in the future.

– I don't believe him.

– But he wouldn't lie to us, surely ...

– That's what I find confusing. Why would he lie about a thing like this?

I shared Zaq's feeling. Something didn't feel right. Not in my wildest dreams did I ever think our quest[2] would end so suddenly, with an unmarked grave in a shrine. Zaq said nothing more all day. He lay on his mat, facing the conical thatched roof, a second bottle in his hand. To my questions he gave only monosyllabic grunts. I slept and woke up around 5 p.m. I picked up my camera.

– Where are you going?

– Taking a walk.

– I think you should go meet that nurse.

– Gloria.

– Ask her what she knows about the English woman.

– What if she doesn't want to talk?

– Didn't I tell you she likes you? Hold her hand. Kiss her. Just get her to talk. It's very important. Don't you like her?

– She's a very pretty woman, Zaq.

I took pictures of the cemetery, making sure I had a close-up of the fresh mound of earth, then I turned my lenses to the sculptures.

1 mess with sb. (infml): start an argument or a fight with sb. **2** quest: search

Afterwards I walked about aimlessly, hoping to catch a glimpse[1] of Gloria, but I did not see her anywhere. I went and sat on the hill to stare at the water and the faraway gas flares that emerged suddenly from pillar-like[2] pipes, holding up their roof of odious black smoke. I thought of so many things, of the priest's words, of the white woman, dead and buried all this while, of Zaq's offer. When I got tired of thinking I descended to join the worshippers for dinner. I found Gloria in the spot where we'd eaten yesterday.

– I was just coming from your hut.

She looked beautiful, her smile cheerful.

– Did you meet Zaq?

– Yes. He was quite chatty[3] today. I think he's recovering very well. Just keep him away from the bottle.

I wondered what she and Zaq had talked about. I wondered what her story was, why she wasn't married, or if she had been married before.

– Have you eaten?

– No. Actually, I've been cooking and I was going to invite you and Zaq to come and eat at my place. But Zaq said he wasn't hungry.

– So –

– So you have to eat for both of you. Come on, let's go.

I followed her through a path in the woods and after a few metres it was as if we had stepped into a different dimension, away from the sea and sculptures and huts and worshippers. The tall iroko trees shaded the sun completely, and whenever a single ray found its way through the million leaves and branches and fell on our skin or on the dead leaves below, it looked so pure and startling, as if it had been refined[4] through a thousand sieves[5]. But at last we came out of the foliage into the busy village: sudden, noisy, alive with movement, and with smells from a hundred pots in a hundred kitchens.

1 catch a glimpse of sb./sth.: see sb./sth. for a short moment **2** pillar-like: resembling a column **3** chatty (infml): talkative **4** refine: purify **5** sieve [sɪv] (n) : tool with tiny openings on the bottom that only allow smaller parts or liquids to fall/flow through

The roads were dusty and open, the houses few and well kept – they had verandas at the front and narrow windows that let in the noise and dust. We passed men seated on chairs, their heads bent, their mouths open, sleeping away the afternoon as chickens poked around for tit-bits[1] between the legs of the chairs.

Gloria's room was in a huge, rectangular compound with a leafy gardenia tree in the centre. She said there were very few such tenement houses in the village, since there wasn't much need for them, the village being without any form of industry[2] to attract outsiders. Almost every house was a family home. The shrine was the main industry, and after it came fishing. Sometimes outsiders visited the shrine and took pictures of the sculptures. Sometimes they rented a room for the night in the tenement compound. None of her co-tenants seemed to be about: the thick wooden doors were shut and silence hung in the air like the black smoke from the faraway pillars.

It was a tiny room, and, seated in the only chair, I constantly had to move my feet out of the way as she bustled about[3] to get me something to eat. In a corner was a table with a few jars[4] of body cream, and a hairbrush, and a mirror and a cup with toothbrushes and a tube of toothpaste. The wind through the small square window played with the flimsy curtain.

– So, tell me about Zaq.

– What do you want to know?

– Have you two known each other long?

– No, not really. This assignment is the second time we've met.

– He told me that ... that ...

– That what?

She turned away, avoiding my eyes, moving about as she spoke, picking up things and putting them down again. She placed a plate of jollof rice before me.

– He said you told him that you think I'm attractive?

– Well, yes. I think you're attractive.

1 tit-bit: *Leckerbissen* **2** industry: (here) business **3** bustle about: move around busily **4** jar (n): small glass container open at the top

She smiled and shook her head and for the first time she stopped moving. She wiped her hands on the kitchen towel she was holding, then she hung the towel on a hook. I went over to her. I put my hand round her waist and drew her against me. She turned her face as I tried to kiss her and my kiss landed on her cheek. She looked at me.

– I'm much older than you, you know. And –

– And?

– I have a fiancé[1]. In Port Harcourt.

Slowly I let my hands slip down from her waist. But she took my hands and put them firmly around her hips, pulling me against her.

– Are you so easily discouraged? Aren't journalists supposed to be very, very persistent[2]?

I tried again, and this time she let my lips descend on her open mouth, her eyes fixed on mine. I spent the night with her, in her narrow bed, and all night long she held me tight, as if to stop me from slipping away in the dark. I woke up once and saw the wind lightly shaking the flimsy lace[3] curtain on the window, and I felt as if the wind were blowing through the fields of my mind, gently stirring up[4] particles in forgotten corners. Then I went back to sleep.

– Tell me about the English woman.

It was morning. I had dressed but she was still lying in bed, the sheets drawn up to her neck. I could see the outline of her breasts beneath the sheets.

– Naman told me you were going to ask me that.

– And?

– And he said to tell you all I know.

– We're reporters, Gloria. It's our job. You'll be helping us. Zaq and me.

She sighed and stared at a hanger[5] on the wall over her bed bearing her nurse's uniform, white and crisp[6], waiting to be worn.

1 fiancé (fiancée) [fiˈɒnseɪ]: man (woman) sb. is engaged to **2** persistent: not giving up easily **3** lace: decorative cloth **4** stir up sth.: *etwas aufwirbeln* **5** hanger: curved item for hanging clothes **6** crisp: (here) freshly washed

– Well, what do you want to know?

– Tell me about the woman. You attended to her when they brought her here.

– Yes. She was in the room where you're staying now.

– Naman showed us her grave. Could she have died from natural causes?

– She was weak and dehydrated[1]. But that wouldn't have killed her.

– Did she talk to you, anything in secret, anything at all?

– No. I attended to her only once. There were men holding guns in that room. Wearing masks. I was too scared even to look at her properly. I wouldn't recognize her if I saw her again.

– Then what?

– Well, afterwards one of the men walked me out and told me if I talked about the woman or about the men to anyone, terrible things would happen to the community, and it would be my fault.

– How many were they? Did they talk to you?

– About ten of them. They stayed for only two nights, and they kept to themselves. They talked only to Naman. They left not long before you first arrived.

– I don't know what your plans are, but her death could mean big trouble for the community. As soon as we report it, the police and army will be here. They're sure to arrest some of your people as accomplices[2]. You have to think of leaving here, at least until this thing blows over. Think about it.

She appeared unhappy talking about the kidnappers and the white woman.

– It just doesn't make sense.

– What?

– Her death. It was so sudden. She didn't look like she was dying.

– Maybe they killed her accidentally. Maybe she attempted to escape. I have to go now. Zaq will be waiting for me. We have to decide what to do.

1 dehydrated: having lost much water **2** accomplice: partner in crime

– Will I see you later?

– Yes.

That night, around midnight, Zaq woke me up holding a lamp close to my face. He sat down beside me.

– Our job is to find out the truth, even if it is buried deep in the earth.

I watched him, an ominous feeling creeping up my chest. He had a crazy look in his eyes, I could smell the drink on his breath, and he hiccuped[1] as he gave his little speech.

– This is something we must do. You have no choice. Without this our mission will be incomplete. Come with me.

And, half excited, half petrified[2], I followed him. The night was silent, broken only by the faraway sound of waves beating against the shore, and what might have been the call of bats or owls or other night birds. We walked through the ranks[3] of the staring statues, which was rather like running an ominous gauntlet[4], a staring match with the unblinking, unmoving figures. At the edge of the sculpture garden was a tool shed whose rusty lock Zaq effortlessly broke with a single twist. He handed me a pick and a shovel and we set out for the cemetery. I was cold, whether from the chill air or from nerves, I wasn't sure. Zaq's portly[5] frame strode[6] before me purposefully, holding up the lamp as if it were a shear[7] cutting through the dense foliage of night. When we got to the white woman's grave he squatted down beside it, the lamp still in his hands.

– Dig.

As I dug he took out the whisky bottle from his pocket and filled his mouth, and when I paused for breath he handed me the bottle.

– Drink.

I drank.

1 hiccup (v): *Schluckauf haben* **2** petrified: (looking/feeling like) turned into a stone **3** rank (n): row **4** run the gauntlet: *Spießruten laufen* **5** portly: corpulent **6** stride (v): walk with long steps **7** shear [ʃɪə(r)] (n): two connected shears make up a tool that resembles a large pair of scissors

I drank to make myself insensitive[1] to the accusing ghost eyes in the light's fringes[2], eyes whose glow seemed to pierce through my body to my very soul, and with every mouthful, every shovelful, I grew as excited as Zaq, and in my mind I repeated his phrase: Our job is to find out the truth, even if it is buried deep in the earth. I giggled, tickled at my own cleverness. Already I could see the inch-high headline: kidnapped briton discovered in shallow grave. Not as aesthetically accomplished as his nuts-and-bolts headline, but, word for word, much more compelling.

It was a shallow grave, too shallow to cover a body, I saw that right away. In my mind I had already braced myself[3] for the smell of rotting flesh, the sight of a worm-infested corpse, but all we found was a stone. A huge, round boulder[4] sitting insensate[5], incognizant[6], like a corpse. Whoever made the false grave had a sense of humour, it seemed. Zaq surged[7] forward when my shovel hit the stone with a dull metallic sound that resounded like a gunshot in the quiet night air. I collapsed onto the mound of earth I had created, breathing noisily through my mouth, the warmth from the fresh earth rising up my body, soothing, reassuring me that the punishing dig was over. I watched him put down the lamp and, like a dog unearthing evidence, he got down on his hands and knees and carefully pushed aside the sandy soil around the stone.

– Take pictures.

I took pictures.

– You knew there was no body?

We headed back to our hut.

– I suspected.

I could feel the exhilaration in his voice, in his jaunty steps. In the room, after we had washed and settled on our mats, he kept tossing

1 insensitive to sth.: (here) unable to feel sth. **2** fringe: edge **3** brace oneself: prepare oneself (for a difficult situation) **4** boulder: rock **5** insensate: having no feeling/consciousness **6** incognizant: unable to know or understand anything **7** surge (v): (here) move quickly

and turning and getting up to walk up and down. At last he lay down and closed his eyes.

– I'd better get a good rest. Tomorrow we leave. We may not be safe here any more.

– I don't think the priest would do us any harm ...

– No, not the priest, but what if he's being watched? He was lying on his back, staring up at the roof, taking occasional swigs[1] of his whisky.

Finally, he blew out the lamp.

– Get some sleep, Rufus.

1 swig (n): large gulp/swallow

14

The soldiers led us to the lock-up when the sun was setting over the land. They walked behind us, their guns raised and aimed at a point between my shoulder blades; Zaq was walking slightly ahead of me on the narrow path leading to the little hut. The lock-up was at the farthest end of the square, next to the water, and as we approached we could see the mosquitoes rising in a thick cloud over the water. I was worried about Zaq. His early-morning alertness[1] had gradually given way to bad-tempered enervation[2] as the sun went down, and now his legs dragged, his shoulders slumped as he walked, and even from here I could hear his breath wheezing out of his nose. I had tried to convince him to let me go alone to the lock-up, but he wouldn't hear of it.

– This is what I came for. Besides, how would you explain my absence to them?

– I'd tell them you are not feeling well.

– No, that won't work. We mustn't leave anything to chance[3]. Besides, I feel strong.

And I couldn't argue any further without telling him bluntly[4] that he was dying, and even if I did, it was no guarantee he'd budge[5]. The soldiers opened the door and threw us in, then they closed it. We felt our way to the wall and we sat against it. Immediately Zaq slumped against me, his head sliding down my shoulder and lolling[6] helplessly. And for a moment I asked myself, what if he died, right here, right now? Best to pretend things were the same as before, that Zaq was all right, and we would interview these people, and we'd go back

1 alertness: (here) state of being awake and attentive to things that happen
2 enervation: weakness, exhaustion **3** leave sth. to chance: *etwas dem Zufall überlassen* **4** blunt: straightforward, direct **5** budge (infml): move **6** loll (v): hang down in an uncontrolled way

to write the story. I even tried to fashion a headline that would be worthy of such a great story, the perfect, inevitable[1] headline, the one that gets your story on the front cover, an inch high, the one that compels the most indifferent[2] reader to stop and pick up the paper.

When my eyes got used to the gloom in the shed, and when I had controlled the dizzying, nauseating effect of the petrol smell that rose off the men's bodies and clothes to cast a miasmatic[3] shadow over the tiny room, I saw Tamuno and Michael huddled together[4] in a corner. The boy was asleep, his head resting on his father's scrawny[5] shoulder, his feet stretched out straight before him. I realized the old man was staring at me, and in his posture I saw an embarrassed apology, as if he was trying to say sorry that things had ended up like this, and I wanted to tell him that it was I who should be apologizing for leading him into this.

Most of the men were lying on the floor, some with faces turned towards the wall. I didn't know how long they had been the Major's prisoners, or what other punishment they had endured in addition to the petrol drenching, but they all looked exhausted and dispirited[6]. In a uniform, spastic choreography they scratched and twitched and rubbed their dry skin where the petrol had scalded them, where it still burned. Only one of them sat without the mad twitching; his head was bowed, but he did not seem defeated or fatigued[7], like the others; he looked like a man lost in thought, a man seated against a wall in his own compound. I crawled towards him, and as I neared him a huge paw from behind grabbed me by the neck and pulled, and suddenly I was staring at two red eyes that bore into me, unblinking, expressionless. The thinking man raised his head and motioned to my captor[8].

– Let him go, Taiga.

1 inevitable: impossible to avoid, (here) absolutely fitting **2** indifferent: disinterested **3** miasmatic [miæzˈmætɪk]: smelling unpleasantly and unhealthy **4** huddled together: staying close to each other **5** scrawny: very thin **6** dispirited: without hope **7** fatigued [fəˈtiːgd]: tired **8** captor: person or animal that captures another person or animal

I couldn't breathe until the fist released me, then I was gasping, sucking in the fumy[1] air, rubbing my neck, which felt broken. I sat next to the man.

– Thanks.

– Did you think he was going to kill you? We're not murderers, my friend, regardless of what you guys write about us.

– My name is Rufus, and that's my colleague Zaq.

– So, what are you doing here?

– We're prisoners, like you. The Major doesn't believe we're innocent journalists.

– Well, are you?

– What?

– Innocent journalists?

– Of course we are. I work for *The Reporter*, and Zaq works for the *Star*.

– Is he the Zaq who used to be with the *Daily Times*?

– Yes, he is –

– Let him speak for himself!

Zaq coughed and sat up straight.

– Yes, my friend. It's me. What's your name?

– Henshaw.

– Glad to meet you, Henshaw.

– We came to find out about the British woman. Is she still alive?

– Is that all you want from me, to tell you whether some foreign hostage is alive or not? Who is she in the context of the war that's going on out there, the hopes and ambitions being created and destroyed? Can't you see the larger picture?

Henshaw sounded educated and very confident, so perhaps the best way to make progress was to appeal to his reason. Zaq must have sensed that as well. I waited for Henshaw to speak some more, but he didn't. He kept his head inclined, as if slumbering[2], already bored by that little exchange. After a while I cleared my throat. I could feel Zaq in the dark, waiting, willing me to go on. I was aware

1 fumy: full of fumes **2** slumber (v): sleep lightly

that time was passing: soon the night would be over, and who knew what the morning would bring? How long would the revived Zaq remain coherent[1], lucid[2], how long would he remain alive?

– Does your group have a name?

– No! We used to have a name, but no more. That is for children and idiots. We are the people, we are the Delta, we represent the very earth on which we stand.

– Are you with the Professor?

– No. I have never met the Professor. We're a different group, the four of us. That man is with the Professor. Perhaps he can tell you about the white woman. Hey you, talk to the reporters. Go on, talk.

The scratching and twitching and pain-filled groans had stopped as everyone strained to listen to our talk. Even the mosquitoes had somehow stopped singing around my ears. I turned to look at the man. He was seated by himself near the door, his back pushing into the wall, away from all the eyes suddenly turned on him. He began to shake his head as I crawled towards him, and when I was in front of him he turned his face away.

– Look, you heard what I told him. We're impartial[3] reporters. All we want to know is where the woman is, if she's alive.

He mumbled something, his voice coming out like a sob. I leaned closer to him.

– What?

Now he turned to me and even in the dark I could see how young he was – between fifteen and twenty. His face was smooth, hairless.

– His name is Gabriel. He was here before we came, at least two days.

The voice came from one of the faces seated around Henshaw – possibly from the one named Taiga.

– Gabriel, I'm Rufus. Have you heard anything about the woman? We saw the battle with the soldiers – were you there? Did

1 coherent: reasonable, (here) conscious **2** lucid: clear, (here) conscious
3 impartial: independent, not supporting the one or the other side

you hear any of your friends talking about it? We saw dead bodies. Were you there? Were you captured, did you surrender?

– Come on, man, stop whimpering like a girl and talk. Talk! Taiga, make him talk!

The threat did the trick. For the first time the boy nodded his head instead of shaking it. He raised his head and looked into my eyes and now his words came out coherently. He'd been there, at the battle. But he didn't say anything more after that, and when I threw more questions, he looked defiantly from me to Taiga.

– Why don't you find out, since you're a reporter?

I crawled back to where Zaq lay and sprawled out beside him. I didn't feel as if I had gained much information. I still hadn't found out anything new about the woman. Had she escaped? I hoped not, because she had no way of surviving out there in the swamps by herself: first of all, her skin would be her worst enemy, it'd emblazon[1] her presence like lightning in a dark night wherever she went, and she might escape from one kidnapper only to end up in the hands of another.

Towards morning, when a pink light stitched in through the million micro openings in the roof thatch, Henshaw crawled over to my side and shook me awake. I sat up beside him, our shoulders touching. Outside, the bugle[2] sounded.

– I know exactly what they're doing out there: right now the soldiers will be in line, shoulder to shoulder, all twenty of them, one sergeant, two corporals, and the rest privates[3], all standing at attention, and he'll be telling them why they must hate the militants, why they must fight to keep the country safe and united. Ten minutes of that. I've been here four days now and I know exactly what they do every minute of the day. I can tell you what they eat, what they think, who is tired of the Major's demented patriotism and just wants to go

1 emblazon sth.: give emphasis to sth. **2** bugle [ˈbjuːgl]: horn used for giving signals **3** private (n): *Gefreiter*

home. We'll outlast[1] them. That's all we need to do. Sit tight. Wait. This land is ours, after all.

He paused, his eyes closed. All the other faces were staring at him, but their ears were focused on something further off, somewhere close to where the bugle had sounded, waiting. And yes, there was a distant sound of a voice, firm, authoritative. Too far away for the words to register. After what seemed like ten minutes, he resumed[2] his commentary.

– Now he's walking in their midst, putting a hand on this one's shoulder, reprimanding[3] that one for a smudge[4] on his boots – imagine reprimanding a soldier for a smudge here in the jungle … and now he is dismissing them. Five of them are coming this way, guns firmly clasped in both hands, trotting, and here they are.

Footsteps came to a stop in front of the hut, and Zaq and I waited to see what was going to happen. The door was kicked open, and two soldiers entered in a splash of morning sunlight. The others waited outside.

– Oya, stand up. Single file. Proceed outside.

It was the tallest of them speaking. They didn't kick or hit the prisoners, they just stood there, their guns ready, waiting for the men to get in line.

1 outlast sb.: live longer than sb. **2** resume sth.: continue sth. after an interruption **3** reprimand sb.: scold sb., rebuke sb., severely critize sb. **4** smudge (n): stain

15

The Major waved his hand towards the approaching shoreline, but his voice was drowned out by the noise from the helicopter, which suddenly appeared above us, like a bird of ill omen. The Major looked up, then he took out his radio and put it to his ear. When he finished speaking his face had a satisfied grin.

– Be prepared for what you are about to see. Irikefe is now mostly ashes and rubble[1], bombed by the gun helicopter over there. Not a hut is left standing ...

– What of the people?

– Most of them would still be there, I suppose. But expect a lot of casualties[2], unavoidable, of course. This is a war zone ... Look, look, you can see the smoke from here.

We descended from the boat into the restless water. On the shore was a line of soldiers in battle gear[3], pointing their guns at us. They led us towards the trees and then to a field of rubble, which I saw was all that was left of the sculpture garden. Memory is nothing but a view through a car window, fast changing, impressionistic. Of all the things that I saw that day, and all the words that I heard, what made the most impression was the sight of the broken statues. The arms and legs and heads sundered from the body. I recall a face, its expression of terror so life-like, the eyes so mobile staring up at me as I passed, its nose broken, its mouth half open and eager to share its secret.

The fighting was over when we got off the boat, but the earth was still smouldering[4] with the remains of battle, the huts still gave out smoke, and soldiers still fired guns sporadically into the air as

1 rubble: mass of broken stones and bricks **2** casualty: person killed or injured in a military conflict **3** gear: equipment **4** smoulder: burn lightly with no visible signs except smoke

they corralled[1] the villagers into one big clearing, trying to determine who among them was a militant and who wasn't. I couldn't recognize the hut where we once slept, and the log on which I once sat. Zaq sat down heavily on the first surface he found. I couldn't sit – I mingled with[2] the worshippers, trying to see if I could find a familiar face, Gloria, or Naman, and yes, here was a familiar face, even though half of it was swollen and covered with blood. It was the man who'd been seated with Gloria and Naman, eating dinner, and if I hadn't been looking keenly, peering almost rudely into the faces, I wouldn't have recognized him. His once pure white robe was now patched with the green of crushed leaves and the rust and red of blood, and the one side of his face capable of expression looked vacant[3], vague, tired, like a man after a long trek, thirsty, but unsure where to look for water or rest. When I stopped next to him and took his hand and introduced myself, he licked his chapped[4] lips and tried to smile.

– Ah, the reporter. But what are you doing here? This place is very dangerous for you. You shouldn't have returned.

– Where's Gloria, and Naman?

He pointed vaguely and continued walking, his eyes looking around for something in the rubble. A woman took me to Naman. He was surrounded by a group of women, all weeping and holding each other, and he went from one to the other, calming them down. I shook his hand and he told me to sit beside him. Like the others his white robe was covered in blood, maybe his, maybe not. I couldn't think of anything to say. I pointed.

– The statuary[5] is all gone.

– It is the nature of existence. A thing is created, it blooms for a while if it is capable of blooming, then it ceases to be.

He said that two days ago the militants had arrived. The worshippers were as usual having their morning dip, chanting their hymn

1 corral (v): *zusammentreiben* **2** mingle with (a group of people): move among (a group of people to get to know them) **3** vacant [ˈveɪkənt]: empty
4 chapped: rough, cracked **5** statuary: group of statues

to the sun, and the next thing they knew they were surrounded by gunmen. Of course they had been visited by the militants before, but nothing like this – usually they came for food, or for medical supplies, or for clothes; once they attempted to abduct a woman worshipper, but Naman had stood in front of the woman and said they had to shoot him first, and of course when their leader, the real Professor, who was a gentleman, found out, he had publicly punished the militant and personally apologized to the community. A good man, the real Professor. But this time it was the other leader, a younger one, and he gathered everyone into the worship hut and said he wanted all the worshippers to swear allegiance[1] to him – imagine that. When Naman said that wasn't really necessary, he placed a gun on his chest and told him to shut up. Then he said he had discovered that traitors, informers, had been giving information to the soldiers. Someone here at the shrine, on the island, must have given them away to the soldiers just before they arranged to meet with the reporters on Agbuki. He said he and his men would spend the night here and tomorrow they'd be on their way, but before they left they'd take a hostage, just to make sure of the worshippers' cooperation. And then he pointed at Gloria, and said, You will come with us tomorrow.

But the soldiers came early the next morning. First they came in a boat, and there were only five of them. They were on routine patrol; they hadn't known the militants were here, and they ran into an ambush – it was a massacre. They were all killed, instantly. The militants had machine guns and grenades. It was awful. But the soldiers must have called for back-up because this morning the helicopter came and started shooting at everything beneath it, indiscriminately[2]. People running and jumping into the water. It was awful. Awful. The water turned red. Blood, it was blood. But in the confusion the rebels slipped away and left the villagers to face the soldiers.

1 allegiance: loyalty **2** indiscriminate: without making any distinctions

– Now, see, everything is in ruins. Nothing left, it is a miracle so many are still alive. A miracle.

He kept repeating it: a miracle.

– And Gloria, where is she?

– They took her away like they promised. She was crying and screaming, but they dragged her away.

*

– A lady was here just now, looking for you. She said she was your sister. Do you have a sister?

– Boma. Here?

Zaq looked about, raising his head from the grass. He was exactly where I'd left him over two hours ago, in the grass under a tree, but now he was fully stretched on his back, his head propped up on the tree's protruding root.

– I told her to walk about, that you were somewhere out there. Maybe she's with the women over there.

I wasn't sure what to make of that news. What would Boma be doing here? How did she get here? I left Zaq and headed for the group of women. The camp had segregated itself, with the men on one side, closer to the water, and the women camped where the tree line began. The women were seated in groups, the fit ones tending to the wounded, while the children crawled between their legs and rolled about in the grass, oblivious of the moment's gravity. And on the outskirts[1] of the two groups were the soldiers, their guns raised, their eyes alert to any movement over the water. I found her sitting by herself on a log, looking absently at two urchins wrestling in the grass. She had a smile on her face, and she looked pretty. I was looking at the good side of her face, and suddenly I was back many years to the last time I'd seen her like this, without the scar. I had returned from Port Harcourt after my apprenticeship with Udoh Fotos; Boma and John had started going out then and were already talking of get-

1 outskirt: area farthest away form the centre (e.g. of a city)

ting married someday. John had pointed at the entire town of Junction with his hand. – But we have to get out of here first.

On the day I left, John and Boma had walked me to the bus station, and as the bus pulled away Boma waved and waved and the sun fell on her smooth face, just as it fell now. Smooth and unmarred[1].

– What are you doing here? I know, don't tell me. You're hoping to find John in the forest, waiting for you.

My voice rose as I spoke, and I felt it rising even higher. I pointed around.

– Look, they're fighting a war here. You could get killed, Boma. And all for what, for a man who walked out on you because he couldn't bear to look at your face any more? It's time to move on. He's never coming back. He's gone. Accept it.

She was staring at me, her head inclined, as if she were watching a stranger. But I was remorseless[2]. I was tired, and all I wanted was to be as far away from here as possible, but her presence only added to the weight on my shoulders.

– I came to look for you, not for John.

I sat down beside her.

– You were supposed to be gone for only a day. I went to your office to see if they had any news and they said no. Nothing. And then your editor said to tell you not to bother to show up at the office.

– He said that?

– Yes.

How quickly things change. It seemed like only yesterday I was seated at the Chairman's right hand, being toasted[3] by the staff, and now I had no job.

– How long have you been here?

– I got here yesterday; the fighting began just after I arrived. The kids wrestling in the grass were now eating out of the same bowl, placed before them by their mother, who stood watching over them as they ate. She was a tired-looking woman with her hair in knots;

1 unmarred: not disfigured **2** remorseless: merciless **3** toast sb.: drink to sb.

she held her grimy white robe bunched up at the hip, lifting it clear of the muddy grass. Her exposed calves were thick and chunky[1], merging into her ankles without definition.

– I was worried about you.

I felt tired. I felt ashamed at my outburst. I tried a joke when I saw how crestfallen[2] she looked.

– I'm the lucky one, remember? Nothing will happen to me.

– Have you found the woman?

– What woman?

– The white woman you were looking for.

– No.

– I met your friend, Zaq, over there. What's wrong with him?

– He's not well. He's dying.

– He's dying?

– That's what the Doctor said.

– So, what are you going to do?

– Find a boat, and take him to Port Harcourt. They have to evacuate these wounded people soon anyway.

I sat up all night beside Zaq. Boma was curled up on her spreadout wrapper close to us, fast asleep, her head resting on her arm, her face beautiful in the glow of the fire someone had started not too far away. I listened to the anxious murmurs of the men around the fire as they sat hunched forward, still in their white frocks[3]. Some of them would look up and stare at me and I'd look back at them, my face full of questions, but I got only silent head shakes. Some shrank from me, as though I were an interrogator brandishing[4] tools of torture. From the women's section came the cries and whimpers of children, from the waterfront came the crunch of soldiers' boots on the hard pebbles of the beach. I watched the fire burn bright and die. I was exhausted but I did not sleep. Instead I let my mind remember the many conversations we had had, right here on this island.

1 chunky: (here) solid, heavy **2** crestfallen: sad **3** frock (n): dress **4** brandish sth.: show sth. as a warning

*

Once Zaq had asked me:

– Rufus, what books have you read?

I mentioned a few journalism books, but he shook his head impatiently.

– You must take a year off, one of these days, before you're old and tired and weighed down by responsibility. Go away somewhere, and read. Read all the important books. Educate yourself, then you'll see the world in a different way.

It was the day after we had dug up the empty grave. We had gone to sleep exhausted by all the excitement; perhaps that was why we didn't hear them the next morning when they opened our door. They came very early. We didn't hear them enter, but the sun on my face woke me up. It was a wafer of a ray, flattened by a narrow crack in the door that directed the sun squarely on my face. I opened my eyes, then, seeing the three men standing solemnly just inside the doorway, I sat up. Zaq, like me, was just waking up, but already his eyes looked alert, and he was getting to his feet.

It was Naman, with two other men I had never seen before, but who, from their clothes, seemed like priests. They stood with their hands clasped behind their backs, the gravitas[1] around them as solid as a rock. Naman, in the middle, was tall and upright; the others were shorter, stooped and older. One was thin and bald and moustachioed[2], and the other was portly with a fine head of hair.

– These are my fellow priests, and together we represent the entire community.

Zaq stood up and faced them.

– You are welcome, but did you have to wake us up like this?

1 gravitas [ˈɡrævɪtɑːs]: seriousness **2** moustachioed [məˈstɑːʃiəʊd]: having a moustache (beard on the upper lip)

– You have committed a grave ill, by going to the burial ground and digging up a grave last night, you have desecrated[1] the place and now –

– Hold on. What are you talking about? Who said we were at the burial ground last night?

Zaq tried to outstare the unblinking priests, but there was neither power nor conviction in his eyes and voice. I said nothing. I sensed a certain change in Naman: this wasn't the same man I had talked to yesterday. He seemed more distant, sadder, and yet there was a determination, a coldness I had not noticed before in him. He was here to carry out a task, and he was going to do it, though he found the task unpleasant. Now he suddenly stepped forward and before I could draw back he took my right hand and raised it up to Zaq. I was taken by surprise and quickly curled my fingers, trying to hide the tell-tale[2] red earth that my hasty washing last night hadn't removed from under the chipped nails. Zaq's stare wavered. He sighed.

– Well ...

– Our head priestess died this morning. And now we cannot bury her because your activity last night has disrupted the balance of things. A purification[3] ceremony has to be carried out. In the meantime, please remain in your hut. The elders will hold a meeting and decide what is to be done.

– We did what we did because you lied to us.

Naman turned to him fiercely. – I didn't lie to you. I told you all I knew. Please stay here till we send for you.

– No. We're leaving today.

– You can't leave till after the burial.

– When is the burial?

– After the purification ritual.

– And when is that?

– We don't know.

1 desecrate sth.: destroy the religious purity of sth. **2** tell-tale (adj): revealing sth. that is not meant to be known **3** purification: act of making sth. pure

– What do you mean?

– We don't know how long the ritual will take, we don't know what the ritual will be, because we have never been faced with such a situation before. No one has ever desecrated a grave before today.

– But it wasn't even a grave, there was no body in it ...

– But what if there had been a body?

At last the bald-headed elder spoke, his voice as whispery as a ribbon of smoke. His voice was almost pleading, but in his rheumy eyes there was a threat. – We are having a meeting of all the elders today. Please don't leave your hut till you have permission.

Naman turned to go, then he stopped and looked at us, and when he spoke his voice was a bit softer. – In any case, there will be no ferry to take you off the island. There will be no movement or activity till after the burial. The whole community will be in mourning[1].

– If we attempt to leave, will we be stopped?

– How can you leave? Will you swim, Mr Zaq?

– We'd rather you didn't force our hands. This is a moment of great sorrow for us.

And they left us. Zaq stood at the door, watching the men disappear into the trees.

– Do you think they're serious?

– They seemed serious about the ferry not coming.

He returned and sat down on his mat. After a while he lay down on his back, facing the roof, his arms folded under his head. I sat down and tried to imitate his calm, but my mind was an ocean, choppy and turbulent and roaring with a million thoughts. My job wasn't the best in the world – I thought I should receive more recognition and encouragement for the effort and enthusiasm I put into it, for instance – but it was the only one I had and I certainly didn't want to lose it. The only way to keep it was to get to the office as soon as I could. And suddenly I noticed the white robe over Zaq's mat, hanging from a nail. He still hadn't returned it. I saw myself in

1 mourning (n): expression of grief and sadness (usu. when sb. has died)

it, disguised[1] as a worshipper, walking quietly into the woods and onto the path between the trees, I saw myself standing at the waterfront, waiting for the next ferry, a fishing boat, anything to take me away to Port Harcourt. Zaq watched curiously as I slipped the robe over my head.

– I'll be back.

I stepped out, hesitant. But everything was as it used to be, men and women in robes came and went, and there were no sentries[2] lurking behind trees watching our door. Perhaps my disguise was working, or perhaps Naman felt his warning had been stern enough to deter us from attempting to escape. I slipped unnoticed into the woods, taking the path between the tall trees and walking fast towards the waterfront, my head bowed, purposeful. But even from afar I could see the usually busy waterfront was empty today. Where were the fishermen setting out or returning in their long narrow boats with their jute nets at their feet and their sturdy oars in their hands? And where were the women waiting to buy the fish fresh from the water, talking to each other and to the fishermen at the top of their voices, now bantering[3], now flirting, but always bargaining? There was no ferry waiting to take passengers back to Port Harcourt and to the dozens of tiny islands dotting the endless water that now appeared so daunting[4] and so foe-like[5]. I was a lone figure in a white robe walking on the beach, looking about, and when I finally got tired I headed back to the village centre. What I needed, I realized, was an ally in the enemy camp, someone who could tell me how serious the elders were about detaining us here, and how long the detention might last. Gloria.

The tenement house was not far from the waterfront. Two women were standing at the front entrance, one with a plastic bucket in her hand, the other holding a baby in her arms. They moved aside

1 disguise as sb.: change one's look to appear as sb. **2** sentry: guard **3** banter (v): talk in a humorous way **4** daunting [ˈdɔːntɪŋ] (adj): intimidating **5** foe (n): enemy

as I approached, not pausing in their breathless discussion. My disguise, so far, was holding. But Gloria's door was locked with a big Yale padlock[1].

Zaq was still lying on his back, his eyes staring at the roof, when I returned.

– We can't get away. There are no boats coming or going, and the whole village is staying home. Nothing is happening.

– You should rest. Save your energy.

– But we're trapped here. We could be here for days, weeks …

– Nothing we can do about it, so we wait. Conserve our energy.

I sat on my mat and stared at the open door. At midday two women came in and gave us lunch, avoiding our eyes, evading our questions. At sundown they returned with dinner. I had no appetite. I watched Zaq eat the boiled yam and oil with gusto[2]. Then I slipped out again as soon as it was dark. Surely Gloria would have heard about our situation by now? Why hadn't she tried to communicate, send us a note? Perhaps she had been warned to keep away from us. I entered the woods, walking fast, almost running, and soon I was out of the trees and once more entering the tenement house. I almost expected to find the two gossiping women still standing by the entrance, but the space where they stood was now empty, the front door ajar. I went inside. The wind stopped suddenly, as if cut off by a switch. Gloria's door was still locked. I decided to wait. For the first time I noticed the rows of doors to my left and right. Some were half open, and sounds from radios drifted out faintly from behind fluttering curtains. A door opened to my right and a woman came out, a bucket in her hand. She glanced at me as she passed, then she went to a corner and I heard the sound of tap water falling into her metal bucket. I turned and left.

The next day I sat on my mat, staring at Zaq, saying nothing, eating when the women brought food, going to the outhouse when I was pressed. When the sun had travelled all the way across the sky,

1 Yale padlock: lock manufactured by the US company Yale **2** with gusto: enthusiastically, with appetite

and still nothing had happened, no one had come to talk to us, I lay on my back and closed my eyes. I conserved my energy, as Zaq had suggested. Boma would be worried by now, wondering what had happened to me.

– If we were to go after the woman, all the way, how would we get off the island? We don't have a boat, we don't know where the militants are camped ...

Perhaps I spoke out of desperation, knowing that my job might not be waiting for me when I got back to Port Harcourt. Or perhaps I was swayed by Zaq's promise of starting a real paper, or maybe a secret part of me had always been waiting for a chance like this, I didn't know, but suddenly I was excited. I wanted to go after the kidnapped woman, to find out what really happened, to interview the Professor ...

– But we have money.

Zaq was smiling as he brought out his brown envelope. – I'm sure we can get some local guide, some fisherman who knows his way around.

– And then –

– The rest we will deal with when we come to it.

But, as it turned out, we didn't have to go looking for a boat – one came to us. Early in the morning, before the cocks began to crow, there was a tentative knock on the door. Zaq and I jumped up at the same time, but I got there before him. I stared at our visitor with disappointment. It wasn't Gloria. It was the old boatman, looking as unobtrusive[1], as natural, as the grass and the trees outside. The morning light fell on his frayed homespun shirt and bare feet, and on the long oar in his hand, held against his chest.

– What do you want?

– Oga Naman send me. He say make I carry[2] you go where you wan go, but you must come quick quick.

1 unobtrusive: not very noticeable **2** He say make I carry (NP): He said I should carry

Zaq and I looked at each other and we didn't wait for him to repeat his offer. We followed him to the boat and soon Irikefe Island was behind us, swallowed by the distance and the darkness of the mist that rose like smoke from the river banks. Mid-river the water was clear and mobile, but towards the banks it turned brackish and still, trapped by mangroves in whose branches the mist hung in clumps like cotton balls. Ahead of us the mist arched clear over the water like a bridge. Sometimes, entering an especially narrow channel in the river, our light wooden canoe would be so enveloped in the dense grey stuff that we couldn't see each other as we glided silently over the water.

16

It felt almost surreal to be back again on the island, trapped again, but this time not by harmless priests and worshippers, but by the Major and his soldiers. Many times in the night Zaq had woken up agitated and sweaty, looking at me as if trying to remember where he had seen me before. Then I'd hold his hand and shout his name, attempting to penetrate[1] the fog in his eyes, but they just looked at me, confused and teary, growing cloudier every minute. And at last, when Zaq went back to sleep, I let go of his hand and sat with my head bowed. I felt cold and nauseous. Perhaps I was coming down with a fever. I wanted to stay awake, but every so often I'd nod off, only to be jerked back to consciousness by Zaq's voice, low and faint, coming from a measureless distance, asking for a drink.

– A drink. Just a sip. One sip, please.

It'd be a miracle if he lasted the night. I felt the tiredness and the hopelessness weigh down on me and, not knowing what I was doing, I turned to him and grabbed his hand, my arm shaking as badly as his.

– What are we doing here, Zaq? It makes no sense. No sense.

Towards dawn I fell asleep, and when I woke up I found Zaq and Naman whispering together, and I couldn't conceal my surprise at how fresh and rested they both appeared. Zaq still looked a bit fey[2], but he was sitting without help, and talking lucidly. He smiled at me.

– Hello.

– Where is Boma?

– Somewhere about.

The soldiers herded us to the water to do our morning ablutions[3], the women behind a huge boulder away from the men. I

1 penetrate sth.: (here) get through sth. **2** fey (adj): strange **3** ablution (n, fml): washing

watched the men wade in and out, dipping their faces into the water and washing under their armpits, their faces blank, their motions mechanical. Some tried to wash the blood spots off their white robes, without much success. I sat with them on the beach as they waited for their robes to dry, some dressed only in their trousers and some in underpants, their eyes lost, faraway. After a while I noticed that the people were moving back to the campsite. Ahead a soldier was waving them forward towards the Major, who was making an address. He was standing on a huge, still smouldering log, looking over the heads of the people, his uniform and his boots as spotless as ever. He raised his rifle and pointed around with it, calling for silence.

– It has come to our attention that the militants who killed our men yesterday, and who caused this massive destruction upon your island, are still out there, not far from here, perhaps planning another attack.

The men looked at each other wearily, while the women pulled the children closer.

– We are also aware that among us here, there are some who are sympathetic to the militants, who are in cahoots with[1] them. We will find you and we will deal with you. We will return fire for fire. As long as you do what we tell you, you will be safe. Nothing will happen to you. You will be confined to[2] this island for at least one week. No going, no coming. You have enough food here on the island. And for those of you who are wounded, we have a doctor. He will be brought here today to attend to your wounds. He is good, he saved my life once when I –

A murmur began among the people and it soon turned into an uproar. The Major stopped talking and looked down at the people. His men raised their rifles nervously and the uproar died out as quickly as it had started. The Major lowered his rifle and turned his back on the crowd.

1 be in cahoots with sb. (infml): work together with sb. **2** confine sb. (to an area): limit sb.'s movements (to an area)

– You are dismissed.

– You can slip away quite easily if you want to.

I looked at Zaq. He and Naman had been in a huddle since we returned from listening to the Major, and I had been wondering what it was they were whispering about, but now I knew. Far away, next to the rubble that had been the communal kitchen, a sort of field kitchen had been set up, supervised by the women who were in turn supervised by the soldiers. A line of hungry men, women and children had formed in front of the triangular[1] hearths.

– Slip away and go where? Besides, my sister is here. I have to look after her. And you, Zaq, we have to get you to Port Harcourt. – I'll be fine, and so will your sister. The worst is over, I think. Boma was with the group of women at the hearth. I could see her from here, her red blouse standing out in the cluster of white robes around her. She was laughing as she bustled about, organizing the children into a neat line, ladling[2] the porridge from the pot into cups and bowls. She looked really happy, and for a moment I almost started to believe that the worst really was over.

– What do you want me to do?

– It's not what we want you to do, it's what must be done, and the truth is, you are the only one in a position to do it.

– What do you want me to do?

– Slip away. Go to Port Harcourt and tell the editors what's happening here. We're trapped here for at least a week – you heard what he said. No one out there knows what's going on here. These people need help. Soon, in a day or two, if they don't get it, they'll start dying ...

– My editor won't listen to me. I've lost my job.

– Go to Beke, my editor. He is a resourceful[3] person, he has his faults, but he can talk to the other editors. He has good contacts in

1 triangular (adj): shaped like a triangle **2** ladle sth.: pour sth. out with a ladle (*Kelle*) **3** resourceful: able to solve problems

Lagos. Tell him what's going on here. You have to do it, you have to do it now.

Escaping the camp was easier than I had expected. I put on the white robe Naman gave me and kept my head low. I entered the woods and went towards the cemetery, all the while keeping half an eye on the soldiers, but none of them seemed interested in me. Only later did I discover the reason for this lack of attention: there was simply no means of leaving the island by boat, even if one escaped the camp. All the boats had been systematically riddled with[1] bullet holes by the soldiers, and the narrow, dug-out canoes had been chopped[2] to bits and were being used as firewood. I did as Naman instructed, and once I left the cemetery I headed north, making for the water. I swam towards the centre of the river, and then took a deep breath and dived. Naman said the current[3] here was strong, that all I had to do was let myself be carried by the water and I'd end up near the pier where the fishermen kept their canoes, and once in the canoe, I wouldn't even need to paddle – the water would carry me down to Tamuno's village and there Chief Ibiram would help me get to Port Harcourt.

But as I dived and touched bottom, everything went dark. I lost consciousness. When I opened my eyes I was on the shore, my legs in the water and my head in the sand, and above me the sun was harsh, burning into my face. I stood up, looking around, trying to determine where I was and how long I had been unconscious. I dragged myself to the line of trees. To my left I could see the fencing around the cemetery, so I had really not gone very far at all in the water. The pier was still way off, about a kilometre away. I decided to walk through the trees, keeping the water in view till I got to the pier. I was so hungry and weak that I fell down after taking only a few steps. I was definitely coming down with something, hopefully not the same fever as Zaq, but I didn't want to think about it. I forced myself up and resumed walking, sitting down sometimes for

1 riddle sth.: make many holes in sth. **2** chop sth.: cut sth. **3** current (n): (here) movement of water in a particular direction

over thirty minutes to rest my wobbly legs, and as I got nearer to the pier, I kept my eyes open for the canoes, and for the soldiers who might be out there, patrolling, looking for stray villagers or invading militants.

Much later, driven by hunger, I came out of the woods and headed for the village centre, ducking behind a tree whenever I heard a noise. I passed houses with wide open doors through which I could see the empty compounds. Some of the houses had broken walls and roofs, with smoke still issuing from the rafters, yet some were surprisingly untouched. At Gloria's tenement I found the front door was kicked in, and it now lay beside the doorway, its zinc sheet twisted and torn. I went in, slowly, staying close to the walls. The central space in the compound was littered with all sorts of objects abandoned by their fleeing owners: a lady's shoe, a magazine, a shattered earthenware[1] pot by the kitchen door. The door to Gloria's room was open, and I entered. I looked at the broken pieces from a mirror on the floor, and the open wardrobe, and the cracked window, and I imagined her being dragged out by the men as she cried and begged to be spared. I sat on the bed where we once made love. Over there was the seat where she had entertained me with a bowl of jollof rice. At the thought of food my stomach rumbled, my knees felt weak, and I knew that I might have to return to the shrine and admit to Zaq that I had failed. But first I needed rest. I lay back and closed my eyes; when I opened them again it was dark. I was sweating and shaking, my mouth was dry, and I could feel the heat rising off my skin. I was definitely coming down with something. I curled up in the bed, watching the compound through the open door. I was too weak to care any more if I was discovered by the soldiers.

1 earthenware: made of clay

17

Outside the sun is bright. I am talking to Zaq in the hut; it is one of those days when he looks spry[1] and full of energy.

– Did you really love Anita? Can you continue to love a person regardless of such shortcomings[2]? Maybe because you hope to save them? Or because you can't help it? Isn't that what love is all about?

Zaq says nothing. He turns his face away, but just before he does so I see the pain, the bitterness on that face. The sadness seems so out of keeping with the beautiful day outside, and I feel sorry I introduced a sad note into such a glorious day, but I want to hear his answer desperately, for some reason. He speaks softly, sadly.

– What's the point? It is all memory now.

Anita died in a detention centre[3] in London. She hanged herself in the bathroom. The news didn't make the front pages of the Lagos papers, just a single column in the back of one or two provincials.

*

Voices. Whispers. Soldiers, perhaps. Then the cry of a child, and I thought I was imagining it. I got off the bed and crawled on all fours to the door. It was dark, the voices were coming from one of the many broken-down doors on either my right or my left. I waited, controlling my breathing, and suddenly I saw a flicker of light, and then it disappeared. Not soldiers – they would be more brash[4] and noisy than this. I stood up and moved towards the room, but just as

1 spry: lively **2** shortcoming: fault **3** detention centre: facility where immigrants are held until it is decided whether they can stay in the country
4 brash: *dreist*

I got to the door my leg kicked against an empty tin, which elicited[1] a brief scurrying sound from the room. Then silence.

– Hello.

Silence.

– Is anyone there? I'm a friend. I know you can hear me. My voice shook, my legs were bowed, and I had to hold onto the door frame with both hands to remain upright.

– I'm a friend. I'm coming in. Here I come.

It was a moonless night and the room was nothing but vague outlines and humps[2]. I held my breath and waited, and after a while I heard breathing, movement. I braced myself, half expecting something to whizz[3] out of the darkness and connect with my face, but instead a match was struck and a face emerged behind the glow. A candle was lit. It was a man, in the corner, crouched on the floor. He raised the light, moving his face sideways, trying to see my face. I stepped in, and in the corners still cloaked in shadow I could hear other figures moving about, staring at me.

– My name is Rufus. I'm alone.

I spoke without thinking, trying to give as much reassuring information as possible. I couldn't see his face: he shaded the candle with his hand so that the light fell only in my direction.

– I'm a reporter.

– A reporter?

It seemed the man turned to look into the dark part of the room, as if to communicate his surprise to the others in the shadows.

– Yes. I'm a reporter from Port Harcourt.

– What are you doing here by yourself?

Now I knew he wasn't dangerous.

– Listen, do you have anything I can eat? I'm very hungry. He got up and disappeared behind the light, then I heard whispering, a

1 elicit sth.: cause sth. **2** hump (n): *kleine Aufwölbung* **3** whizz out of sth.: move quickly out of sth.

woman's voice, low. He came back with something in his hand and gave it to me. It was meat, dried, rubbery, gamy[1].

I sat down on the floor and ate, all the while staring into his glowing, watchful eyes, and when I finished he gave me a cup of water that I drank in a single gulp. He seemed to want to get rid of me as quickly as possible, but I wasn't ready to leave him just yet, I was curious to see who was with him, and I had questions that needed to be answered, like where to find a boat.

– I escaped from the fighting. Who are you?

A figure rose from the corner and entered the light, and I saw a woman in a boubou[2] and wrapper, a head-tie covering most of her face. More figures came forward. It was a whole family: father, mother and three children. The youngest, who looked to be about three, was crying, her face running with tears and snot, blotchy[3] from insect bite and grime. The mother and children had been huddled beneath a large blanket, and now the children peered at me from outside the light's circumference, and their expression told me they felt more pity for me than fear. They had been here a whole day now. They had locked themselves up in the toilet when the shooting began, and afterwards they had moved to this tiny room, coming out only to go to the toilet or to look for food. The husband was a tall, distracted-looking fisherman and he jumped at the slightest noise, clearly scared witless for his children's safety. I wondered if there were similar families in the other houses, huddled beneath blankets, stifling[4] their children's cries, waiting for the storm to blow away. Revived by the water and dry meat, I stood up.

– You'd do better if you joined the camp. The soldiers are not letting anyone off the island for a few more days. You can't survive here that long.

1 gamy: having a strong smell like meat from hunted animals **2** boubou: long garment worn in West Africa **3** blotchy: covered with marks **4** stifle sth.: suppress sth.

The wife shook her head, grabbing her children to her bosom. He looked at me and then at his wife and the children. I guessed he'd do whatever she said.

– Where can I find a boat?

He looked at her and she nodded. Crawling from house to house, dashing forward, then stopping, he led me back into the woods. He took me near the waterfront, and between two thick trees, in a deep gorge[1] that led all the way to the sea, cleverly covered by grass and sand and rocks, he unearthed a boat and two oars. He helped me push it to the water and pointed me in the right direction. The sea was very narrow here; all I had to do was cross it and on the other side I'd find the river that led inland.

I waved as the boat pulled away, and he stood there a long time, waving back. For a moment he had put aside the enormous responsibilities of protecting his family, and now he had to return. And soon I had no need for the long oar – the water was swift, the waves were high and then low, and it wasn't long before there was as much water in the boat as in the sea. The waves flashed at me, white and swift and startling, carrying me away.

On a spit of dry land in the middle of the sea – that was how they found me, they told me. There was no sign of my boat, and I was semi-conscious[2] and spitting out water. I was discovered by a group of villagers venturing far from their little village to where the fishing was better, and if they hadn't gone that far, or if they had been an hour late, I'd have died, exposed, cold, belly up, like a beached fish. It seemed I had made it to the river, more by accident than by my own efforts. I woke up in a little room filled with smoked fish left to dry on racks. A single lamp hung from the roof on a long hook. In its weak, smoky light I saw that everywhere was covered with fish, and the only space left was where I was lying on a mat against the wall. The smell of fish got me crawling to the door and emptying my stomach on the doorstep.

1 gorge: small canyon **2** semi-conscious: half-conscious

They didn't ask who I was and where I was going and why I was here; they only asked if I was strong enough to move on. These were dangerous waters, and I could be an escaped hostage. The last thing they wanted was a boatload of gun-wielding militants berthing[1] on their shore. If I was going to get out of here, I had to regain my strength. I slurped the thick rice porridge they gave me with superhuman concentration and then went outside and threw up. I asked for more, my hands shaking. There were four people peering down at me: an old man seated on a rickety[2] hand-carved stool, fair-skinned with hairs all over his face and growing like tendrils out of his nostrils and ears and armpits and the top of his singlet[3]; a fat woman standing over him, the hair on her head white and knotted; and two silent men standing in the shadows behind the fat woman, not saying much, not much hair on their heads. A smoky lamp on a hook hung from the roof. The woman took the bowl from my hands and shook her head.

– No more.

I slept for a half-hour or so and didn't even notice the fish smell. When I woke up I was strong enough to eat a whole fish. Cat fish[4], the whiskers[5] on its intact face looking like the hairs on the old man's face. I told the old man I was a journalist and I was on my way to Port Harcourt.

– Ah, Port Harcourt, very far from here.

He pointed up with his hand, and from the way he pointed, and the vague, uncomprehending look on his face, Port Harcourt might have been on the moon. The others nodded.

– Can you help me?

– Everybody wan go Port Harcourt. You go enter ferry from Irikefe.

– I've come from Irikefe. There's fighting going on there.

Again, they didn't ask for details, though surely they must have been aware of the fight? News travelled fast on the water, from island

1 berth (v): tie (a ship) up to the quay **2** rickety: in bad condition **3** singlet: sleeveless undershirt **4** cat fish: *Wels* **5** whiskers (pl): (*hier*) *Barteln*

to island, from creek to creek, boat to boat, hut to hut. They continued to stare at me in silence, and the lamp grew smokier above us, making my eyes water. It took a while before I registered something odd in the man's comment.

– What do you mean everybody wants to go to Port Harcourt? Who else wants to go there?

They looked at each other, their eyes expressed their debate, whether to trust me – a stranger who had just washed up on their shore – or not.

– I'm a journalist. You can trust me.

The woman spoke first. She said a white woman was here three days ago, wanting a boat to go to Port Harcourt.

– Was she alone?

– No. One man dey with am[1]. Him name na Salomon.

Isabel Floode. And Salomon, the wanted driver, the primary suspect. The two had arrived in a boat, the woman's face blackened with pigment, dressed in a man's clothes, her hair covered in a hat, but there was no hiding the blue eyes when she came closer, nor was there disguising the voice, the speech. She didn't look very well, her arms were covered in bug bites and rashes, and she looked weak, but she was pretty determined to go to Port Harcourt at once. They spent the night here because they had arrived very late. They didn't say much about where they were from, or who they were, but they did promise the villagers a lot of money if they would help them get to Irikefe in the morning, from where they'd get the ferry to Port Harcourt. But then the fighting had broken out.

– Where is she now?

– We send her to Chief Ibiram.

– Chief Ibiram?

– Yes. Him place no far from here.

I looked around the little room, the three faces staring at me. I tried to imagine the woman here, her life in the hands of Salomon and these simple fishing folk. Until now I had only thought of her as

1 dey with am (NP): was with her

a subject, if I thought of her at all, but now, perhaps because of my weakened state, I found myself trying to imagine what must have gone through her mind. How did she manage to escape, coming so far, only to discover the fighting at Irikefe? But why didn't she go to the soldiers? I looked outside at the forest and the abandoned boats on the water, the few thatched huts, and I thought, what could fate possibly want with her on these oil-polluted waters? The forsaken villages, the gas flares, the stumps[1] of pipes from exhausted[2] wells with their heads capped and left jutting out[3] of the oil-scorched earth, and the ever-present pipelines, criss-crossing the landscape, sometimes like tree roots surfacing far away from the parent tree, sometimes like diseased veins on the back of an old shrivelled hand, and sometimes in squiggles[4] like ominous writing on the wall. Maybe fate wanted to show her first-hand the carcasses[5] of the fish and crabs and water birds that floated on the deserted beaches of these tiny towns and villages and islands every morning, killed by the oil her husband was helping to produce.

– Listen, you must take me to Chief Ibiram now. He is a friend. I have to meet the white woman.

They looked at each other and shook their heads.

– Chief Ibiram don go[6]. E no dey[7] here any more. E say e no wan[8] stay here any more, because of so so[9] fighting and because of bad fishing.

– So where is he going to?

They all pointed in the same direction: northward. That meant Port Harcourt, and that explained why they had sent the woman to him: to hitch a ride[10] on one of his boats – it was her best chance of getting there. With the whole clan on the move, she could travel with them undetected.

1 stump: remaining part after sth. has been removed **2** exhausted: (here) yielding no more oil **3** jut out: stick out **4** squiggle: curved handwriting **5** carcass [ˈkɑːkəs]: dead body of an animal **6** don go (NP): has gone **7** E no dey (NP): He is not **8** E say e no wan (NP): He said he didn't want to **9** so so (NP): all the **10** hitch a ride (infml): get sb. to take you somewhere in her/his vehicle

18

It was not easy: first I had to convince them I was strong enough to leave, then I had to convince them we could catch up with Chief Ibiram if we left immediately. When words failed I waved my big wet wad of James Floode's money before the hirsute[1] old man, and he nodded. Two young men, Charles and Peter, eager and full of questions, set out with me in one of the village's few sea-worthy boats, and we headed north, hoping Chief Ibiram and his clan hadn't already put too much distance between themselves and us. Charles, it turned out, was the one who had taken Salomon and Isabel to Chief Ibiram. He said Chief Ibiram and his people had left their settlement late yesterday night, preferring to travel under cover of darkness, and by his estimate that put them at least ten hours ahead of us, but because they had children and women they'd be forced to stop often. If we went hard without a pause – we carried two extra gallons of petrol to avoid stopping for refills – we should be able to catch up with them before sunset.

As we passed the flood plain where Chief Ibiram's village had once stood, I told the two men to slow down for a minute. The place looked desolate: the only signs that a community had once thrived here were a few sticks jutting out of the water, pieces of straw from roof thatches scattered in the mud and a pile of garbage under a tree, that was all.

We caught up with them very late in the afternoon – and by now I was almost fainting from fatigue and weakness. My guides had offered many times to stop and rest but I had insisted we keep going, and now they had to hold me under the arms as I got off the boat.

1 hirsute ['hɜːsjuːt] (adj, fml): very hairy

The group were camped in a forest not far from the river, where their boats, laden with their meagre belongings, waited near the trees and rocks on the banks. They had set up tents and sheds, and curious faces peered out of the doorway slits[1] as we passed, some nodding in recognition. Young men and women and children sat under trees, eating, or playing, or just idly waiting for nightfall, when they'd be on the move again. Chief Ibiram's tent lay a few metres from the others.

– Good to see your face again, reporter.

– You too, Chief Ibiram.

He was seated on his reclining chair[2], his radio on a side table; I sat on the mat, facing him, and for a second it seemed time had not moved an inch since that day when the old man and his son had first brought Zaq and me to this community. The same cloth chair, the same radio by his side, and somewhere in an imaginary back room I could hear women and children talking and laughing. Only this time there was no Zaq, and this time it was I who was slumped and bowed like Zaq had been that day, and all alone. And the old man, Tamuno and his son Michael, where were they?

– They returned safely. They are fine. They are out there, somewhere.

– Good to hear that.

– And where is your friend, Zaq?

– I left him at Irikefe. He's not well.

– You also don't look well, reporter.

– I'll be fine. I'm on my way to Port Harcourt, where I'll see a doctor. And you, I see you are on the move again.

– Yes, we couldn't remain there any more. My people, they are frightened, the violence gets closer every day. We've heard of a place not too far from Port Harcourt, the people there are friendly, most of them are refugees like us. My people could get some sort of work in Port Harcourt.

1 slit (n): narrow opening **2** reclining chair: comfortable chair with adjustable back rest

His voice was hopeful, but his eyes were pessimistic, cloudy. Gradually the community was drifting towards the big city, and sooner or later it would be swallowed up, its people dispersed, like people getting off a bus and joining the traffic on the city streets. He sighed.

– You came for the white woman, didn't you? Do you want to see her now?

– Can I?

At last I was going to see Isabel Floode, and I didn't even have a pen or a notepad or my camera. I tried to control my nervousness as I followed Chief Ibiram out of his tent into the heat. She was in a tent by herself, seated on what looked like a folded trampoline; beside her was a half-covered bowl with a half-eaten meal in it. She was staring out to the trees through the door slit, and she didn't seem at all surprised to see us; perhaps her recent experiences had exhausted her capacity for surprise – which I could understand. Now she looked up with a dull, locked-in expression, waiting for us to speak.

– This is Rufus, a journalist. He's come to see you.

At the mention of 'journalist' a spark of interest entered her eyes. His job done, Chief Ibiram nodded at me, turned and left us. Now I saw how thin she looked. Her hair had been chopped off and the jagged edges hung unevenly over her ears. An old red blouse that didn't seem to belong to her hung from her shoulders, and her collar bones[1] jutted out, stretching the skin. Her face was covered in rashes; the skin was still slightly discoloured from whatever dye[2] she had used to disguise herself while making her escape from her kidnappers. But it was her eyes that expressed her situation best: they looked hollow, lustreless[3], and even when they rested directly on you, they did so bluntly, never cutting below the surface. She was about forty years old, but right now she looked ten years older.

1 collar bone: bone between shoulder and neck **2** dye [daɪ] (n): substance used to change the colour of sth. (e.g. of hair) **3** lustreless: without glow, (here) lifeless

– My name is Rufus. I'm from *The Reporter.*

– Hello. I'm Isabel Floode.

– Yes. Mrs Floode, your husband sent me ... us. Me and a friend, though I'm alone here at the moment. We've been searching for you for more than two weeks now.

– James sent you?

– Yes. He sent us to see if you were alive and well, and if possible to negotiate your ransom ... but now that you are free ...

– Yes, yes. I'm free.

I noticed that her attention kept wavering. Her eyes were still fixed at the little slit through which a line of light came into the tent, and I wondered what she was staring at outside, or if she was expecting something to come charging in. I felt awkward, unsure how to behave with her, what to say or ask. I had always imagined she'd be surrounded by gun-toting[1] militants when I met her, and I had always assumed Zaq would be there with me and he'd do all the talking; not in my wildest imaginings did I ever see myself sitting less than a metre from her, alone in a tent by the river, carrying the burden of the conversation. But I was a reporter, and this was what reporters do – improvise, look confident and poised.

– Mr Floode really wanted to be here himself, but because of security ...

She said nothing, and kept staring at the same spot.

– I know you're tired; if you'd rather rest ...

Now she turned to me and I saw how my unexpected comment had taken her by surprise. She shook her head.

– No. I can talk. What do you want to know?

– Well, how did you do it? How did you manage to escape?

– It wasn't that hard. Salomon was able to overpower the guard. He bashed him on the head with a stone, and we slipped away. I guess they weren't expecting us to try something so crazy.

– Yes, Salomon, why did he help you escape? He kidnapped you in the first place, didn't he?

1 tote sth.: carry sth. (heavy)

– It's complicated.

– What do you mean?

– He didn't actually kidnap me.

– He didn't? Well, the police are looking for him. He's their primary suspect.

– Look, you'll have to ask Salomon for some of the details of what happened that day. He's out there somewhere. What I can tell you is what I know.

– Okay. That's all right. Please go ahead, Mrs Floode.

– Sorry ... I didn't mean to snap[1] at you, but everything is so ... I expected to die back there, you know. I still find it hard to believe I'm here, almost safe, on my way to Port Harcourt. When I decided to come to this country, the last thing on my mind was getting kidnapped. Of course I had been advised about the risks of coming to Nigeria, to Port Harcourt. The embassy had shown me all the newspaper clippings[2] about abducted foreigners, but I didn't pay much attention. I was coming on a special mission. I was coming to save my marriage. Things were not good between me and James, and I wanted to make one last effort to fix them.

She paused and looked at me, her eyes still expressionless. I had read somewhere that she was a schoolteacher – perhaps her husband had told me – and her eyes made me feel like an erring[3] student, waiting for judgement.

– Rufus, I'm telling you all this just to put everything into perspective. I know you must have risked a lot to be here, so you deserve to know everything. Perhaps my husband has told you some of it already, but it doesn't matter. Though I expect you to use your judgement to know what to print and what to leave out.

I nodded. She turned away and continued her story.

She had met Floode at university. He was in his final year, and she was a year behind. They got married a year after she graduated. The first years were happy ones. He worked for a chemical company in

1 snap at sb.: speak to sb. in a rude, aggressive way **2** newspaper clipping: cut out article from a newspaper **3** err (fml): make a mistake

London, but then he got his present job, and that was when things began to change. He was a gifted petroleum engineer, and his skills were in great demand. He began to travel a lot, and over the past three years he had lived in five different countries: Hong Kong, Indonesia, Canada, the Netherlands and now Nigeria. At first she happily went with him to each new place, but after Canada she suddenly lost interest. Why go all that distance only to stay at home watching TV, or shopping at the mall, never seeing him till late in the evenings? So when he got posted to the Netherlands, they decided it was best if she stayed with his mother in Newcastle. But six months later he was out of the Netherlands and on his way to Nigeria. When she asked him if he was happy with the way things were, if he would perhaps think of another line of work for the sake of their marriage, he told her Nigeria would be for only two years, and then he would retire. He was being paid a lot of money to go there because of the dangerous conditions. But then she met someone else. It was nothing serious, nothing actually happened, but it got her thinking.

– I realized how lonely I had been all this while. What we had, me and James, couldn't really be called a marriage. At first we used to phone every day, but then many days would pass without a word from him. He always claimed that the infrastructure in Nigeria was just awful. Well, I had a brilliant idea. I was going to have a baby. I was going to go to Nigeria on a surprise visit, get pregnant, and everything would be fine.

At first he appeared happy to see her, and every day he came home early from work; there were invitations from other families for cocktails and garden parties, and trips to Lagos and Abuja – in the evenings they'd sit out on the veranda, with its view of the distant sea, and eat, refreshed by the sea breeze. But then, abruptly, things changed. A bomb exploded at his office, and the next day an Italian worker was kidnapped. He started coming home late, saying things were crazy at the office, and he had to be there all the time. After a month of waiting for things to change, of going to the club to play tennis with some of the wives, of sipping sherry under umbrellas by the pool, alone, she realized that was it, and things were not going to change.

– When, in desperation, I told him about my intention to get pregnant, he said it was out of the question. And that was when he told me he was seeing someone else. He didn't tell me whom, and I assumed it was one of the many expatriate women I always saw at the club. He told me he wanted a divorce.

I kept nodding, keeping my expression pleasant and interested, comparing what she was telling me with what her husband had told me. I tried to calm my excitement: I was being handed a major scoop, and, though I had no pen or recorder, I was storing every word, every inflection[1] of her voice.

– Well, he said the affair had been going on for a while, and ... and that she was pregnant. You can imagine how I felt, the shock. It was as if a cloud had risen in the room, roaring and blocking out every other thing. I couldn't see. I needed to be alone, to think. It was late at night and I didn't know the roads very well. The driver, Salomon, always took me out, but I didn't care. I took the car and went to the club. My plan was to leave for London the next morning.

But she was surprised the next day when Salomon came to look for her there. At first she thought he was waiting to drive her home, but then she noticed he wasn't wearing his blue-and-black uniform.

– Hello, Solomon ...

– Salomon.

She realized she had always referred to him as Solomon, and he had never corrected her, till now.

– Oh, sorry.

– It's okay. No problem.

– Did James send you?

– No, madam. I came to talk to you about something serious.

He looked and sounded different. He was wearing a jacket – a bit tight around the shoulders – and it gave him a more formal air than the uniform ever did; and he wasn't speaking the usual pid-

1 inflection: change

gin English that she found so irksome[1] and that always had to be explained to her. Today he spoke a grammatically faultless English, and even the accent was modified, easy to understand. Later she discovered that he was actually a university graduate who, like a lot of young men in the Delta, had been forced to take a job far below his qualifications while he waited for that elusive[2] office job with an oil company. She gave him the car keys and they drove – she had no idea where they were going, but she didn't care. Something told her what she was about to hear wasn't going to be pleasant. He said nothing as he drove but she could feel him watching her in the car mirror. Finally they stopped at what looked like a roadside motel.

– Can I get a drink here?

– Yes. My uncle owns this place.

– Good. I'll have a whisky.

He led her into a deserted bar, and they sat in a dark corner. The bartender glanced briefly at them and returned to reading his magazine. Salomon went to the bar and came back with her drink.

– Thanks. Aren't you having anything?

– No, madam. I'm fine.

– Okay, what is it?

– It's about Koko.

– Koko? What about Koko?

Koko was the maid. She cooked and cleaned three days a week.

– Koko is my fiancée. Yesterday she told me she was pregnant.

He looked mournful, uncomfortable. He sat stiffly on the edge of his seat, and he avoided her eyes as he spoke.

– Well, Salomon, congratulations, but I'm in no mood to celebrate –

– No, not by me. She is pregnant by the Oga.

She didn't feel anger or sadness; she had already exhausted that emotion the night before. She only felt surprised that she had been unable to detect what was going on, right under her nose, and she felt sadness, not for herself but for Salomon.

1 irksome: annoying **2** elusive: (here) difficult to obtain

– Do you love her?

He nodded, the bitterness now plain on his face, making his mouth twist at the side, and his eyes turn red and teary.

– I love her.

– I'm sorry.

– It is not fair. How can the Oga do this to me? I respected him. I trusted him, and see what he did to me. Why? I want to know why, can you please tell me?

– And, suddenly, I didn't feel like seeing James again. I didn't want to go home; I couldn't. I told Salomon to take me to any good hotel, and he suggested I stayed there, at his uncle's motel.

– And you weren't scared of staying there? You trusted Salomon that much?

– I guess I did. I had known him for over six months by then, and ... it was a good motel, really. It was quite clean, but, most importantly, it was the last place James would come looking for me.

– But why didn't you go back to the club?

– Because that was the first place James would come looking for me. And I didn't want to see them, my fellow expatriates, with their phoney[1] smiles, laughing at me behind my back. I just wanted to be alone ... I gave Salomon a note for James. I told him to give Salomon my things, that I was leaving the next day, that I would call him when I got to London. And –

She was interrupted by a hand parting the door slit open and a face peeping in – it was the young girl, Alali, and she entered with a single item of clothing held gingerly[2] in her hand. Isabel took it – it was a blouse – and put it beside her on the mat. She smiled up at the girl, who smiled back and skipped[3] out of the tent.

I waited for her to resume where she'd stopped, and as I waited my nervousness returned. She had told me a great deal, but there was still a lot more to tell, and what if she didn't want to go on – how should I persuade her to finish the story? So far all I had was one half

1 phoney (adj): fake **2** gingerly (adv): carefully **3** skip (v): jump, (here) move quickly

of a story. What would I do with it if I didn't get the other half? She closed her eyes and held one palm to her forehead – she wasn't well, it was obvious.

– Mrs Floode ... are you all right? Do you need a rest? We can continue later ...

She nodded gratefully.

– Yes, please. I have a crushing headache ...

I left. It was a long way to Port Harcourt and I was sure there'd be another opportunity to finish the interview. Besides, I was also feeling tired. The initial burst of energy I'd felt when she granted me the interview was dissipating. I met the girl outside and she took me to Tamuno and Michael. They were by the water, stripped to the waist, working on their boat, patching holes[1] with tar[2] and scraping mud from the bottom. Other men were equally busy getting their boats ready for departure. The old man took my hand and pumped it energetically. The boy wrapped his arms round my waist and for a moment I was reminded of how he had done the same to Zaq when Zaq agreed to take him back to Port Harcourt. Now I wondered if that promise would ever be kept.

– But where Oga Zaq? You come alone?

I sat next to them and told them about Irikefe, about the fallen statues and the burned houses, about the injured worshippers held more or less as prisoners by the occupying soldiers. They worked as I talked, and the water in the river flowed, and the men came and went, calling out to each other, and for a moment I believed that my adventure was over, and that by this time tomorrow I'd be in Port Harcourt, perhaps writing my story, safe, and wiser from my experiences.

1 patch a hole: *ein Loch flicken* **2** tar [tɑː(r)] (n): black substance often used for making roads

19

But that was a dangerous thought, an illusion – like a drowning man letting down his guard at the sight of shore, deceived by the promise of safety, and drowning as a consequence. We were still deep in militant territory and, as if to remind me of this, the militants came. They must have been watching us and waiting, as we were, for nightfall. They waited until all the boats were loaded and everyone was on board and about to sail before they appeared. The roar of their speedboats was deafening, the glare of their flashlights blinded our eyes and threw the women and children into panic and confusion. Some started to jump into the shallow water, some threw themselves below the benches, but, above the cries and wails of women and even men, one voice rose and tried to maintain calm – it was Chief Ibiram's, from the lead boat. I could see his silhouette as he stood up, his arms raised.

– Calm down. Sit still. Everybody, sit down.

The militants said nothing and continued to circle in their boats, blocking all avenues of sudden escape, and then at last, when the noise had gone down a bit, a man in one of the boats stood up and shouted over the water:

– We want the white woman now. Give us the white woman and her driver and we won't harm you. If you don't we will sink all your boats and set fire to your things. If you tink say na joke[1], try us.

I was in Tamuno's boat with Isabel and Salomon. We were sitting side by side, and behind us father and son watched and waited in silence. I waited. And then the man started a countdown:

– One, two, three ...

The third count was accompanied by gunfire aimed into the cloudy night sky. Isabel stood up, holding onto my shoulder for bal-

1 tink say na joke (NP): think we are joking

ance, and I could feel how her hand shook. And when she spoke her words were almost a sob

– I … am here. Please … don't shoot. I'm here.

The light fell on her. She removed the black scarf covering her chopped hair, and with the other hand she covered her eyes from the blinding flashlight.

– Bring her here. Now!

This was accompanied by another wild gunshot into the sky. The old man lowered his oar into the water and rowed, and slowly we went past the other boats, past the neutral space between our men and the militants, and then we were with them. Two men jumped out of a boat, still holding their guns on us, and helped Isabel out and into their boat.

– Where is the driver?

Salomon stood up and, in trying to get out, fell into the water and came up again, gasping for breath. The two men pulled him out and pushed him onto a seat next to Isabel, and then, when we thought it was over, the leader of the militants let off another shot into the sky.

– Chief Ibiram, why did you do this? Are you now on their side? Are you trying to take her back to get a reward, is that so?

– It is not so. We are only trying to help her. She came to us and begged –

– She came to you, then you should have known what to do. Tell me, what should you have done when my prisoner escapes and comes to you? I can't hear you. Louder!

– I should have come to you. I am sorry. This will not happen again.

– You are right, it will not happen again. To make sure it doesn't I will take one of you with me. Just as insurance. When we are sure you haven't gone to the government soldiers to betray us, he will be released. You decide who.

I noticed Tamuno inching closer to his son and putting a protective arm around him; I was sure that behind me, in the other boats, mothers were wrapping their arms around their children, and fathers were lowering their heads in anxiety.

– Chief, we are waiting. One, two, three …

Again a flash and the rude sound of gunfire, followed by silence. I could imagine Chief Ibiram in his boat, and the million things going through his mind.

– Well, since no one is willing to come, we will take this boy here.

And again the two men jumped into the water and came to our boat.

– Nooo! Abeg[1]. Please! Noo!

The cry came from the old man as the men approached our boat; he threw himself at them as they began to drag Michael out of the boat, his puny[2] arms rising and falling ineffectually against the men's burly[3] frames, but still he fought them, his rage churning[4] up the water. The boy held tightly onto my arm, screaming for his father. I saw a gun rise and then descend on the old man's head and he slumped against the boat and then into the water. Slowly I stood up, my arms raised. An image of the boy proudly scrawling his name in the earth came to my mind, and it seemed just like yesterday. The old man had served us diligently[5] in the hope that we'd take his son to Port Harcourt and a better future, and instead we had led him to incarceration[6] and being doused in petrol. Now the old man lay face up in the water with a cracked skull, and his son was about to be taken away.

– I will go. Take me. Leave the boy alone.

I got into the water and helped Tamuno back into the boat. Then the two men took my arms and we waded to their boat, where they shoved me in beside Salomon and Isabel.

They were the masters of the waterways – they knew every turning, every shallow[7], every rapid[8]; many times I expected our boat to

1 abeg (NP): please **2** puny: small and weak **3** burly: large and strong
4 churn up sth.: stir up sth. **5** diligent [ˈdɪlɪdʒənt]: making a great effort
6 incarceration: imprisonment **7** shallow (n): area of low water **8** rapid (n): area where the water's current is very strong

crash into some shadowy form looming[1] suddenly in front of us – a tree, a rock – but our boat would effortlessly curve away into the darkness and into an open expanse[2] of water and the men would let their guns roar as if in defiance[3] of danger and death. There were about five boats with four men in each, all armed, all eager to shoot off a few rounds at the slightest opportunity. Salomon and Isabel and I hung on for dear life as the boats ate up the darkness. I had expected a blindfold[4], but nobody paid me or my fellow prisoners any attention once we left Chief Ibiram and his people.

Our destination turned out to be closer than I had anticipated – we got there in under thirty minutes, and even in the dark I could appreciate how impregnable[5] the approach to land was. It was one solid slab[6] of granite rising sheer[7] from the water, and not till we left the boats did I see the tiny steps cut into the rock face; they looked no more than hand- and toe-holds, but they were cut in a curving zigzag, making the climb easier than one would have expected, yet still daunting to someone not fully recovered from a fever, and hungry, and prodded by guns in the back, and unsure of whatever lay in store. Our arrival was announced by more gunshots and whoops[8] and calls, but the camp was clearly asleep. A few fires burned to illuminate makeshift sheds and tents, and two sentries appeared suddenly from behind trees, looking as one with the night, their presence indicated only by the inevitable cigarette between the lips. Salomon and I were dumped under a tree, while Isabel was led away to a group of tents. Although we couldn't see a guard in our immediate[9] vicinity[10], I knew they were there, shadowy, watching, waiting. I turned to my companion, but he had dragged himself to the foot of the tree and was seated with his back against it, his head lowered onto his knees, and after a while I realized he was sobbing.

1 loom (v): come into sight (usu. sth. menacing) **2** expanse: large, open area **3** in defiance of sth.: refusing to accept sth., facing up to sth. **4** blindfold (n): scarf tied around the head to cover sb.'s eyes **5** impregnable: (here) difficult to pass **6** slab: thick flat piece (e.g. of rock) **7** sheer: (here) very steep, almost vertical **8** whoop (n): loud and excited shout **9** immediate: (here) closest **10** vicinity: surrounding area

– Salomon, are you all right?

He said nothing, and I decided to let him cry in peace. I could imagine how terrified he must be. After all, he had helped the woman escape, and he knew a terrible punishment awaited him in the morning. I hoped he would be composed enough to grant me an interview before they came for him ... for us. I was aware that unless I could prove I was a journalist, and that I could be useful to the militants with my piece, my fate wouldn't be any better than Salomon's. I lay on my back and closed my eyes, but that night sleep didn't come easily.

In the morning I was awakened by a kick in the ribs. I sat up, holding my aching side, and saw a man with a gun standing over me. He said nothing, only motioned with his gun. He wanted me to stand up. I stood up. Salomon was already on his feet, and from his swollen and bloodshot eyes I could tell he hadn't slept much last night.

– Let's go.

Another gunman appeared and led the way through the centre of the camp. The militants were already awake and busy. Men and a few women crawled in and out of canvas[1] tents; others sat or stood under trees, in groups, talking and smoking and cleaning their guns. All seemed to be dressed in black, some wearing head bands, and some wearing masks.

– Keep walking.

We went deeper into the camp, away from the river, and as we went the trees grew denser, our path grew narrower, and I kept looking around trying to spot Isabel, or Gloria. We passed a group standing before an open fire, and when the smell of the meat they were roasting reached me my legs almost buckled[2]. I hadn't eaten since yesterday. We passed another group standing in a circle, singing in loud, discordant voices, and when I recognized the song as one from my long-ago Sunday school[3], I did so with shock. A tall man

1 canvas: *Segeltuch* **2** buckle: give way **3** Sunday school: class on Sunday that teaches children the Bible

with grey hair stood in the centre of the circle, frenziedly[1] waving a Bible in the air, his eyes closed, leading the song. Our escorts finally led us to another group sitting under a leafless tree standing by itself in a large circular clearing. There were already about half a dozen men sitting under the tree, and they all looked abject and forlorn. At the edge of the clearing I saw two militants sitting on boulders, guns lying in the grass beside them.

– Sit here.

I was glad to sit, for my legs could barely support me. When I regained my breath I turned to the men around me, and they all stared back at me. Prisoners, like me. I wondered if they were being held for ransom, or if they had simply fallen foul[2] of the Professor and were being kept here in the open as punishment. As I turned away from their faces I noticed a footpath leading away into a densely wooded area, and now I could hear voices coming from that direction. I wondered if it was an extension of the camp, and if there were more prisoners being held there. We sat for hours, we watched the shadows under the trees shift and grow longer and longer, and still no one came to talk to us. We watched the camp going about its regular business. Every once in a while a militant would step forward and release a shot into the air, almost casually, and his friends would cheer him briefly before resuming whatever they were doing. Salomon still sat away from me, his head bowed. At last I stood up and faced the guards, and one immediately stepped towards me, his gun raised.

– I need to stretch my legs. I have cramps.

I went over and stood next to him.

– My name is Rufus. I'm a reporter. It's very important that I speak to the Professor – I have an urgent message for him.

He looked at me, and I could see he was trying to decide whether I was joking or not. He was young, about twenty, he had cross-eyes[3] and I couldn't tell if he was staring unblinkingly at me or at some-

1 frenzied: uncontrolled, hysterical **2** fall foul of sb.: get into conflict with sb.
3 have cross-eyes: *schielen*

thing else, but his gun was without doubt pointed at my gut. He didn't look threatening, and he even smiled at me when I asked him his name.

– Joseph. People call me Joe. Which paper you work for?

– *The Reporter.*

– So you be reporter and you work for *Reporter.*

– Yes, funny.

He nodded, smiling widely.

– I really have to see the Professor.

– No worry, you go see am[1]. He dey[2] busy right now.

Joseph continued to stare over my shoulder and to point the gun at me. When I got tired of standing I sat down again. One of the men dragged himself over, carefully reclining on one elbow, and, as I turned away from him, he tapped me on the shoulder. I was surprised by the sudden show of interest.

– Are you really a journalist?

– Yes.

I raised my head to see a line of about ten men emerging from the path – they were talking excitedly, and all carried sacks over their shoulders.

– They are getting ready for something big.

– What?

Now I turned to the man and looked at him closely for the first time. His hollow eyes were like those of a holy anchorite[3] who has fasted for days and reached that stage of numbness from which there is no return, unless perhaps by electric shock. Without thinking I stood up and made for the narrow path. The guards, surprised, didn't react till I had gone a few metres, then Joseph ran to me and held me by the hand, the wide smile still on his face.

– I have to see the Professor.

Joseph was roughly pushed aside by the other guard, a short, stout fellow with red, merciless eyes, who stood firmly in my path.

1 you go see am (NP): you will see him **2** dey (NP): is **3** anchorite: person living in isolation for religious reasons

He threw away his cigarette into the bush and moved closer to me till his gun made contact with my chest.

– Where you tink say you dey go[1]?

– I have to see the Professor. I'm a reporter –

– Go back before I blast you to hell!

I went back. The reclining man tapped me again on the shoulder.

– Well, you are a very brave man.

He stared directly at me, as the light fell on his face through the few tree branches, leaving blotches of light and shade where the shadow mixed with light.

– What do you mean?

– You don't seem to be afraid of their guns.

– Who are you? Why are you seated here? Are you prisoners, hostages?

– We are militants, just like them.

– Then why are they guarding you?

– We have a slight problem, that's all. Each of us is here for a different reason. Those two sitting right under the tree, they are from a different gang and they want to join this gang, so they are being watched for a day or two to make sure they are who they claim to be. That one next to them, in the blue shirt, he is being punished. He used to be one of the Professor's top men, he was sent to buy boats from a foreign dealer, and somehow he lost a lot of money in the transaction, I don't know how much, but the Professor is very angry with him, very angry. See that one over there, near the path, sitting by himself, well, he made a mistake. He brought back the wrong hostage.

The man he pointed to was seated on the very edge of the patchy shade cast by the tree's branches. He was a fair-skinned, balding man, dressed in green military fatigues, mostly now torn and dirty, his head bowed between his knees, exposing the round bald spot at the back of his head.

1 Where you tink say you dey go? (NP): Where do you think you are going?

– The Professor needed to raise money quick quick to pay for a consignment[1] of guns he was expecting from overseas, so he sent that guy over there, his name is Monday. His assignment was simple: take some of the boys, and enough guns and boats and everything you need, go to one of the oil companies in Port Harcourt and kidnap one foreign oil worker and bring him back. Well, he went, and he returns with this cheerful-looking man who keeps saying they are making a terrible mistake in kidnapping him. Well, they didn't listen to him. They lock him up in one of the tents over there reserved for such purposes. They send their ransom demand, and they wait for the company to get in touch so they can begin negotiations, but surprisingly, the company shows no interest. Meanwhile the hostage is treated like all other hostages, very good food, everything he need, they even bring a doctor to see him when he has a problem. Well, eventually they discovered what was wrong. The hostage was not a white man at all, despite his very fair skin. You know what he was, an albino[2]! And here he was eating the best food and sleeping all day, as if he was on vacation. Very funny, isn't it?

– What do they call this place?

– Forest. And you, what is a reporter doing here?

– I was taken by force, together with that man over there. If I can talk to the Professor, I can prove who I am.

– Don't worry, the Professor will see you, eventually. His men will tell him what you said and he will want to verify[3] if it is true. I just hope you can prove you are who you claim to be.

And, having said that, the man suddenly lost interest in me. He went back to his spot and to his ruminations[4].

1 consignment: shipment **2** albino (n): person with a condition that, among other things, causes the skin to appear very white **3** verify: check **4** rumination: intensive thinking

20

I was somewhat cheered by the man's assurance that the Professor would definitely see me, and even further cheered when a team of women appeared with food in a big basin[1] and then proceeded to ladle out portions on plastic plates to each of us. The food wasn't remarkable – rice immersed[2] in a mess of beans – but it was filling. After eating I decided to tackle Salomon right away – I had given him enough time to recover, and perhaps what he needed to snap him out of his self-pity was conversation. I went over and sat next to him, and he looked up but said nothing. He was a tall, angular[3] beanpole[4] of a man. His skin and clothes looked as if they hadn't touched water in a long time, and he gave off a musty smell that was quite overpowering, even in the open air. He kept licking his dry lips as he waited for me to speak, and I saw his hand shaking slightly. He kept darting glances[5] at the guards, who were now watching us intently.

– Hi, Salomon.

– Hello.

– We need to talk ...

– I don't want to talk. Leave me alone, please.

– Look, Salomon, I know you're scared of what might happen to you here. I'm scared too. But by talking to me, you'll be doing yourself a favour.

– How?

– Once I have your story, they wouldn't dare do anything to you, because they know when I go out there I will print it, and the world will know you are here, kept against your will ...

1 basin: large bowl **2** immerse sth. in sth.: completely cover sth. with sth. **3** angular: (here) with clear-cut body shapes **4** beanpole (infml): tall, thin person **5** dart glances at sb.: look aggressively at sb.

– Nonsense.

– What?

I thought I was doing so well, and for a moment I was telling myself that even Zaq would be proud of my persuasiveness, but obviously the driver wasn't persuaded.

– These people, they no care. They have killed before, and I know nothing is going to save me ... nothing ... The Professor is a madman. I have seen what he can do. A few days ago, just before we ran away, he shot a man over there. Point blank[1]. He said the man was giving away information to the soldiers, he screamed at him and called him a traitor, then he took out his gun and boom! He shot him and said, Throw him into the water for the fish to eat. Just like that.

I refused to let my perturbation[2] show. If I showed no fear, nothing would go wrong. I renewed my effort, and as I spoke I was aware my words were also aimed at myself, at my quaking[3] heart.

– Well, but isn't that another good reason why you should tell me everything? Isabel told me what happened, about your fiancée, and her husband. The police have everyone thinking you're some crazy kidnapper – don't you want to put the record straight? This might be your only chance, you know. Don't you want your family and friends to know the truth, the real truth?

– It is a long story ...

– I'm very patient, and it doesn't look as if we're going anywhere soon.

– What do you want to know?

– Your side of the story. Why did you kidnap her?

– I didn't kidnap her ...

– Well, okay. Tell me about you and Koko.

I saw his eyes darken with anger, and he started to rock himself back and forth, back and forth, his arms wrapped tightly round his knees.

1 point blank: (shooting) from a very short distance **2** perturbation: agitation, anxiety **3** quake (v): shake

– Well, I knew she was pregnant. We lived together, and we were happy, well, I thought we were. I was happy. I was looking forward to being a father. I never suspected she was cheating on me, how could she? It was I who brought her to Port Harcourt from our village. She wanted to be a nurse, she took the exam, and as we waited for the results, she begged me to help her look for a temporary job, just till the results came out. And so I talked to my Oga. He was always good to me. A nice man. And he said, yes, why not? And that was how she started working in that house. I did everything for her. If only I'd known things would turn out like this. I should have realized something was wrong when she got her exam results and she said she wasn't going to nursing school any more. She said we needed the money for the wedding, and for the coming baby.

Salomon paused, as if to go on would be just too painful. He continued to rock, back and forth, back and forth, the harsh sun overhead forcing the sweat to drip down his face, but he didn't seem to notice.

The day she told him about James Floode, he had returned early from work. The madam didn't need him for the rest of the day, so he went to his two-room tenement house and turned on the TV. Usually Koko was home from work earlier than him, but today she didn't return till after nightfall, and he had started to worry. He saw that something was wrong the moment she entered. She looked distracted, and she went into the bedroom without a word. When he followed her he found her lying in bed, her eyes closed. When he asked her what was wrong, and if they were not going to eat, she threw off the sheets and started raging at him. It was as if she had been waiting to do this for a very long time.

– You this man, why don't you leave me alone? Don't you know where the kitchen is? Or don't you have hands?

– She had never behaved that way before, and I thought it was the pregnancy, so I said nothing. I just turned to go back to the living room, but then, as I turned, she made that sucking noise through her teeth and said, *Mumu*. I couldn't believe my ears. I asked her, What did you call me?

– *Mumu.* Fool. *Mumu.* You heard me right. And I want to tell you, I am moving out tomorrow. No more marriage.

– Koko, have you been drinking? Is it me you are calling a fool?

– Yes. All this while I have just been pretending with you. And this pregnancy that you think is yours, it is not. It is the Oga's pregnancy.

– I don't understand.

– What is there to understand? Me and the Oga, we are in love. He is getting a divorce from his wife, and he is going to marry me. He will take me to London with him when his contract[1] finishes.

Salomon didn't know what happened; he said he saw himself standing over her, his fist raised. He must have hit her, but she didn't cry, in fact her eyes were glowing with triumph, and she was still hissing at him. She said if he touched her again, he would not only lose his job, but she would make sure the Oga had him arrested. Slowly he lowered his hand. He went out to a nearby bar and he drank till closing time, and when he came back she wasn't there – she had packed a bag and left.

– The next morning I decided to go meet the madam and tell her what had happened. She was very friendly, unlike the other *oyinbo*[2] women I had worked with, who only shout orders at you. I remember the day she arrived, I had picked her up from the airport, and she told me how tough it was getting through customs, and how they asked her to open all her bags, and how they had put their hands all over her things, including her underwear, and that a few of her things had been confiscated for further examination. She said to me in her soft English voice, I'm sure I'll never see them again. Will I, do you think? She was like that when we drove around, asking questions, leaning forward in the back seat and talking to me.

– At the house I was told by the guards at the gate that madam wasn't at home, and I decided to check the European Club, even though it was I who always took her there. When I found her, she

1 contract (n): (here) job contract **2** oyinbo: term used in several Nigerian languages to refer to white people

seemed very sad, and I knew she was dealing with the same problem as myself. But later, at my uncle's motel, I realized she didn't know it was Koko her husband was leaving her for.

He stopped his narration suddenly and stared past me at the sun that seemed to be hanging on the edge of the island, all orange and red and purple, as if it were only a hand-span away.

– Reporter –

– Call me Rufus.

– You know why I am telling you all this, Rufus? It is because some of us might not live to see another sunset like this one.

– Everything will be fine. You're doing the right thing by talking to me.

– You must write it down exactly as I say, because I am the only one who knows everything that happened. I had a hand[1] in the kidnapping, at first, but later I took care of her very well, otherwise … she wouldn't be alive right now.

– What happened after you left her at your uncle's motel for the night?

– It is a long story …

– I'm listening.

– I went back to my room, but I couldn't rest. My mind was still worried. Later, when my neighbour Bassey came back, we sat down to drink and when he asked me where Koko was, I told him everything. When I left him, he went and told his friend Jamabo, a police officer, and it was Jamabo who came up with the kidnapping idea. Late that night they came knocking on my door. I listened as they laid out the plan. Jamabo said as a police officer he had seen many cases of kidnapping and it is like plucking money off a money tree – that was how he put it. And when I asked, What if we get caught? He said there was no danger of that: usually the police prefer to stay out, leaving the oil company to handle things its own way, which is what it prefers. But what of the woman? I said. She has done nothing wrong, will she be all right? Jamabo said nothing would happen

1 have a hand in sth. (infml): be involved in sth.

to her. She would remain in the motel room, we'd treat her well, and we'd let her go as soon as we had the money. It wouldn't take more than two days in all. He said technically it wasn't even kidnapping; I'd just be collecting payment for all the pain these people caused me, a refund[1] for all my investment in Koko. And that was what convinced me. The Oga had insulted me badly, he'd taken away my pride, my dignity[2], my manhood, and all the time I was serving him honestly, diligently. I trusted him. And another point, the money wasn't even coming out of his pocket: the oil company always pays the ransom, and Bassey said that if you thought about it carefully, you'd realize that the money came from our oil, so we would be getting back what was ours in the first place. Well, I started to really think. This was the chance of a lifetime. And, like Jamabo said, it wasn't a real kidnapping. So we all agreed. We were going to ask for one million dollars. Over three hundred thousand each. We would be rich. With that kind of money I could get out of the country and no one would ever find me.

And so, their plan carefully prepared, the three went to the motel early the next morning. Isabel looked surprised to see not just Salomon but also two men with him, one carrying a duffel bag[3], but she let them in and turned to Salomon for explanation. Salomon just stood there, unable to speak, unable to look her directly in the eye. But when Bassey pushed him aside impatiently to face her, Salomon found his voice.

– I will tell her.

He took her into the next room and told her the two men outside would stay with her until her husband paid ransom for her. He said if her husband cooperated, she would be free in a day or two. Slowly she sat down on the bed, shaking her head.

– No, Salomon, you're doing the wrong thing. Listen, they'll catch you and you'll go to prison – do you want that? I know you're doing this because of your fiancée, but this is wrong.

1 refund (n): financial compensation **2** dignity: *Würde* **3** duffel bag: travelling bag mainly used by sailors

He turned and left the room, locking the door behind him, but Jamabo went in again and inspected the windows, making sure they were all firmly secured. The men stayed in the living room all day, playing cards, and when night finally fell, Salomon checked on her once more to make sure she was okay – there was a fridge in the bedroom, with water and fruit and bread in it – and then he left. However, a big shock awaited him when he got home and turned on the TV.

– The first thing I saw on the screen was the madam's face, she was missing, and then my own face, the last person she was seen with when leaving the European Club in her car. And I remembered I had left the car at the motel, and I began to worry. What if somebody stumbled[1] upon it, my uncle or one of his workers?

The same story was on all the stations: Isabel Floode, only six months in the country, abducted on the way home from the European Club, her driver, Salomon, wanted for questioning. He felt trapped in his room, unsure what to do. The plan had been for him to take the ransom note to Floode's office in the morning, and to drop it there without being seen; Jamabo had drafted[2] the note with clear instructions as to where to bring the money and how to get the woman back. But this was now too dangerous and would have to change.

He couldn't stay in his room any longer, so he quickly gathered together a few things and took a bus back to the motel.

– I went straight to No. 19 and knocked on the door. I could see the curtain shake as a figure observed me from inside. I shouted, It is me, Salomon, open up quickly. Jamabo opened the door and dragged me inside, telling me to keep my voice down. I looked around and he was alone. I went to the adjoining[3] room where the madam was, and it was empty. Jamabo is sitting on a chair in the first room, waiting for me. Sit down, he told me, there is a change in plans. What do you mean there is a change in plans? I shouted at him. Who is

1 stumble upon sb./sth.: come across sb./sth. by chance **2** draft sth.: write down the first version of sth. (a text) **3** adjoining (adj): situated next to sth.

making the plans, is it not me? He said, Sit down, I am making the plans now. Listen, we think the million dollars you are asking is too small for this operation. But that is bigger than you are ever going to earn in all your life as a policeman, besides, this is not a real kidnapping, I said. Isn't it? he asked. My friend, kidnapping is kidnapping. Did you see the news? I am thinking that is why you came back so quickly, isn't it? Where is she? I asked. Don't worry, she is being taken somewhere safe as we speak. I saw the news and I knew she couldn't stay here any longer, so I called a friend of mine who owns a boat and now he is taking her to an island not far from here. No one can find her there. We'll soon join her. But before we go, I want to make sure you are with us. This is not a game any more. That is why we are asking for three million instead of one. Last week, a foreign family was kidnapped, a man and his wife, their company paid three million ransom for them. Cash. This woman is worth nothing less than that, but if they decide to negotiate, we can go down to two million. Are you coming with us? You decide. But, I said to him, this is not a real kidnapping. But it is, he said, we will get the same prison sentence regardless of how much we ask for. You are a kidnapper already. Well, I had no option. And we left. First I went and checked out of the motel room, as if nothing was wrong, then we took the car and dumped it in front of a supermarket, then we set out for Agbuki Island. That was where she was being taken by Bassey.

– I know the place. I was there with other reporters. We met nothing there but dead bodies and burned-down houses.

– We went there in a speedboat, and I was surprised at how glad she was to see me. I promised her everything would be all right. They had locked her up by herself in one of the huts and she looked terrified. Well, in the morning we wrote the new ransom note and sent it to the husband, but we didn't hear back from him, nothing. Two days we were there and by now the lady was beginning to fall sick and the army was out there patrolling the water trying to find her and we didn't know how long we could remain undetected. Jamabo said we should go and meet the husband with a picture of her as proof. He wanted me to do it since I was the driver and the husband knew me. The other two said we should seek help from other gangs, bigger gangs who had done this kind of thing before, like the Professor. There was constant argument and fighting, and all the time, when I go to give her her food, she'd urge me to take her back home, that she'd make sure her husband paid me my share of the ransom money no matter how much it was. She said she'd not mention my part in it. But I told her I couldn't. The others were watching us all the time and they wouldn't hesitate to shoot me if they suspected anything. Besides, I couldn't see myself taking the husband's money like that: I still hated him. Anyway, things were resolved for us the next day when the whole island was surrounded by boats. It was the Professor. His men came out shooting into the air, they shot at goats and dogs and chickens just like that. They went from door to door till they came to us. We were all in the same hut, the hostage and Bassey and me and Jamabo and Paul, the man with the boat who Jamabo hired. Well, the Professor came in and I was surprised to see how small and ordinary he looked. I had read about him in all the papers and I always assumed he would be a big man. He sat down and he didn't look at us, but he said to the madam, Are they treating you well? I hope they are, because if they are not then they will be giving all of us a bad name. Kidnapping is not for amateurs, they make a mess, people get killed, and when they do the papers have a field day. They call us barbaric, and it spoils business for everyone. Jamabo quickly jumped in and said, We are taking care of her very well. Everything is under control. Ah, so you are the leader, the Professor said, turning and looking up at Jamabo. Jamabo nodded eagerly. And you think you can just kidnap people here in my territory, without letting me know? The Professor spoke very mildly, he didn't raise his voice. And Jamabo kept nodding and even smiling, he said, *Haba*[1], Professor, we were going to contact you after everything had been settled. We will give you your share … And the Professor raised his hand and said to his men who were standing there holding guns, Take him out. And they grabbed Jamabo and

1 Haba (NP): expression of surprise and disbelief

took him out and after a minute we heard a scream then a gunshot. Just like that. Well, everyone fell silent. We couldn't believe what had just happened. But we never saw Jamabo again. Not even his dead body. The madam was holding my hand, and she was trying to hide behind me and she was whimpering like this, mmmh, mmmmh, on and on, and she didn't even know she was doing it. He looked at me and at her and he said, We are taking you off the hands of these idiots. But she was still whimpering and shaking her head and holding my hand and saying, Please, please, no. And he said, Believe me, you are more likely to get hurt in the hands of these idiots than with us. We will get in touch with your family and everything will be settled in a few days. We want this over as soon as possible. He looked at me and said, You must be the driver. She seems to trust you, so you will come with us. You are in charge of her welfare. And then Bassey raised his hand and said, Please, Oga Professor, I want to join you too. You are welcome, said the Professor. And we left together. They blindfolded me, and Isabel and Bassey. We were taken onto a boat and then we were on the water. It was a fairly long boat journey and when the blindfold was finally removed, we were on a strange beach with statues facing the water. They call it Irikefe.

I nodded.

– I know Irikefe.

– That day the Professor called me and said, How much were you idiots asking for?

– And I said, Three million, and he shook his head and said, Idiot. She is worth more than that. At least five million. We will send them her hair, that should convince them we have her. If it doesn't, we will send an ear. But I hope it never gets to that, not good for business. She does have rather distinctive hair so the husband should know it is hers. At the moment she is all over the news. That is good. The more publicity, the more money the company is willing to pay; if they refuse to pay they will be seen in a bad light. So, we will send the hair, then we will arrange a viewing. We will call the media to come in two days.

– The plan was to bring you reporters first to Agbuki, and then to Irikefe, where she was being held. And I was left with her because I was the only one she would talk to, and she was really falling sick by now. Vomiting all the time. She couldn't eat the food. The Professor went with two boatloads of his men to Agbuki to wait for the media. He loves the media, he loves talking about his war for the environment and he wanted to receive the media personally and lead them to the worshippers' island. But somehow the army had found out what was going on and were waiting for him when he got there. They thought he was with the woman. Many men were killed. But the Professor got away, they went back to Irikefe and that night we left the island with the hostage and came here.

– And what happened to your other partner?

– Bassey.

– Yes.

– He was killed by the soldiers on that island.

– Now tell me about the escape, how did you manage it?

He said although he was not confined in any way, he soon realized that he was as much a hostage in the forest as Isabel, and he grew scared. And meanwhile the woman grew sicker every day. After the attack at Agbuki, the Professor had raised the ransom money to ten million dollars, he had also grown more cautious, and it didn't look as if she'd be freed any time soon. She grew more nervous, her face grew red and blotchy with insect bites, and her clothes were all torn and dirty – they gave her a jacket to put on when she washed her things. She cried more and more often, and more and more time went by, and at last Salomon gave in. He told her he would try to escape, but they had to plan carefully. The good thing was that even though general security was very tight, only one guard watched over them at any one time, because it didn't seem conceivable that they'd make a break for it[1]. Where would they go?

– But still, it was not going to be easy. If we were able to leave the forest, we'd have to find one of the military camps out there, and

1 make a break for it (infml): try to escape

if we didn't find any, we'd have to find a village that would agree to hide us, and help us get word to the military or to her husband. Hopefully they'd help us if we promised them money. I knew the people were more likely to betray us to the Professor – they fear the militants more than the army. But by now I was as desperate as she was to escape.

– How did you do it?

– One night, when the camp was almost deserted, most of the men had gone on an operation, they do that all the time. I was in charge of her, as always. I knew where they keep the boats, over on that side, in a cave. There are always a few boats there; in case they are attacked suddenly by the army they can get away in the boats. And so that night she put on the military jacket and covered her hair and blackened her face a bit so she wouldn't be recognized. The guard watching us always fell asleep around 1 p.m.; I guess he didn't believe we would ever attempt to run away. So we waited till I was sure he was asleep, then we sneaked out. We almost made it to the boats when we were challenged by a voice right behind me. I didn't think, I just threw myself at him, and luckily he didn't have time to fire his gun. We fought and I bashed[1] his head with a rock. I don't know if he died. We rowed for many hours till we got to a village, and luck was on our side. They were good people. They listened to our story, and they helped us.

1 bash sb./sth.: hit sb./sth. hard

21

When I woke up the next morning a man was kneeling over me, nudging me with his gun. I sat up quickly and the man stood up and moved back. The others were awake, except Salomon, who wasn't anywhere to be seen. After our interview yesterday he had turned away from me and lain on his side, and he didn't get up even when our evening meal was brought by the same group that had fed us earlier. When I called to him to come and eat, he had said no, he wasn't hungry. Now the man with the gun beckoned to me with one hand and turned and started towards the trees. For some reason I knew I was being taken to the Professor, and I was ready. In the time I had been here I had somehow managed to get over my initial fear and nervousness, and had finally come to believe what I always knew in my heart was true and yet had never taken consolation[1] in: the Professor needed the press, and, from all that I had heard about him, he wasn't a madman who shot people for fun. He was a man with an agenda, and anything that could help him in that pursuit he'd treat with respect. I was that thing, and the more firmly I believed that, and behaved accordingly, the safer I would be.

The Professor was lying in a hammock[2] hanging from two stunted mango trees, and he jumped down as soon as I was presented to him. There were about a dozen men around him, all armed, all looking distrustfully at me. Above us, through the tree branches, I could see the sun just breaking out of the eastern clouds. Most of the camp was still asleep.

– Journalist, it is a pity about your friend.

– My friend?

1 take consolation in sth.: find comfort in sth., feel better because of sth.
2 hammock: kind of bed made from a net tied between two trees or posts

– The white woman's driver. Didn't they tell you? Didn't anyone tell him? He tried to run away early this morning. He had done it once, and he thought it was going to be as easy as before, but you can't fool the people all the time. My men saw him and gave chase and he lost his head. He jumped off the cliff and fell on the rocks below. He died instantly.

I closed my eyes.

– His body was taken away by the river. A tragedy, don't you think?

– I find it hard to believe ...

The Professor stepped forward till he was standing right in front of me, but the menace of this gesture was diminished by his short stature – his eyes were just about level with my chin. Two of his men stepped forward with him, and their combined presence forced me to take a step back, and yet I felt no fear.

– Are you calling me a liar, reporter?

– No, Professor. I am not. I don't know you well enough to do that.

He looked at me for a while, and then he turned and hopped back into his hammock, his short legs swinging, his thick military boots clicking together, dropping bits of mud into the grass. He extended his arm and one of the men placed a rifle into the open hand.

– You reporters, you are always clever with words – me, I am a soldier, I know how to fight, and I will never stop fighting till I achieve my goal. Write that when you get back.

– I will do that.

– I called you here to set you free. You can go. There is a boat waiting for you, one of my men will take you to a nearby village, and you will be on your own. We are going out on an operation; you may have noticed the whole camp getting ready. By this time tomorrow, one of the major oil depots will be burning. I want you to write about it, tell them I am responsible. I can't tell you more than that, but I can tell you the war is just starting. We will make it so hot for the government and the oil companies that they will be forced to pull out. That is all I can say for now.

– What about the woman?

– The woman is safe, as you will see for yourself.

There was a movement behind the trees and two men appeared leading Isabel. She looked as I had last seen her, still wearing the same clothes, her hair shockingly cropped[1] short, but in her posture and in her gaze I detected a subtle[2] change, a sort of resignation, a surrender to the strange and obscure forces that sometimes take over our lives, and which it is futile to resist. I made to go towards her but one of the men raised his gun and shook his head at me. My eyes met hers and I nodded, and she nodded, then she turned and was led away by the men.

– Take this envelope to her husband: it contains more of her hair. Tell him his wife is safe, but after two days, if we don't hear from him, we can't guarantee her safety any more. We are getting impatient. Two days, final.

– There is another woman, from Irikefe. Her name is Gloria. Your men took her a few days ago ...

– Ah, the nurse. She is gone. We set her free two days ago. Did you think we'd keep her here against her wish, rape her maybe? We are not the barbarians the government propagandists say we are. We are for the people. Everything we do is for the people, what will we gain if we terrorize them? I am speaking for myself and my group of course. I am aware that, out there, there are criminal elements looting[3] and killing under the guise[4] of freedom fighting, but we are different. Those kind of rebels, they are our enemies. That is why I am letting you go, so you can write the truth. And be careful, whatever you write, be careful. I am watching you. I have people everywhere.

– I will write only the truth.

He jumped down and came forward till his chin was almost touching my chest. This time he reached out a finger and poked me, his eyes locked with mine.

1 crop sth.: cut sth. **2** subtle (adj): slight, small **3** loot sth.: plunder sth.
4 guise (n): pretence

– Write only the truth. Tell them about the flares you see at night, and the oil on the water. And the soldiers forcing us to escalate the violence every day. Tell them how we are hounded[1] daily in our own land. Where do they want us to go, tell me where? Tell them, we are going nowhere. This land belongs to us. That is the truth, remember that. You can go.

I sat under the tree and watched the men come and go, some of them busy comparing guns, rolls of bullets draped around their shoulders like scarves. Some carried metal boxes that they passed down to the boats waiting in the river. They were on the war path, and I was free. Soon I had to set out on my own path, yet a heaviness lay on my heart, and I felt no exhilaration or joy or relief. I just felt tired, and hungry. I kept looking in the direction in which I had seen Isabel disappear, and I was tempted to go after her and assure her I would deliver the silent message she had passed to me with her eyes, and I would waste no time doing it. But she knew that already, I was sure.

Our boat's prow[2] broke into the dense, inscrutable[3] mist, making for open water. It was an old wooden boat with an outboard motor that looked just about capable enough to take us to the next settlement. I looked back to the shore we had just left. A few militants stood in the mist, guns dangling by their sides, staring after our slowly disappearing boat. My escort left me on the other river bank with a plastic bottle full of water. Before me was a dense forest and my heart quivered[4] just to think that I'd soon be traversing its depth on my way to the other side, where, he told me, I'd find a village and a boat to take me to Irikefe. The river curved in a big U, and the ground I'd be covering was the middle of the U; on the other side I'd meet the river again where it joined the sea.

1 hound sb.: hunt sb., harass sb. **2** prow: front part of a boat **3** inscrutable: impossible to see through, mysterious **4** quiver: shake slightly, tremble

When I came out of the forest, I had no problem getting a boat on the other side, and after a ride of over two hours on the sea we arrived at Irikefe. I got down and thanked the men. I joined a group standing by the water watching three fishermen in a boat slowly pulling up a big net full of wriggling[1] fish. We cheered as the net came up, and then I left the group and headed for Gloria's house.

I found her at the standpipe[2], bent over an iron bucket filled with soapy water and dirty clothes. I stood over her, unable to speak, and when she looked up and saw me, she straightened up slowly. Then she smiled and I thought it was the most beautiful sight I had ever seen. She took my hand and led me inside, making me sit on the bed. She knelt down and took off my shoes, and then she went out and returned after a few minutes.

– I have taken a bucket to the bathroom for you.

She gave me a towel and I went out. After the bath she gave me a bowl of hot pepper soup and I drank. Then I slept. She was lying beside me when I woke up, her eyes closed. The window was open and the wind was shaking the curtain and it was as though it was riffling through a field in my mind. I sat up and gently shook her arm till she opened her eyes. She smiled.

– I was watching you sleep, and then I fell asleep. You slept for five hours.

She told me Zaq was dead. He'd died before the militants brought Gloria back to Irikefe, setting her free on the shore. I let her words sink in, not interrupting. When she came back she found the military pulling out, and the villagers, led by Naman, who was now the head priest, engaged in rebuilding the shrine and the huts and salvaging[3] anything that they could. First she joined her co-tenants to make their house habitable, scrubbing[4] the floor till her hands ached, repainting the walls and finding a strange pleasure in watching the grime disappear forever beneath the cover of

1 wriggle (v): move with small, quick movements **2** standpipe: vertical water pipe **3** salvage sth.: gather up sth. that can still be used **4** scrub sth.: clean sth. intensively

fresh new paint, then nailing back the windows onto their hinges and finally throwing away whatever was beyond repair. Afterwards she felt like Christians must after being baptized[1]: born again. Then she joined the worshippers who were putting together the statues piece by piece; when they were through, an uninformed observer would never be able to guess that only a week ago the figures had been knocked down and broken by the soldiers. Even the chips[2] and holes in them only added to their dignity.

Boma was still on the island. She had joined the worshippers, walking with them in a procession every morning and every evening to immerse herself in the sea and sing a hymn to the rising and the setting of the sun. And since Gloria had returned, the two had been inseparable. Every morning they would stand at the waterfront, looking hopefully at each in-coming boat, waiting for me to return. When she told me Zaq had been buried on the island, at the little cemetery near the sculpture garden, I stood up and put on my shirt.

– I have to go and say goodbye.

Although the doctor had prepared me for this, and although I had been with him most of last week and seen him ailing[3] and declining daily, I still felt totally disoriented by the news of his death. I didn't know there were tears on my face till I felt them fall on my arm. Gloria held my hand and pulled me back into bed.

– Rest. You have a slight fever. You'll be stronger tomorrow. We will go together tomorrow.

– Tomorrow I have to be in Port Harcourt; a woman's fate rests in my hands.

– You can do both tomorrow. I'll come to Port Harcourt with you … if you want. I could ask the Doctor for a few days off.

– What doctor?

– Dr Dagogo-Mark.

1 baptize sb.: pour water over sb.'s head in a ceremony to welcome her/him to the Christian church **2** chip (n): (here) thin peace of wood that has been chipped off **3** ail [eɪl]: be sick

She said he had arrived on the island the day I left, and he had opted[1] to remain after the soldiers had pulled out. Already he had set up a dispensary, and he was now talking about starting a proper hospital with wards[2] and an operating theatre[3].

– He is a good man.

– I know.

We sat down side by side on the bed and watched the darkness grow, not bothering to turn on the light.

– What about your fiancé?

– I haven't thought about him in a long time.

We set out for the shrine with the first light. Gloria left me at the sculpture garden and went to look for Boma. She was right – though the number of statues had greatly diminished, those that now stood looked as if they had always been like this. Their scars and punctures seemed to have been put there by time and weather, and not by random weaponry. There were two men walking among the statues, picking up loose stones, wiping off the final traces of the violence from the figures. They nodded at me and I nodded back. Zaq had been buried in the empty grave he and I had once dug up in the dead of the night, intoxicated by whisky and feverish with the prospects of uncovering a major scoop. A wooden cross stood at the head of the grave, and attached to the cross was a square of wood bearing the simple inscription:

zaq. journalist. august 2009. rip[4]

There were over a dozen new graves surrounding Zaq's, their mounds rising like freshly prepared furrows in a field, raw and dark and fecund, waiting for seeding. I sat in the dirt and stared for a long

1 opt to do sth.: decide to do sth. **2** ward (n): part of a hospital **3** operating theatre: operating room **4** rip: rest in peace (common inscription on gravestones)

time at the simple grave, not sure what to do. I wished I had a bottle of his favourite Johnnie Walker so I could pour him a libation[1]. I wondered what he would have made of it all, he who had travelled so far, and seen so much, and suffered so much, only to end up in this strange place, with such a plain epitaph[2]. I remembered he once told me of his time in Ouagadougou[3]. It was in the last days of General Abacha, when the pressure on journalists and pro-democracy activists was at its pitch, and he had escaped to Burkina Faso to lay low, to wait for Abacha's inevitable downfall. He was telling me this the day after we had dug up the empty grave, the day Naman had forbidden us to leave the island. He was drinking, lying on his mat, staring at the ceiling, and he asked me, as he always did, Did you ever think in your wildest moment that you'd be here, in this hut, detained by some nature-worshipping priest? Ah, such is life. Of all the places I have been to, only one place still stays in my mind. You can't guess where, not in a million years.

– London? New York? Paris? Johannesburg?

– No. Nothing so fancy. Ouagadougou. If I could return to any one period in my life, one place, it would be Ouagadougou.

– Ouagadougou? Why?

– I met a woman there, and we lived together for four months.

And he closed his eyes, his face pointed at the roof, and I waited and waited for him to go on, but he didn't. The smile stayed on his lips till he fell asleep. Perhaps he was there right now, in Ouagadougou, taking a last detour to revisit friends before passing on to eternity, wherever that is.

I passed the two men on my way back, and once more they paused and nodded to me, and I nodded back. Boma was waiting for me at the edge of the sculpture garden. She was wearing the long white robe. I stopped and pointed at the robe.

– Gloria told me you were here now ...

1 pour a libation: *Trankopfer darbringen,* (here) pour a drink **2** epitaph: inscription on a gravestone **3** Ouagadougou: capital of Burkina Faso

– Yes.

She looked well. There was a smile on her face.

– Well, you look healthy, happy.

– I'm happy to see you back in one piece. You left without telling me.

– I'm back now.

– And the white woman?

– She's still there. I have a message for her husband from the kidnappers.

– Will she be all right?

– Yes. I'll meet with her husband today, and I'm sure he'll do the right thing. We have only a few hours before the ferry gets here. You have to get ready.

She turned and looked towards the shrine, where a few worshippers were beginning to line up, getting ready for their morning procession to the sea. She turned back to me. – I've made up my mind to stay.

– Stay here?

She nodded. – I like it here, I like the people, and I can feel myself relaxing in a way I haven't in a long time. My spirit feels settled.

– Well, if you're sure ...

She came forward and hugged me, then she left to join the procession. I made my way to the little hill overlooking the sea. The ferry wouldn't be here till afternoon. Gloria and I would have lunch with Boma and Naman before we left, but until then I would sit and watch, perhaps for the last time, the worshippers process to the water. In the distance, at the edge of the clearing where the huts began, I saw a portly figure in a white jacket talking to Gloria; it was Dr Dagogo-Mark.

Far away on the horizon the flares were still sending up smoke into the air, and for a moment I imagined, somewhere on the river, a refinery up in flames, sabotaged by the Professor and his men – if nothing had happened last night to stop them. I imagined huge cliffs of smoke and giant escarpments[1] of orange fire rising into the atmosphere, and thousands of gallons of oil floating on the water, the weight of the oil tight like a hangman's[2] noose[3] round the neck of whatever life form lay underneath. I thought of Isabel out there in the forest, waiting. She might not have long to wait. This could all be over by tomorrow, and then another period of mental healing would begin for her, but by then she would be somewhere far away, among her people. A fortnight hence and she'd look back and this would all be nothing but a memory, an anecdote for the dinner table. And her husband, James Floode, I wondered what his future plans were: but I would have a chance to ask him later today when I saw him.

Now the worshippers were in the water, swaying and humming; I strained my eyes, trying to determine which of them was Boma. She'd be happy here, I was sure. This was a place of healing and soon she'd forget John, her scars would recede to the back of her mind, and one day she'd look in the mirror and see they were gone. I had felt the same optimism three days ago when I looked back from the militants' boat at Chief Ibiram and his people. They were a fragile flotilla[4], ordinary men and women and babies, a puny armada[5] about to launch itself once more into uncertain waters, braving the darkness in order to get to the light. That day I didn't get a chance to wave goodbye to them: Tamuno and Michael and Ibiram and Alali and all the nameless ones. Now alone on the hill, I raised my hands and waved and waved – down below someone waved back, it looked like Boma, but it was too far to say for sure. I turned and began my descent.

1 escarpment: steep side of a hill, (here) clouds of smoke that look like a hill
2 hangman: person who carries out an execution by hanging **3** noose: rope put around sb.'s head for hanging **4** flotilla: group of boats **5** armada: group of armed boats

ADDITIONAL MATERIALS

Rape of A Nation: An Eco-critical Reading of Helon Habila's Oil on Water *Solomon Edebor*

Edebor, a researcher at the Nigerian Afe Babalola University, in his 2017 essay reads Habila's novel from an ecological standpoint and investigates how literary texts like Oil on Water *illustrate environmental concerns.*

[...] Rufus, the narrator of events in the novel, throws light on the disturbing contamination and degradation[1] of the Niger Delta nation due to oil spillage and gas flaring. He, in fact, paints a dark picture of a nation trapped in irredeemable[2] ruins, showing the roles played by the military, the government (and its officials), the transnational companies and the militants on one hand; while also showing the grim effects of the reckless actions and inactions of these forces on the environment, the society (man), and other living things (animals, fishes, etc), on the other hand.

Perhaps, as a way of making the reader have an in-depth comprehension of his pity for the unsympathetic actions of human beings towards nature, Habila presents us the pristine[3] state of the Niger Delta physical environment, foregrounding[4] the benefits accrued[5] to man in the process. He, in this context, celebrates nature and foregrounds the ecological wisdom in ensuring that the earth is not damaged in any way. The air, for instance, is presented as having healing powers to cure all manners of diseases. This is evident in the speech of Naaman, the Chief Priest of the shrine at Irikefe village. When Rufus expresses a misgiving regarding Zaq's decision to stay back at the shrine in spite of his failing health, Namaan interjects: 'We have a nurse here and she will attend to you (Zaq). But perhaps

1 degradation: damage **2** irredeemable: (here) destroyed forever **3** pristine (adj): in its original state, untouched **4** foreground sth.: emphasize sth.
5 accrue to sb.: *jemandem zuteilwerden, jemandem zufallen*

you won't need her. The air alone will heal you. I have seen it happen'.

Again, during the conversation that ensues[1] between Rufus and Gloria, Gloria emphasises the healing powers of the uncontaminated sea, which, as a consequence, has drawn the attention of many worshippers. In fact, the Irikefe villagers believe so much in the powers of nature that they worship the sun. Rufus' sister, Boma, also finds comforts in nature. Following her ordeals in life and in marriage, she decides to stay with other worshippers at the shrine in Irikefe. [...]

Habila's depiction of the healing powers of the air and the sea, as well as how people worship nature (the sun) in this context is very revealing. Apart from proving that protecting our environment is protecting our lives, it seems he is implicitly pointing attention to how industrialization is gradually destroying our world, particularly with the daily emission of poisonous gases into the atmosphere resulting in air pollution; and also the release of harmful waste substances into the seas, leading to destruction of much beauty and extermination of countless fellow species. That people worship the sun signifies the reverence that people have for it – their love, admiration and belief in nature. To the people, nature is meant to be hallowed[2], not desecrated.

Besides, Habila establishes the strong interdependence existing between man and nature, demonstrating how it, together with all the living things therein, sustains and helps man in achieving his numerous goals. For the Niger Delta people who are fishermen, they mostly make 'their living on the river that poured its water into the sea'. [...]

Rufus draws a sharp contrast between the present state of the physical environment of the community and the one known to him in the past, noting how unrewarding[3] the villagers' efforts at seas are as they merely succeed in catching 'a handful of thin wiggling fish'.

1 ensue: follow **2** hallow sb./sth.: treat sb./sth. as holy **3** unrewarding (adj): not paying off, not worth the effort

[...] Gloria later adds her voice, stating that many islands around her used to be a big habitat for bats, but now have a few dozen due to the gas flares that kill them. [...] At every direction now, one sees '... dead birds draped over tree branches, their outstretched wings black and slick with oil; dead fish bobbed white-bellied between tree roots. ... The patch of grass growing by the water was suffocated by a film of oil ...'.

[...]

Apart from revealing the terrible effects of environmental degradation on the survivals of animals, fishes, birds, grass, rivers and creeks, Habila poignantly[1] reveals some of the dire consequences of the activities of the oil companies on the host communities. These include: sicknesses, unwarranted[2] loss of lives, severe accidents, poverty, lack of means of self-sustenance[3], extermination of communities, loss of faith and moral piety, hopelessness, displacements of people, broken homes/marriages, and lack of unity, among others. [...]

From: Solomon Edebor, 'Rape of A Nation: An Eco-critical Reading of Helon Habila's Oil on Water', *Journal of Arts & Humanities* 6.9: 2017, pp. 41–49

1 poignant: moving, touching **2** unwarranted (adj): unjust **3** self-sustenance: state of being able to support oneself without external help

Oil Spills Occur Almost Weekly In Nigeria – Interview with Julia Baird *Neil Conan*

Since drilling began over 50 years ago, millions of barrels of oil have spilled into the Niger Delta. Julia Baird, deputy editor of Newsweek, talks about the environmental and social impact of the spills, which occur almost every week.

NEAL CONAN, host: [...] Julia Baird is deputy editor at Newsweek and wrote the piece 'Oil's Shame in Africa' and joins us by phone from Philadelphia. Nice to have you with us today.

Ms. JULIA BAIRD: (Deputy Editor, Newsweek): Thank you very much, Neal.

CONAN: And can you describe the kind of damage that has occurred in the Niger Delta?

Ms. BAIRD: Yes. It's quite shocking, and it's gone on for several decades. Ever since they began drilling there in 1958, we've had five decades of extensive and ongoing spills. Really, experts estimate that approximately each year, there's a spill the size of the Exxon Valdez[1] in the Niger Delta, which is home to 31 million people, the world's third largest area of kind of wetlands[2], which is mangroves and fish and shellfish[3].

And I think a lot of the problem is that the spills just aren't cleaned up quickly. They aren't attended[4] to sometimes at all or there's a very paltry[5], you know, effort put in and there's 2,000 sites there which still need to be cleaned up.

CONAN: Two thousand sites that need to be cleaned up?

Ms. BAIRD: Yes.

1 Exxon Valdez: The oil tanker 'Exxon Valdez' ran aground off the coast of Alaska in 1989 and spilt hundreds of thousands of barrels of oil, causing a major ecological desaster. **2** wetlands: swampy area **3** shellfish: *Schalentier* **4** attend to sb./sth.: take care of sb./sth. **5** paltry (adj): (here) small

CONAN: What kind of damage is that causing? You mentioned marshlands. Obviously, we're aware of the kind of damage that can cause from our recent experience in Louisiana. But as you mentioned, there's an awful lot of people who live down there too.

Ms. BAIRD: Well, that's right. I mean, you know, in terms of the health problems that are reported, a lot of children especially talk about lesions[1] on their skins, problems breathing. And, look, life expectancy in the area has gone down. Obviously, that's something that's very difficult to measure. There's a number of factors. There's extreme poverty. But we certainly know that this is a contributing factor to health and illness. And of course, there's livelihood.

When there's entire kind of villages and populations that have depended on fishing, shellfish, you know, even wildlife and crops[2], and suddenly, you know, their entire farm is wiped out[3] and they're never really compensated for it, that obviously is going to play into a lot of health problems as well.

CONAN: Nigeria has a popularly elected government. And from reading your article, they appear to have done very little here.

Ms. BAIRD: Well, yes. The aptly[4] named Goodluck Jonathan has his work cut out for him[5]. Obviously since the time – since independence, they've been run largely by military dictators. So – and there hasn't really been a lot of effort to either respond to the spills, listen to the people or return some of the vast amounts of money which have been got from the oil production. Six hundred billion dollars so far. And kind of return that back to the people in any way.

And that's where we've seen a real kind of anger and, you know, uprising amongst a lot of Nigerian people. There's a lot of terrorists now. There's an independence movement that's engaging a lot of sabotage and kidnapping. I just think, just for so long there was such a discrepancy in terms of wealth and the ongoing oil problems that

1 lesion: damage, injury **2** crop (n): agricultural plants **3** wipe out sth.: destroy sth. **4** apt: fitting **5** have one's work cut out for oneself (infml): have a lot of work to do

now, you know, it's a complete disaster for a lot of the oil companies, and even functioning there.

CONAN: You mentioned the resistance movement and the secessionist[1] movement and terrorism. That is indeed the source of some of these spills.

Ms. BAIRD: Yes, well, that's right. And how much are the source is under dispute. It's obviously growing. You know, according to an Amnesty International report from last year, up until the mid-1990s, companies were saying, look, about roughly 50 percent, yes, it's our fault. It's due to corrosion, infrastructure problems, all those kinds of things. Now what is the dispute now is how much of it actually due to sabotage. We know it's a problem. The companies are saying it's about 80 percent.

A lot of the Amnesty workers on the ground found that some things were being called sabotage when there was actually parts falling apart and so on. But I do think that, you know, if sabotage is an issue and, obviously – I mean, it's a terribly violent atmosphere for a lot of oil workers to be operating in – then the companies need to actually have ways of responding to sabotage attempts very quickly, you know, if not kind of putting up – you know, putting things in that it would prevent them in the first place. So I think they kind of have to – instead of being victims of sabotage, they need to actually address that aggression more assertively[2] themselves.

CONAN: Wouldn't the protection be the responsibility of the government?

Ms. BAIRD: Well, yes. But would regulation be the responsibility of the government? I mean, absolutely. I mean, I think they need to be working together. I mean, part of the problem is is that the regulatory agencies which have been looking after, you know, the monitoring of the situation and the spills has been reasonably toothless. And effectively, a lot of the companies are left to regulate themselves.

1 secessionist (adj): fighting for independence **2** assertive: confident

Yes, you'd think they would work in concert with the government to deal with the violence. But, you know, then they obviously also need to be responding very quickly to the spills as they happen. I mean, the sabotage that we've – the companies are claiming that the production went down by 20-odd[1] percent between 2006 and 2009 due to sabotage efforts alone. So it is a very real problem.

CONAN: You're saying that if the oil companies are effectively a law unto themselves and regulate themselves, they ought to be the order unto themselves too, and provide for that as well?

Ms. BAIRD: Well, I mean, look, if it's costing them so much and it's causing so many problems, then certainly you would think they would be more assertive, you know, front-footed[2] in working with the government to ward them off. I mean, they are – look, Goodluck Jonathan has been trying. He's been issuing cautions, you know? I think the problem is the punitive[3] measures haven't been particularly punitive. And there's been kind of a growing kind of feeling, especially since people have watched, and Nigerians have been watching what's happened in America[4], and the response to the Gulf and the interest in the president.

And there had been a couple of, you know, court cases recently where companies have been ordered to pay compensation for spills going back as far as 1970. So there is kind of a move – mood of accountability. But unless actually they're severely punished for it, I mean, the environment of, you know, self-regulation in inverted commas is going to continue. I mean, this problem, it's a very complex and difficult issue, but I think there's a lot of human rights of the local people at stake and since their access to health – sorry, access to water and to food and their basic health.

[...]

1 20-odd (infml): about 20 **2** front-footed: taking the initiative **3** punitive (adj): serving as punishment **4** Baird is referring to the explosion of the oil platform 'Deepwater Horizon' in 2010 that led to a massive oil spill in the Gulf of Mexico.

Oil on Water by Helon Habila – Bernadine Evaristo on a topical[1] and urgent tale of environmental and rights abuses in the Niger delta

Evaristo, a novelist and reviewer of fiction for the Guardian, *comments on Habila's novel, calling it an illuminating narrative that brings to light an 'overlooked story of environmental and human rights abuses'.*

A huge chasm[2] exists between Nigeria's multibillion dollar oil revenue and the standard of living for most Nigerians, the majority of whom are dirt-poor. When oil was discovered in the Niger delta in the late 1950s, Nigeria was on course to become the richest country in Africa. But for over 50 years the corrupt collusion[3] between the multinational petroleum corporations and the Nigerian government has meant that profits are siphoned off[4] into Swiss bank accounts, while the rest of the country can go hang itself.

And when the renowned novelist Ken Saro-Wiwa led a movement of non-violent protest against the environmental damage in the region, the government did indeed hang him, after a kangaroo trial[5] in 1995. International outcry brought the plight[6] of the Niger delta, home[7] to 20 million people, to public attention. Yet interest soon waned[8], and today little has changed.

Helon Habila's third novel is therefore topical and urgent, as it ambitiously tackles the collision between the oil companies, the people of the delta whose lands are exploited and ruined, the military who patrol the region, the militants or freedom fighters who are there to disrupt business as usual, and the media who are supposed to observe and record the 'truth'.

1 topical: currently relevant **2** chasm: gap **3** collusion: secret (usu. illegal) agreement **4** siphon sth. off: pump sth. off **5** kangaroo trial: unfair trial **6** plight: difficult situation **7** bring sth. home to sb.: make sth. clear to sb. **8** wane: decrease

All this is refracted through the eyes[1] of a young journalist, Rufus, on his first serious job accompanying his idol, Zaq, a once-celebrated hack[2] who is now a pathetic[3] alcoholic. They are sent into the delta to find the kidnapped wife of a British oil company engineer. En route they endure and witness imprisonment, violence, murder, sickness, deprivation and destruction. When they venture up river by canoe, in scenes reminiscent of Conrad's *Heart of Darkness*, the oilfields are a hellish place.

The narrative oscillates[4] between past and present, tracking the two journalists' assignment in the delta as well as digressing[5] into their respective pasts, but the most powerful and interesting character in the story proves to be the fetid[6], viscous, menacing landscape. Habila's prose perfectly evokes the devastation of the oil-polluted wetlands. Animals lie decomposing, drowned in oil, the poisoned river water is 'foul and sulphurous', abandoned villages have an 'indefinable sadness in the air, as if a community of ghosts were suspended above the punctured zinc roofs', and always in the distance, in the darkness, are the burning flames of the toxic gas flares that many villages crave because of the short-lived prosperity they bring.

In the most poignant passage, a community is overjoyed that its land has finally been turned into an oilfield. They become night people – holding meetings, markets and mass by the light of the god-like 'unquenchable orange flare'. Within a year they and their livestock fall sick and die. Elsewhere, a chief who refuses to sell his land to an oil company is murdered by the police.

In this climate of exploitation, vulnerability, violence and avarice[7], the freedom fighters seek, like the government and oil companies, to make themselves rich. The army major policing the region is a sadistic thug. The desperate locals, 'who endure the worst condi-

1 refracted through sb.'s eyes: seen through sb.'s eyes **2** hack (n, infml): writer
3 pathetic: pitiful **4** oscillate: move back and forth **5** digress: *abschweifen*
6 fetid: smelly **7** avarice (n): greed

tions of any oil-producing community on Earth', resort to[1] illegal oil-tapping[2] as a means of survival. And the husband of the kidnapped woman, the voice of the omnipotent[3] oil companies, seems to live on another planet, bemoaning the fact that 'our pipelines are vandalised daily, losing us millions ... These people don't understand what they do to themselves.'

The big difference between 'conflict diamonds' and 'conflict oil' is that one is a luxury and the other a necessity, which means the international community turns a blind eye. *Oil on Water* brings to light this overlooked story of environmental and human rights abuses. In the delta, the leader of a militant group tells Rufus: 'A war is just starting. We will make it so hot for the government and the oil companies that they will be forced to pull out.'

From: Bernadine Evaristo, 'Oil on Water by Helon Habila', *The Guardian*, September 25, 2010

1 resort to sth.: do sth. because you have no alternative **2** oil-tapping: (illegal) pumping of oil from pipelines **3** omnipotent: all-powerful

Interview with Helon Habila *Henning Steinfeld*

HENNING STEINFELD: You created a somewhat gloomy and pessimistic image of the Niger Delta with corrupt army officers, poor people and polluted landscapes. Were you ever afraid that stereotypes of Africans could be reproduced?

HELON HABILA: I think there are two types of stereotypes. Some stereotypes degrade people and put them into boxes, those are negative. Then there is a kind of stereotype that you try to go beyond. You get the reader with a certain trope[1] that the reader is familiar with and then you take it from there to open the reader's eyes and show him that there is actually more. So, in that way you educate the reader. There is no way you can avoid stereotypes because the things mentioned in the question are present in the Niger Delta ... there's poverty, violence, all that. But what do you do with that? Do you pretend it is not happening or do you try to willfully change reality? So, you can use a stereotype and ask, why is it there, why do people have these difficulties? A negative stereotype is telling you that these people have no willpower, no volition[2]. What I am trying to do with my book is to show that these people are actually trying to take their fate into their hands, even though there are some historical factors against them and it is really hard.

STEINFELD: The shrine seems to have a central function in the narrative. Please tell us a little more about traditional life in the Niger Delta villages and which role it played in people's lives when you visited and did your research in 2007.

HABILA: My idea is to show community life and create this sort of imaginary place that is almost out of time. It almost takes you back into history, to an ideal village and what it might have been like: a village that is not effected by oil pollution, a village that is still holding on to these traditions and cultures. I am kind of idealizing the actual villages. There are also other villages that are suffering

1 trope: expression, image **2** volition (fml): will

and are invaded, which I outlined in the book. In 2007–2009, when I was doing my research, different things were going on: kidnappings, the military invading and destroying villages. There was a real war taking place. During my research at that time, we traveled through these creeks on a boat and we saw all these military encampments with their guns pointing at us. They were able to wipe out a village at any given minute if they suspected the presence of militants.

The military operations, the violence, the pollution have destroyed these villages and pushed them back developmentally. You can also say that about colonialism. If people hadn't left their cultures and their traditions, they could have been worshipping and praying and living the kind of life that I depicted in Irikefe Island. It is a kind of imaginary idealization of an African setting that is outside colonialism, outside modernity, with its own kind of civilization.

STEINFELD: The community of worshippers and their new member, Boma, teach us a lot about eco-critical standpoints. Do you think that Western readers can learn from pre-colonial life in the Global South?

HABILA: I think it is possible. If you look at activism and the need for change, the West tends to think that they know everything and that they are leading the way and these Third World Countries do not know how to move forward at all. But they lived sustainable lives, and in the past, they developed their religion and their culture around nature. You can not separate man from nature. Everything they did was sustainable, even their farming techniques. They moved from farmland to farmland to enable the soil to regenerate. When they hunt they do not go trophy hunting but hunt for food. So, these are lessons we could all look at and learn from. These people may not have the words that environmentalists use but they have an intuitive understanding of how nature works. You have to live in coexistence and you have to respect nature.

These people look at trees and say that these trees have spirits. One could say that they are superstitious[1] because trees do not have spirits. But one could also look at the trees and say you can not cut them down because they also have spirits and are essentially like us. So, if you want to cut down a tree you need to have an elaborate ceremony and invite the whole village to show respect to nature and save trees. So, I think there is a lot to be learned.

There are other Africans as well, such as Wangari Maathai, the Kenyan Nobel laureate, who tried to show the world that Africans have always had sustainable ways of living. The West often tries to teach too much, although it is the place that has the industries that destroy the environment in the first place.

STEINFELD: Religion plays a significant role in Nigeria, as you indicate with the arrival of Brother Jonah and Pentecostalism[2]. Does religion make people's lives worse or does it help Nigerians?

HABILA: Religion has its place and its own uses if it is not abused. But it is often abused. It helps some people get rich. Religion is a reflection of politics because they have similar hierarchical structures. You have the pastor, who can not be questioned and is, essentially, getting rich. These pastors have private jets and own palaces in Europe and America. And people keep going to church and giving them money. At the same time, these people who claim to be religious will go to their office and take bribes and give the money to the church and think they will go to heaven. You just don't understand the logic of it.

However, when politics and society do not work and when there is no law and order or justice, people turn towards religion because they think it offers the perfect society they are hoping for. In the church, everything seems to work ... there is a hierarchy, people come and sing, there is a structure. Some churches are located in the centre of settlements, in the centre of a community. These churches have houses, security and thus resemble a government.

1 superstitious: *abergläubig* **2** pentecostalism: Christian renewal movement

Since the actual government does not work, these churches give the people hope.

It's the same with Boko Haram[1] ... people are so fed up with the politics and corruption that they say they want to form a society that is going to be perfect and is going to provide justice. And even if they die they go to heaven, so it's a win-win-situation, there is no loss. It's a kind of denial syndrome[2] because you are living as if you're in heaven although you're actually on earth. You are closing your eyes to all the things you could change and escape into this illusion of another life in heaven. That's Nigeria for me.

STEINFELD: *Oil on Water* draws a complex image of post-colonial Nigeria. What is Nigeria for you nowadays?

HABILA: Nigeria will always be home. Sometimes, home can be a hostile environment. Sometimes, home can be welcoming. Home can be many things at the same time but it is always going to be home. Home is never perfect. I have been outside of Nigeria for about 15 years and many things have changed. I go back every year to visit and maintain contact.

The most important thing is that Nigeria is a source of my memories, a place that has made me who I am. It is a complex place that inspires my stories, keeps me rooted in tradition and culture. I like the food, the music ... the way I see the world has been formed and shaped by the education I achieved when growing up in Nigeria. But as one moves on, one realizes that there are many cultures and many good and bad things about your home. When you move out of your place, you realize that your place has its own problems. But it does not have to be perfect, that's just the way it is. One has to love it, with the good and the bad. So, for me, that is what Nigeria is.

STEINFELD: In your work, you capture the violence we find in Nigeria and try to identify what caused it. Oil companies, the mili-

1 Boko Haram: fundamentalist Islamic terror group active mainly in the north of Nigeria **2** denial syndrome: medical condition that makes sb. deny the reality of unpleasant facts in her/his life

tary, Boko Haram ... What has to change so that Nigeria can become a better place in the future?

HABILA: There is so much injustice and inequality. Sometimes, you hope for a good leader, or even a messiah ... but you realize that is never going to happen. Nigeria has a class system. There is an entrenched[1] group that benefits from the chaos and corruption. They benefit from that and will never change the country. If the country changes and there is justice, they will no longer get the benefits. People dying, children not going to school, violence and kidnappings ... that's perfect, that works for them. So, I think there has to be more education of the common people, more effort towards democratization. We need to have grass roots organizations[2] who work with the people. That is going to take a long time. I thought this would happen in my life time. But every election comes and nothing really happens. You realize it takes time.

But here and there you see little signs of hope, especially in the civil society. There is activism around elections, publishing companies are doing well. People are actually publishing and reading books. There are all these compensatory activities. Sometimes, we take a step back and a step forward. To be honest, sometimes one gets pessimistic and tired. But what can you do? You just keep hoping for the best and try to contribute. I try to contribute what little I can, through my writings, my speeches, whatever I can do.

Henning Steinfeld, 'Interview with Helon Habila', unpublished manuscript, August 26, 2019

1 entrenched: firmly established **2** grass roots organization: political organization formed by average citizens

Background Information on Nigeria

Nigeria's diversity

Kidnappings, ethnic clashes, military coups, oil spills – in the media Nigeria is often portrayed as a 'failed state', but only rarely it is explained why exactly the 'Giant of Africa' with its estimated 200 million inhabitants often has to struggle to live up to its own diversity.

Religion

There is hardly a place in Africa where religion plays a more significant part in people's lives than in Nigeria. The nation's various ethnic groups have for centuries practiced their own traditional set of beliefs with their very own cosmologies, ethics and customs. Contact with Europeans, however, has led to fundamental changes. The colonialists, who saw the south of today's Nigeria mainly as a resource to be exploited and turned many coastal places into centres for the global slave trade, utilized Christianity as a handy instrument to justify the subjection of non-Europeans. At the same time, the introduction of Islam between 1100 and 1400 CE transformed the northern lands into a predominantly Muslim region. To date, the South has remained essentially Christian and the North mostly Muslim (Sunnite).

Ethnicity

Ethnic boundaries are a major source of conflict in Nigeria. Roughly 250 ethnic groups live in Nigeria. The Yoruba, Igbo, Fulani and Hausa people, Nigeria's four most important ethnic groups, all number around 30 to 40 million each and make up about 70 % of Nigeria's overall population. Each group has its own social organization and language, which is why many people communicate in Nigerian Pidgin, a lingua franca making use of English words and grammar. Ethnic affiliation may be considered just as relevant or even more important than (Nigerian) nationality, which is why the country has seen many clashes that are, at least to some extent, based on ethnic tensions. The Biafran War (1967–70), following the state of Biafra's attempt to gain its independence, or the latest conflicts in northwestern Nigeria, for instance, cannot be explained without referring to the nation's ethnic divisions.

Political system

These ethnic dividing lines also affect the nation's political system. On paper, Nigeria may be a democratic republic modelled after the United States. The country's political system, however, is anything but stable. In addition to ethnic conflicts also corruption and the militants active in the state of Borno or the Niger Delta are a serious threat to the nation's stability. Several times, democratic governments have been overthrown by the military, and only in 2007 was power peacefully transferred from one civilian regime to another for the first time in the country's history. Having become a formally independent federation only in 1960, Nigeria is a rather young nation, which may explain to some extent that it is still a somewhat fragile construct that many of its inhabitants cannot fully identify with.

Economy and oil industry

Hardly any Western newspaper will publish an article about Nigeria without at least once addressing the soaring corruption rampant in the economy. Indeed, the informal sector in most places accounts for more than half of all economic activity. For example, it is assumed that in Lagos up to 90 % of the businesses operate outside the law. The country's oil industry, which has been growing rapidly since the beginning of the 20th century, contributes enormously to this gray economy. International companies such as Shell or Total have not only been widely criticized for polluting the Niger Delta, a region with one of the world's largest oil deposits, but have also been accused of fueling the corruption of the political elites when pursuing their economic ambitions.

Environment, pollution, and climate change

The pollution caused by the oil industry (e.g. oil spills) poses a serious threat to the country's rich environment. The Niger Delta, for instance, which is one of the world's largest river deltas, belongs to the coastal plains that mostly have a tropical rainforest climate. Its humidity and constant warmth produce heavy rainfalls which result in misty air. This climate is the basis for a very diverse vegetation with many forest swamps (especially mangrove swamps). But as the Niger delta has become a battlefield of companies, politicians, and militants, many animals and plants can no longer survive. The northern lands, for instance, which are mostly savannah and have less rain, face massive air pollution caused by old cars. And also the effects of climate can no longer be denied, with increasing temperatures and droughts impacting the country's agriculture.

Culture

Despite Nigeria's many problems, it would be a mistake to see the country simply as a failed state. *Naijá*, as most inhabitants call it, has a very rich culture. Many writers and filmmakers refuse to reproduce stereotypes and oversimplifications and try to create a more balanced and realistic image. Nowadays, Nollywood movies dominate the African film market and novels written by Nigerian authors can be found in most Western bookshops. Nigeria's cultural hegemony may therefore contribute to a more complex understanding of the country.

References

Falola, Toyin, and Matthew M. Heaton, *A History of Nigeria*, Cambridge: Cambridge University Press, 2008

Olopade, Dayo, *The Bright Continent. Breaking Rules and Making Change in Modern Africa*, New York: Mariner, 2015

Packer, George, 'The Megacity. Decoding the chaos of Lagos', *The New Yorker Online*, 13 November 2006, https://www.newyorker.com/magazine/2006/11/13/the-megacity

Paehler, Klaus, 'Nigeria im Dilemma des Klimawandels', 19 July 2007, https://www.kas.de/laenderberichte/detail/-/content/nigeria-im-dilemma-des-klimawandels1

Pfaff, Isabel, 'Der Sumpf im nigerianischen Öldelta', *Süddeutsche Zeitung*, 10 November 2015

Nigeria Administrative Map

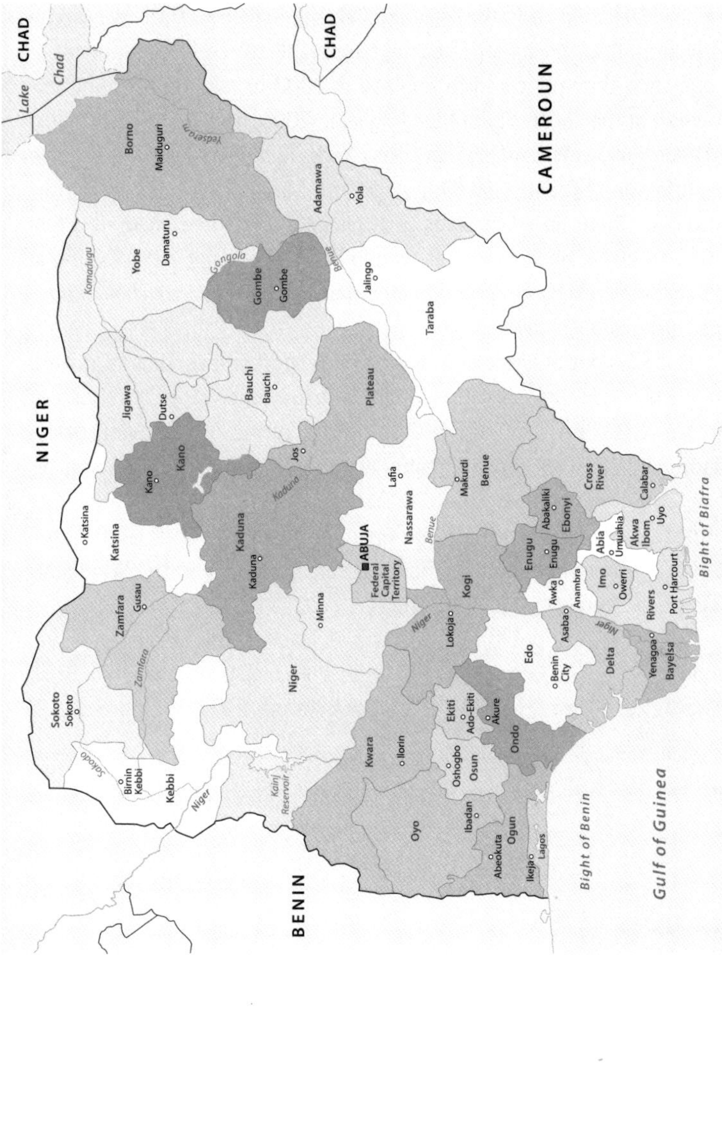

The Author

Helon Habila was born in Kaltungo/Nigeria in 1967. After receiving a B.A. from the University of Jos, he temporarily worked as a journalist in Lagos and then relocated to England in 2002 to take up a writing fellowship at the University of East Anglia. In 2005, he was the first Chinua Achebe Fellow at Bard College, New York. Two years later, he became a professor of Creative Writing at George Mason University in Fairfax, Virginia, where he still resides with his wife and three children. From 2013 to 2014, he worked and lived in Berlin, Germany, participating in an academic exchange programme organized by the *Deutscher Akademischer Austauschdienst*.

Habila is not only the author of various short stories, poems, novels, and articles. He has also taken part in many other projects related to literature, such as editing the *Granta Book of the African Short Story*, participating in an annual creative writing workshop, or founding his own publishing company, Cordite Books. His fiction has won a number of prizes, among them the Caine Prize for Best First Novel (2001), the Virginia Library Foundation's fiction award (2008), and the Windham-Campbell Literature Prize (2015).

Oil on Water, published in 2010, is Habila's third novel and was shortlisted for the Commonwealth Writers' Prize (2011), the Orion Book Award (2012), and the PEN/Open Book Award (2012).